330

my revision notes

Edexcel A-level

ECONOMICS A

Quintin Brewe

Hachette UK's policy is to use papers that are natural, renewable and recyclable products and made from wood grown in sustainable forests. The logging and manufacturing processes are expected to conform to the environmental regulations of the country of origin.

Orders: please contact Bookpoint Ltd, 130 Milton Park, Abingdon, Oxon OX14 4SB. Telephone: (44) 01235 827720. Fax: (44) 01235 400454. Email education@bookpoint.co.uk

Lines are open from 9 a.m. to 5 p.m., Monday to Saturday, with a 24-hour message answering service. You can also order through our website: www.hoddereducation.co.uk

ISBN: 978-1-4718-4213-9

First published in 2016 by

Hodder Education,
An Hachette UK Company
Carmelite House
50 Victoria Embankment
London EC4Y 0DZ

www.hoddereducation.co.uk

Impression number 10 9 8
Year 2020 2019

Cover photo reproduced by permission of Cozyta/Fotolia

Typeset in Bembo Std Regular, 11/13 pts. by Aptara, Inc.

Printed in India

A catalogue record for this title is available from the British Library.

Get the most from this book

Everyone has to decide his or her own revision strategy, but it is essential to review your work, learn it and test your understanding. These Revision Notes will help you to do that in a planned way, topic by topic. Use this book as the cornerstone of your revision and don't hesitate to write in it — personalise your notes and check your progress by ticking off each section as you revise.

Tick to track your progress 

Use the revision planner on pages 4–7 to plan your revision, topic by topic. Tick each box when you have:

- revised and understood a topic
- tested yourself
- practised the exam questions and gone online to check your answers and complete the quick quizzes

You can also keep track of your revision by ticking off each topic heading in the book. You may find it helpful to add your own notes as you work through each topic.

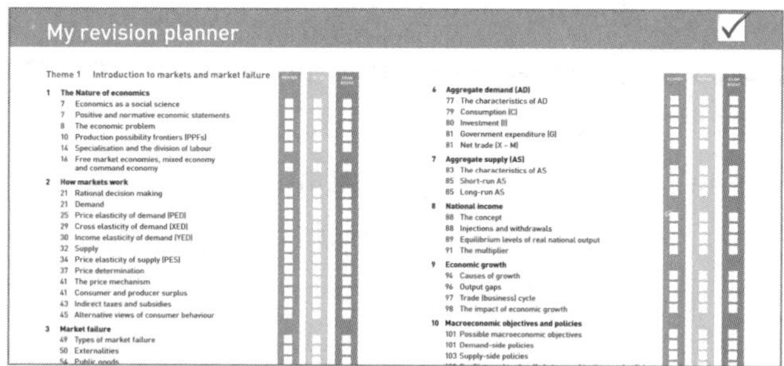

My revision planner

Theme 1 Introduction to markets and market failure

1 The Nature of economics
7 Economics as a social science
7 Positive and normative economic statements
8 The economic problem
10 Production possibility frontiers (PPFs)
14 Specialisation and the division of labour
16 Free market economies, mixed economy and command economy

2 How markets work
21 Rational decision making
21 Demand
25 Price elasticity of demand (PED)
29 Cross elasticity of demand (XED)
30 Income elasticity of demand (YED)
32 Supply
34 Price elasticity of supply (PES)
37 Price determination
41 The price mechanism
41 Consumer and producer surplus
43 Indirect taxes and subsidies
45 Alternative views of consumer behaviour

3 Market failure
49 Types of market failure
50 Externalities
54 Public goods

6 Aggregate demand (AD)
77 The characteristics of AD
79 Consumption (C)
80 Investment (I)
81 Government expenditure (G)
81 Net trade (X – M)

7 Aggregate supply (AS)
83 The characteristics of AS
85 Short-run AS
85 Long-run AS

8 National income
88 The concept
88 Injections and withdrawals
89 Equilibrium levels of real national output
91 The multiplier

9 Economic growth
94 Causes of growth
96 Output gaps
97 Trade (business) cycle
98 The impact of economic growth

10 Macroeconomic objectives and policies
101 Possible macroeconomic objectives
101 Demand-side policies
103 Supply-side policies

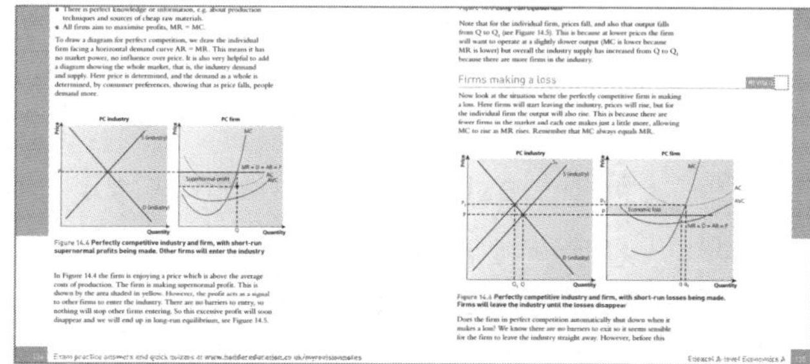

Features to help you succeed

Examiners' tips and summaries

Expert tips are given throughout the book to help you polish your exam technique in order to maximise your chances in the exam. The summaries provide a quick-check bullet list for each topic.

Typical mistakes

The author identifies the typical mistakes candidates make and explains how you can avoid them.

Now test yourself

These short, knowledge-based questions provide the first step in testing your learning. Answers are at the back of the book.

Definitions and key words

Clear, concise definitions of essential key terms are provided where they first appear.

Key words from the specification are highlighted in bold throughout the book.

Revision activities

These activities will help you to understand each topic in an interactive way.

Exam practice

Practice exam questions are provided for each topic. Use them to consolidate your revision and practise your exam skills.

Online

Go online to check your answers to the exam questions and try out the extra quick quizzes at **www.hoddereducation.co.uk/myrevisionnotes**

My revision planner

Theme 1 Introduction to markets and market failure

REVISED | TESTED | EXAM READY

Theme 2 The UK economy: performance and policies

REVISED | TESTED | EXAM READY

Exam practice answers and quick quizzes at www.hoddereducation.co.uk/myrevisionnotes

Countdown to my exams

6–8 weeks to go

- Start by looking at the specification — make sure you know exactly what material you need to revise and the style of the examination. Use the revision planner on pages 4–7 to familiarise yourself with the topics.
- Organise your notes, making sure you have covered everything on the specification. The revision planner will help you to group your notes into topics.
- Work out a realistic revision plan that will allow you time for relaxation. Set aside days and times for all the subjects that you need to study, and stick to your timetable.
- Set yourself sensible targets. Break your revision down into focused sessions of around 40 minutes, divided by breaks. These Revision Notes organise the basic facts into short, memorable sections to make revising easier.

REVISED

2–6 weeks to go

- Read through the relevant sections of this book and refer to the examiners' tips, examiners' summaries, typical mistakes and key terms. Tick off the topics as you feel confident about them. Highlight those topics you find difficult and look at them again in detail.
- Test your understanding of each topic by working through the 'Now test yourself' questions in the book. Look up the answers at the back of the book.
- Make a note of any problem areas as you revise, and ask your teacher to go over these in class.
- Look at past papers. They are one of the best ways to revise and practise your exam skills. Write or prepare planned answers to the exam practice questions provided in this book. Check your answers online and try out the extra quick quizzes at **www.hoddereducation.co.uk/myrevisionnotes**
- Use the revision activities to try out different revision methods. For example, you can make notes using mind maps, spider diagrams or flash cards.
- Track your progress using the revision planner and give yourself a reward when you have achieved your target.

REVISED

One week to go

- Try to fit in at least one more timed practice of an entire past paper and seek feedback from your teacher, comparing your work closely with the mark scheme.
- Check the revision planner to make sure you haven't missed out any topics. Brush up on any areas of difficulty by talking them over with a friend or getting help from your teacher.
- Attend any revision classes put on by your teacher. Remember, he or she is an expert at preparing people for examinations.

REVISED

The day before the examination

- Flick through these Revision Notes for useful reminders, for example the examiners' tips, examiners' summaries, typical mistakes and key terms.
- Check the time and place of your examination.
- Make sure you have everything you need — extra pens and pencils, tissues, a watch, bottled water, sweets.
- Allow some time to relax and have an early night to ensure you are fresh and alert for the examinations.

REVISED

My exams

A-level Economics Paper 1

Date:..

Time:..

Location:..

A-level Economics Paper 2

Date:..

Time:..

Location:..

A-level Economics Paper 3

Date:..

Time:..

Location:..

1 The nature of economics

Economics as a social science

Thinking like an economist

REVISED

Economics is concerned with the ways by which societies organise scarce productive resources in order to satisfy people's wants. It provides a unique and special way of examining many areas of human behaviour which involves using the economist's toolkit of concepts, theories and techniques to analyse economic issues and problems.

Economists often use models to develop theories of behaviour. These models are usually based on assumptions from which certain deductions may be made.

The use of the ceteris paribus assumption in building models

REVISED

When building models economists work on the basis that all other variables are held constant to enable deductions to be made. This is called the '**ceteris paribus**' assumption which means 'other things being equal'. This helps to simplify analysis so that the impact of a single change in a variable can be examined.

Ceteris paribus means that when the effect of a change in one variable is considered, it is assumed that all other variables are held constant.

The inability in economics to make scientific experiments

REVISED

It is impossible for economists to conduct laboratory experiments because economics is a social science involving people. Consequently, economic policies which may have been effective at one time in one country may not have the same impact at another time or in another country.

Exam tip

Analysis is usually based on the ceteris paribus assumption. However, in making an evaluative comment, you may find it helpful to remove this assumption.

Positive and normative economic statements

Positive economics

REVISED

Positive economic statements are based on facts that can be proved or disproved. They include what was, is or will be, and these statements can be verified as being true or false by reference to the date or by using a scientific approach.

As noted above, economists often use models as a way of predicting behaviour. It is possible to make positive statements on the basis of models, such as the impact on price of a product following an increase in demand.

Positive economic statements may be based on official data such as gross domestic product (GDP), prices of commodities, the rate of unemployment, and the exchange rate of one currency against another.

Positive economic statements are objective statements based on evidence or facts which can, therefore, be proved or disproved.

Normative economics

REVISED

Normative economic statements are based on value judgements and are, therefore, subjective. They relate to what:

- might be good or bad, or
- should be or ought to be, or
- would be fair or unfair

Normative economics is usually associated with discussions about economic policy. In this unit, for example, it is concerned with issues such as whether or not there should be:

- a minimum price for alcohol
- subsidies for green energy, e.g. wind farms
- road tolls
- an increase in the tax on cigarettes
- more private sector provision in the health service
- the introduction of a tax on sugary drinks

Normative economic statements are subjective statements based on value judgements and cannot be proved or disproved.

Typical mistake

Answers relating to normative statements often consider them to be opinions. Although this is not technically incorrect, it is much better to use the terms 'value judgements' or 'subjective views' to describe them.

Now test yourself

TESTED

1 Which of the following are positive statements and which are normative statements?
  (a) Taxes on bankers should be increased.
  (b) The GDP of Greece fell by over 25% between 2008 and 2014.
  (c) New technology has caused a fall in the price of mobile phones.
  (d) High energy prices are unfair on the poor.
  (e) Inequality is increasing in the UK.

Answers on p. 215

The economic problem

The problem of scarcity

REVISED

All societies face the problem that wants are infinite but resources are limited in supply. This is the underlying reason for the fundamental economic problem of scarcity. Therefore, choices must be made. The issue of **scarcity** means that societies face a series of questions:

- **What to produce and how much to produce?** This relates to the different types of goods and services the economy should produce and how much of each.

Scarcity exists because resources are finite whereas wants are infinite.

- **How should the goods and services be produced?** Production may be labour intensive, i.e. a high proportion of labour used relative to capital, or capital intensive, i.e. a high proportion of capital used relative to labour.
- **How should the goods produced be allocated?** This is concerned with the distribution of the goods produced and will affect the degree of equality in the society.

Resources

REVISED

The resources of a country are referred to as **'factors of production'**. Four factors of production may be identified:

- **Land:** includes all natural resources, raw materials, the fertility of the soil and resources found in the sea.
- **Labour:** refers to those involved in the production of goods and services and includes all human effort both physical and mental.
- **Capital:** any man-made aid to production including factory buildings, offices, machinery, IT equipment which are used to make other goods and services.
- **Enterprise:** the entrepreneur performs two essential functions:
  - bringing together the other factors of production so that goods and services can be produced and
  - taking the risks involved in production.

Factors of production are resources and include land, labour, capital and enterprise.

Typical mistake

Describing money as capital should be avoided. As a factor of production, capital is something tangible which is used to make other goods.

The distinction between renewable and non-renewable resources

REVISED

Some resources are renewable, i.e. they can be replaced naturally after use, e.g. solar energy, wind power, wood and fish. Such resources are likely to be sustainable unless they are consumed more quickly than they can be replaced. Other resources are non-renewable, i.e. continued consumption will eventually result in their exhaustion. Examples include oil, platinum and copper.

Renewable resources are those whose stock levels can be maintained at a certain level.

Non-renewable resources are those which will eventually be completely depleted.

The importance of opportunity costs to economic agents

REVISED

Scarcity implies that choices must be made. However, each choice involves an opportunity cost. This may be explained as follows: if a country's resources are used to manufacture one product, then it must forgo an alternative product that could have been produced. The next best alternative foregone is called the opportunity cost of what has been produced. Opportunity cost, therefore, is a **real cost** measured in terms of something that is foregone.

Opportunity cost is the next best alternative that is forgone when a choice is made.

Examples of opportunity cost include:

- For a consumer: a woman might have enough money to buy either an ebook or a music download. If she decides to buy the ebook then the opportunity cost is the music download.
- For a firm: it might have to make a choice between its two priorities — buying a new IT system and building a new factory. If it chooses the IT system then the opportunity cost is the new factory.

- For the government: suppose it has £10 million with which to fund one of its two main priorities, both requiring a £10 million investment — building a new hospital or building a new university. If it decides that its first preference is the hospital while the second preference is the university, then the opportunity cost of building the hospital will be the university building.

Typical mistake

Considering opportunity cost in terms of money. This is incorrect: opportunity cost must be measured as a real cost, i.e. in terms of goods forgone when a choice is made.

Economic goods and free goods

REVISED

Economic goods are created from resources that are limited in supply and so are scarce. Consequently, they command a price.

Free goods are unlimited in supply such as sunlight or sand on a beach. Consumption by one person does not limit consumption by others. Therefore, the opportunity cost of consuming a free good is zero.

Now test yourself

TESTED

2 Identify the factor of production in each of the following cases:
  (a) Copper deposits in Zambia.
  (b) A woman who opens a hairdressing salon.
  (c) Machinery used in car production.
  (d) An engineer making computer games for a company.
3 Classify the following into capital and consumer goods:
  (a) A laptop used by a company director for his business.
  (b) A curry eaten by Marie for her lunch.
  (c) A visit to a spa by Kirsten.
  (d) A car used to transport a manager between offices.
4 Why do societies have to make choices about what to produce?
5 If a person's top two priorities are a holiday in Greece and a new a home cinema system but he only has enough money for one of these, what would be the opportunity cost of purchasing the home cinema system?
6 Why does the consumption of free goods not incur an opportunity cost?

Answers on p. 215

Production possibility frontiers (PPFs)

A **production possibility frontier** (PPF) shows combinations of two goods which could be produced by an economy if all its resources were employed fully and efficiently. Figure 1.1 shows a PPF.

A **production possibility frontier** illustrates the maximum potential output of an economy when all resources are fully employed.

In constructing the following PPF it is assumed that the economy can produce either consumer goods or capital goods. **Capital goods** are those required to produce other goods — both capital and consumer goods. Examples include machinery, factory buildings. **Consumer goods** are those that give satisfaction (or utility) to consumers, e.g. smartphones, curry and cars.

Exam tip

To avoid confusion between capital goods and consumer goods, consider how they are used: anything which is an aid to production is classified as a capital good, whereas anything used by someone for final consumption is classified as a consumer good.

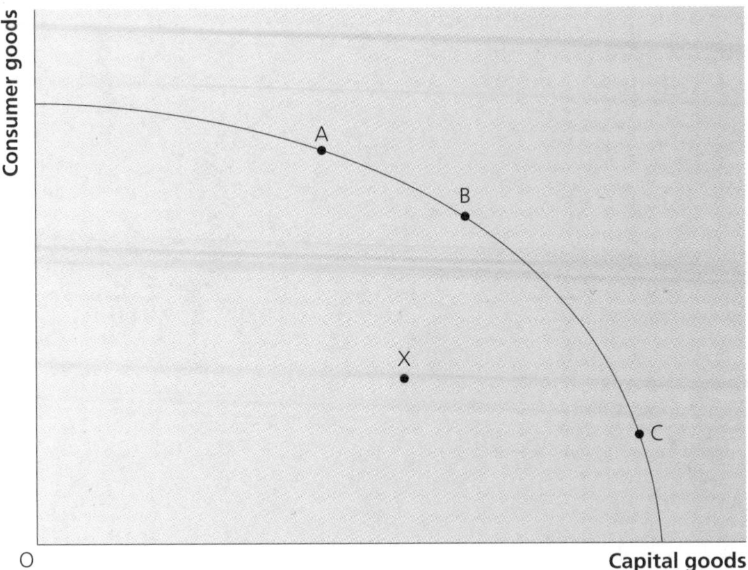

Figure 1.1 A production possibility frontier (PPF)

By definition, any point on the PPF, e.g. A, B or C, implies that all resources are fully and efficiently employed. Therefore, all points on the PPF indicate **the maximum productive potential of an economy and that resources are being used efficiently**.

However, if the economy was operating inside its PPF, e.g. at point X, then it would indicate that there are unemployed resources in the economy. For example, some workers may be unemployed or machinery may be unused. It could also imply that **resources are not being allocated efficiently**.

Possible and unobtainable production

REVISED

Any points inside, or on the PPF, represent combinations of the two products which are obtainable.

However, any points to the right of the PPF would be currently unobtainable. They could only become obtainable if there was economic growth.

PPFs and opportunity cost

REVISED

- The PPF is drawn as a curve (concave to the origin) in Figure 1.1.
- This may be analysed in terms of the concept of opportunity cost and marginal analysis.
- **Marginal analysis** involves consideration of the impact small changes make on the current situation.
- Therefore, a marginal increase in the output of capital goods means that some consumer goods must be sacrificed (the opportunity cost).
- In Figure 1.2, when output of capital goods is increased from 0M to 0S, the output of consumer goods is reduced from 0L to 0R.
- Therefore, the opportunity cost of increasing the output of capital goods by MS is LR consumer goods.
- Since the PPF has been drawn as a curve, it can be seen that as output of capital goods is further increased, e.g. by SV, the opportunity cost rises, i.e. by RT consumer goods. The main reason for this is that some resources will be better suited to the production of consumer

Marginal analysis is concerned with the impact of additions to or subtractions from the current situation. The rational decision-maker will only decide on an option if the marginal benefit exceeds the marginal cost.

Exam tip

If the PPF was a straight line then the opportunity cost would be constant.

goods, while others are better suited to the production of capital goods. Therefore, when more and more capital goods are produced, the opportunity cost in terms of consumer goods will increase.

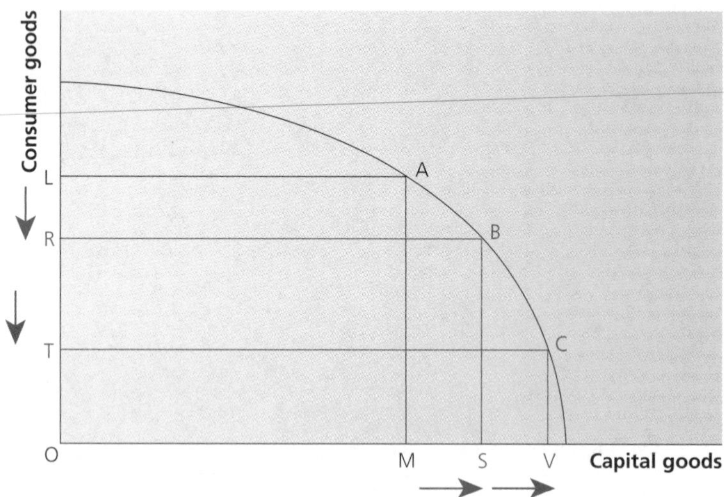

Figure 1.2 **Production possibility frontiers and opportunity cost**

Production possibility frontiers (PPFs), economic growth and economic decline

REVISED

PPFs may be used to illustrate **economic growth**.

- Look at Figure 1.2. Suppose that the economy is currently operating at point A on the PPF with 0L consumer goods and 0M capital goods being produced.
- It is also assumed that the 0M capital goods produced are just sufficient to replace worn-out machinery.
- If there is a reallocation of resources so that the production of capital goods is increased to 0S, then only 0R consumer goods can now be produced.
- Therefore, the opportunity cost of producing MS more capital goods is LR consumer goods.

This reduction in the output of consumer goods implies a fall in current living standards. However, in the long run, there will be economic growth because the extra capital goods will cause an increase in the productive capacity of the economy resulting in a rightward shift in the PPF as shown in Figure 1.3.

Economic growth refers to an increase in the productive capacity of the economy indicating an increase in real output.

Economic decline refers to a decrease in the productive capacity of the economy indicating a decrease in real output.

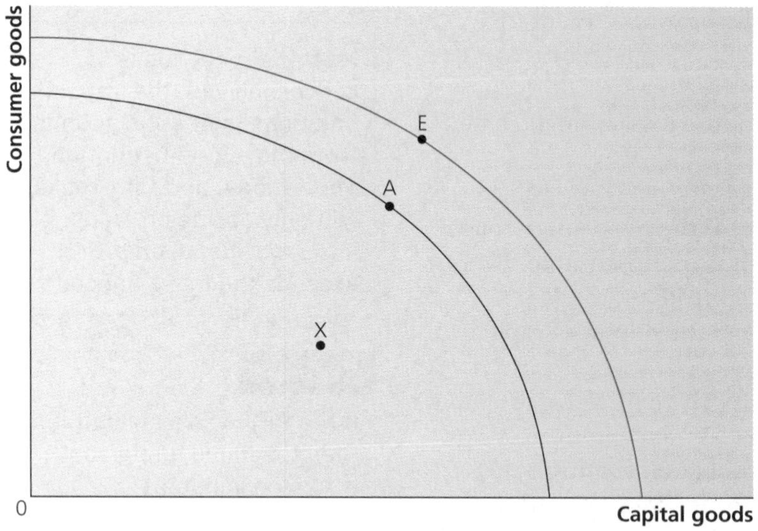

Consumer goods

E

A

X

0

Capital goods

Figure 1.3 **Production possibility frontiers and economic growth**

It can be seen that if the economy moved from point A to point E then more of both capital goods and consumer goods could be produced. In turn, this implies that living standards would increase in the long run.

In contrast, **economic decline** would be associated with an inward shift in the PPF and might have occurred as a result of resources being reallocated from the production of capital goods to the production of consumer goods, e.g. if the production of capital goods was reduced below 0M then there would be insufficient production of capital goods to cover depreciation so reducing the productive capacity of the economy. This would cause an inward shift in the PPF. Other factors causing shifts in the PPF are outlined below.

Movements along a PPF and shifts in PPFs

REVISED ☐

Changes in the combination of the two goods being produced e.g. capital goods and consumer goods would cause movements *along* a given PPF. Such a change might occur if the economy devoted more resources to the production of capital goods and fewer to the production of consumer goods. This would involve an opportunity cost (see section above on PPF and opportunity cost).

There are a range of factors which could cause a shift in the whole PPF. These are outlined in the following two sections.

Factors causing an outward shift in the PPF

REVISED ☐

Factors which might cause an outward shift in the PPF include:

- discovery of new natural resources, e.g. oil
- development of new methods of production which increase productivity
- advances in technology
- improvements in education and training which increase the productivity of the workforce
- factors which lead to an increase in the size of the workforce, e.g. immigration, an increase in the retirement age, better childcare enabling more women to join the workforce

Factors causing an inward shift in the PPF

REVISED ☐

Factors which might cause an inward shift in the PPF include:

- natural disasters, e.g. earthquakes, floods which cause a destruction of productive capacity
- depletion of natural resources
- factors causing a reduction in the size of the workforce, e.g. emigration, an increase in number of years spent in compulsory education
- a deep recession that results in a loss of productive capacity with factories closing down permanently

Exam tip

Remember that the PPF represents the possible outputs of two goods which could potentially be produced. Points on the PPF do not represent what is actually produced unless all resources are fully employed.

Now test yourself

TESTED

7 With reference to the diagram below:

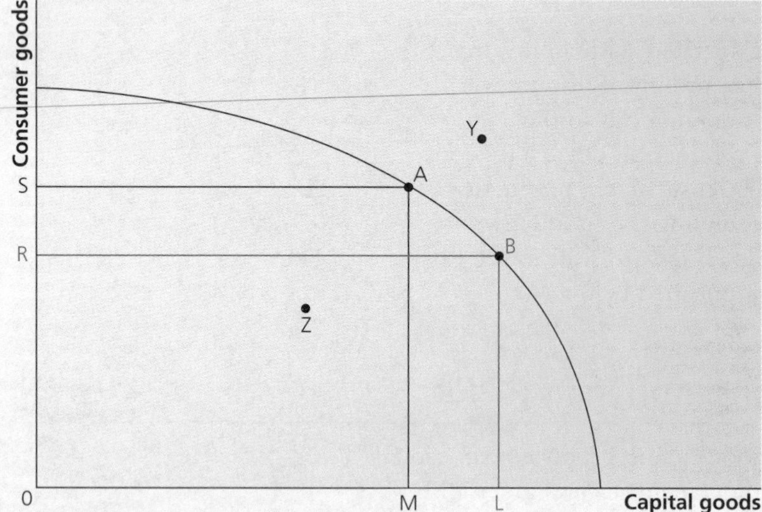

(a) What does point Z represent?
(b) Under what circumstances could the combination of goods at point Y be achieved?
(c) What is the opportunity cost of increasing the output of consumer goods by RS?
(d) How might this affect:
 (i) present living standards, and
 (ii) future living standards?

8 What will be the effect on a PPF of each of the following:
(a) improvements in education and training leading to an increase in labour productivity
(b) a tsunami in Japan which caused the closure of nuclear power stations
(c) an increase in the amount of capital per worker
(d) an increase in immigration of people aged between 16 and 65

Answers on p. 215

Specialisation and the division of labour

The meaning of the division of labour

REVISED

This occurs when workers specialise in very specific tasks, i.e. the work is divided up into many smaller parts so that each worker is responsible for a very small part of the product or service being provided.

Division of labour occurs when the work is split up into small tasks.

Adam Smith and the division of labour

REVISED

In *The Wealth of Nations* Adam Smith set out the view that economic growth could be achieved by increasing the division of labour. This involved the breaking down of a task into many small jobs with workers specialising in a particular task without the need to change jobs during the day. This saved time and enabled each worker to become an expert in that task so increasing his or her productivity.

Advantages and disadvantages of specialisation and the division of labour in organising production

REVISED

Advantages

The following factors help to explain why the division of labour has been widely adopted:

- Each worker specialises in tasks for which he or she is best suited.
- Therefore, he or she only has to be trained in one task.
- Less time is wasted because a worker no longer has to move from one task to another.
- In manufacturing such an approach enables production line methods to be employed and allows an increased use of machinery.
- In turn, this helps to increase productivity and to reduce average costs of production.

Typical mistake

Thinking that division of labour entails increased training costs. In practice, training costs should be reduced because the worker only has to be trained in one particular task.

Disadvantages

Despite the above advantages, certain problems are associated with the division of labour including:

- Monotony and boredom for workers: this could result in a decrease in productivity.
- Loss of skills: workers trained in one particular task have only limited skills. This could be a problem if they are made redundant.
- A strike by one group of workers could bring the entire production facility to a standstill.
- There is a lack of variety because all goods produced on a production line are identical.

Advantages and disadvantages of specialisation to trade

REVISED

Advantages

If a country specialises in the production of certain goods and services and then trades these in exchange for goods and services that it does not produce, then it can benefit from increased output, greater choice and lower prices.

Disadvantages

Such specialisation might mean that a country becomes over-dependent on imported goods and services. If its goods and services are uncompetitive then unemployment could result, and the country's value of imports may persistently exceed the value of its exports.

Limits to the division of labour

REVISED

Certain factors will limit the extent to which the division of labour can be applied:

- The size of the market: if there is only a small market then it will be more difficult to specialise.

- The type of the product: for example, designer fashion products are likely to be unique and not suitable for the division of labour.
- Transport costs: if these are high then large-scale production and the division of labour may not be possible.

The functions of money

REVISED

Money performs various functions which help to facilitate specialisation and the division of labour. The key functions are:

- **As a medium of exchange** enabling people to specialise, exchanging the money earned from doing a specialist job for the goods and services they wish to buy.
- **A store of value** enabling people to save in order to buy goods in the future.
- **A measure of value** enabling people to assess the value of different goods and services.
- **A means of deferred payments** enabling people to buy goods and pay for them on credit.

Money refers to anything that is used as a means of exchange for goods and services.

Now test yourself

TESTED

9 Which of the following would make it more difficult for a firm to adopt a greater degree of specialisation?
(a) increasing sales
(b) new machinery available
(c) falling costs of transporting goods to consumers
(d) production of unique products which are designed to meet individual consumer wishes

10 Explain the importance of money as a medium of exchange.

Answers on p. 215

Free market economies, mixed economy and command economy

Economies may approach the economic problem of scarcity and of answering the questions of what to produce, how to produce, and how the goods produced should be allocated in different ways as described below.

Free market economies

REVISED

The **free market economy** is one in which the above questions are determined by market forces. The main characteristics of such economies are:

- Private ownership of resources.
- Market forces, i.e. supply and demand determine prices.
- Producers aim to maximise profits.
- Consumers aim to maximise satisfaction.
- Resources are allocated by the price mechanism.

In his book *The Wealth of Nations*, written in 1776, **Adam Smith** suggested that when individuals follow their own self-interest, they indirectly promote the good of society. Consequently, the free market economy would result in an ordered market with producers responding to changes in consumer wants in such a way that there was little waste. Smith believed that the role of the government should be limited to providing public goods such as defence and justice.

In the twentieth century **Frederich Hayek** offered a strong defence of the free market along with support for private property. Further, he argued in his book *The Road to Serfdom* that attempts by governments to determine the answers to the questions what to produce, how to produce and for whom, were doomed to failure. State planning would require force and involve restrictions on freedom.

Now test yourself

11 Identify four characteristics of a free market economy.

Answer on p. 215

Command economy

REVISED

The **command or centrally planned economy** is one in which the above questions are determined by the state. The main characteristics of such economies are:

- Public (state) ownership of resources.
- Price determination by the state.
- Producers aim to meet production targets set by the state.
- Resources are allocated by the state.
- There is greater equality of income and wealth than in a free market economy.

Writing in the nineteenth century, **Karl Marx** thought that capitalism was inherently unstable because workers are exploited by the bourgeoisie (the owners of the factors of production). Ultimately, there would be a proletariat revolution in which communism would result.

Mixed economy

REVISED

The mixed economy is a mixture of the free market economy and the command economy. In practice, there are no absolutely free market or command economies: most are mixed economies. In these economies, some resources are allocated by the price mechanism while others are allocated by the state. What differs between countries is the degree of that mix.

Typical mistake

Assuming that there is government intervention in a free market economy.

Exam tip

A **free market economy** refers to all the buyers and sellers of a product or service who determine its price.

A **command economy or centrally planned economy** is one in which resources are allocated by the state.

A **mixed market economy** is a combination of a free market economy and a command economy.

Advantages and disadvantages of free market economies

REVISED

Advantages

The main advantages of free market economies include:

- **Consumer sovereignty** — this implies that spending decisions by consumers determine what is produced.
- **Flexibility** — the free market system can respond quickly to changes in consumer wants.
- **No officials** are needed to allocate resources.
- **Competition** and the profit motive help to promote an efficient allocation of resources.
- **Increased choice** for consumers compared with a command economy.
- **Economic and political freedom** for consumers and producers to own resources.

Now test yourself

TESTED

12 What is meant by 'consumer sovereignty'?
13 Outline three other advantages of a free market economy.

Answers on p. 215

Disadvantages

Disadvantages associated with free market economies include:

- **Inequality** — those who own resources are likely to become richer than those who do not own resources.
- **Trade cycles** — free market economies may suffer from instability in the form of booms and slumps.
- **Imperfect information** — consumers may be unable to make rational choices if they have inadequate information or if there is asymmetric information (see p.57).
- **Monopolies** — there is a danger that a firm may become the sole supplier of a product and then exploit consumers by charging prices higher than the free market equilibrium.
- **Externalities** — these are costs and benefits to third parties which are not taken into account when goods are produced and consumed.

Exam tip

When thinking about the advantages and disadvantages of a free market economy, consider the impact on individuals, businesses and the whole economy.

Now test yourself

TESTED

14 Why does inequality occur in a free market economy?
15 Outline three other disadvantages of a free market economy.

Answers on p. 215

Advantages and disadvantages of command economies

REVISED

Advantages

The main advantages of command economies include:

- **Greater equality** — the state can ensure that everyone can enjoy a minimum standard of living and that no one is extremely rich.
- **Macroeconomic stability** — the state can ensure that booms and slumps are smoothed out.
- **External benefits and external costs** may be taken into account when planning production.
- **No exploitation** — there is no exploitation of workers and consumers by privately owned monopolies.
- **Full employment** — the state can ensure that all workers are employed.

Disadvantages

Disadvantages associated with command economies include:

- **Inefficiency** — the absence of the profit motive and competition may result in an inefficient allocation of resources.
- **Lack of incentives to take risks** — again the absence of the profit motive may reduce incentives for investment.
- **Restrictions on freedom of choice** — people would be directed into the jobs deemed to be needed by the state.
- **Shortages and surpluses** — if the state miscalculates supply and demand then there may be excess demand and/or excess supply of goods and services.

Now test yourself

TESTED

16 Who is responsible for allocating resources in a command economy?
17 Identify two advantages of a command economy.
18 Why might there be inefficiency in a command economy?

Answers on pp. 215–6

The role of the state in a mixed economy

REVISED

The state performs a variety of roles, many of which depend on the political priorities of the ruling party. However, in most economies, the state has a number of key roles which include the following to a greater or lesser degree:

- defence and internal security
- provision of public goods
- provision of essential public services, e.g. education and health
- redistribution of income from the rich to the poor

Revision activity

1 Investigate the characteristics of the North Korean economy and identify which economic system it most closely resembles.
2 Make a list of the characteristics of a mixed economy.
3 Draw up a list of the advantages and disadvantages of a mixed economy.

Exam practice

1 (a) **Statement 1:** 'Child benefit can no longer be received if one person in the household earns more than £60 000 a year.'
Statement 2: 'Only those people on low incomes should receive child benefit.'
Which of the following best describes the two statements above?
A both statements are positive.
B statement 1 is positive and Statement 2 is normative.
C both statements are normative.
D statement 1 is normative and Statement 2 is positive. [1]
(b) With reference to Statement 2 above, explain why economists might disagree about an economic policy. [3]

2 (a) An increase in specialisation and the division of labour is most likely to:
A reduce the amount of machinery used in production
B increase the cost of training an individual worker
C reduce total output
D increase output per worker [1]
(b) Explain the disadvantages to an individual worker of having a highly specialist job. [3]

3 (a) Explain two possible problems faced by a command economy. [3]
(b) One function of the price mechanism in a free market economy is to:
A stabilise prices
B enable the government to set prices
C ration scarce goods
D reduce consumer surplus [1]

4 (a) A reason why a person might switch her energy supplier from Company X to Company Y which is supplying gas and electricity more cheaply is that:
A She believes that prices charged by Company Y will rise in the future.
B She is unable to calculate the potential benefits of switching suppliers.
C Company X, her current energy supplier, will reduce its prices next year.
D She is behaving rationally. [1]
(b) Explain why another person may not switch his energy supplier even though competitors are charging lower prices. [3]

Answers and quick quiz 1 online

ONLINE

Summary

You should have an understanding of:

- What economics is.
- The four key factors of production: land, labour, capital and enterprise.
- The meaning of scarcity and the need to make choices.
- The difference between consumer goods and services and capital goods and services.
- The difference between labour intensive production and capital intensive production.
- Opportunity cost and its significance for individuals, firms and the government.
- The distinction between free goods and economic goods.
- Positive and normative economic statements.
- Production possibility frontiers including the ability to draw them accurately.
- The use of PPFs to illustrate opportunity cost and economic growth.
- Factors which can cause an inward or outward shift in the PPF.
- The meaning of specialisation and the division of labour.
- Advantages and disadvantages of the division of labour.
- Free market, command and mixed economies.

2 How markets work

Rational decision-making

The standard neoclassical analysis makes two very significant assumptions about the ways in which consumers and firms behave:

- Consumers act rationally by aiming to maximise their **utility** (satisfaction).
- Firms also act rationally by aiming to maximise profits.

These assumptions provide a powerful tool for analysis and much of this chapter explores how this can be applied in theory and in real world examples. The analysis that follows is based on these assumptions and can provide some invaluable insights for businesses and governments. However, some economists have criticised the validity of these assumptions, and this has led to the development of a new branch of economics called 'behavioural economics'. This will be considered at the end of this chapter.

Utility refers to the level of satisfaction a consumer receives from the consumption of a product or service.

Demand

Demand refers to the amount demanded by consumers at given prices over a certain period of time. It is important to include a reference to prices and to the time period in a definition of demand.

Demand is not the same as 'want' — 'wanting' a product which cannot be afforded is not demand. Demand must include the ability to pay for the product or service.

Demand is how much is demanded at each price over a certain period of time.

Typical mistake

Confusing 'want' with 'demand': 'wants' refer to desires, and desires may be unaffordable, whereas 'demand' is backed by money.

Shape of the demand curve

REVISED

Figure 2.1 shows that the demand curve is downward sloping from left to right indicating that more will be demanded as price falls.

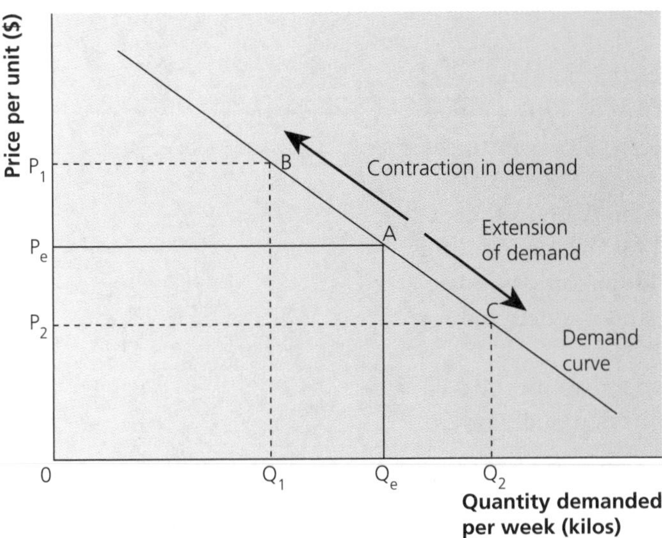

Figure 2.1 Movements along a demand curve

The demand curve demonstrates how a fall in price will cause an increase in the quantity demanded (or an extension in demand) and a rise in price will cause a decrease in quantity demanded (or contraction in demand).

This is based on:

- **The substitution effect:** when there is a rise in price, the consumer (whose income has remained the same) will tend to buy more of a relatively lower-priced good and less of a higher-priced one.
- **The income effect:** when there is a rise in price, consumers will suffer a fall in their real incomes, i.e. purchasing power of their money incomes. With normal goods, the fall in real incomes will reduce the quantity demanded so the income effect reduces the substitution effect.

Movements along the demand curve

REVISED

It may be seen from Figure 2.1 that movements along a demand curve would be caused by price changes. Given that the demand curve has a negative slope, then a rise in price would cause a fall in quantity demanded and a fall in price would cause a rise in quantity demanded.

Revision activity

Construct a demand curve on graph paper based on the following information:

Price per kilo ($)	Quantity of soya demanded per week (kilos)
10	100 000
9	120 000
8	140 000
7	160 000
6	180 000
5	200 000

Shifts in the demand curve

REVISED

Various factors can cause a shift in the whole demand curve. These include changes in:

- **Real incomes.** An increase in real incomes implies that incomes (after discounting the effects of inflation) have increased. This would result in an increase in demand for most goods and services, causing a rightward shift in the demand curve.
- **Size or age distribution of the population.** An increase in the size of the population will cause an increase in demand for most goods and services. An ageing population would cause demand for some goods and services to rise, e.g. sheltered accommodation, and the demand for others to fall, e.g. clothes for teenagers.
- **Tastes, fashions or preferences.** For example, a decrease in the popularity of cabbage will cause a leftward shift in its demand curve.

- **Prices of substitutes or complements.** If there is a change in the price of a related good, it will affect the demand curve for the product. For example, if the price of beef rises, then the demand for a substitute such as lamb will increase. In contrast, if there is a rise in the price of petrol (a complement to cars), then the demand curve for cars would shift to the left.
- **The amount of advertising or promotion.** A successful advertising campaign would cause an increase in demand.
- **Interest rates** affect the cost of borrowing money. For example, a rise in interest rates increases the cost of borrowing money for mortgages, so causing a decrease in demand for houses.

Exam tip

It is only when there is a change in the conditions of demand that the whole demand curve shifts. Price changes cause a movement along an existing demand curve.

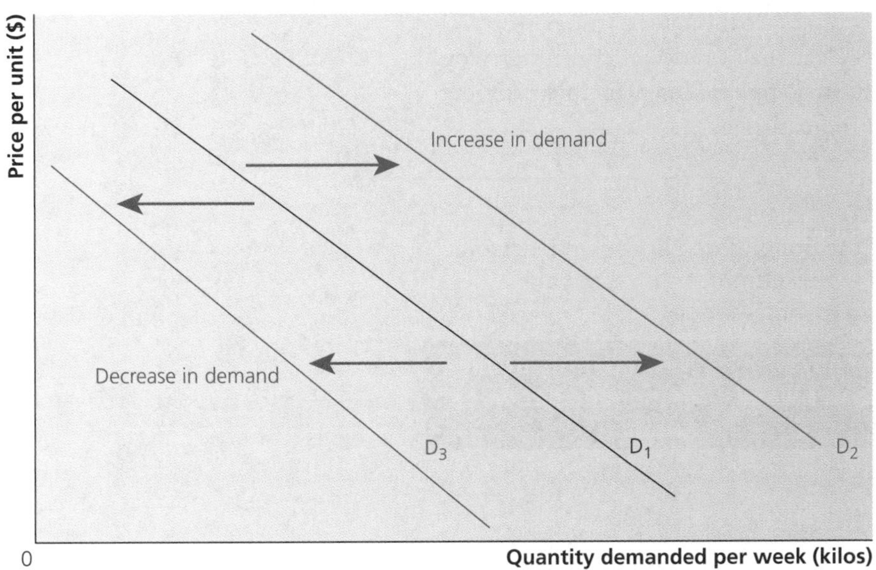

Figure 2.2 Shifts in the demand curve

Figure 2.2 illustrates how an increase in demand would cause the whole demand curve to shift to the right, whereas a decrease in demand would cause the whole demand curve to shift to the left.

The concept of diminishing marginal utility and its influence on the demand curve

REVISED

This principle is based on the idea that consumers gain satisfaction or utility from the goods they consume. **Total utility** represents the total satisfaction gained from the total amount of a product consumed, whereas **marginal utility** represents the change in utility from consuming an additional unit of the product.

The principle of diminishing marginal utility states that, as a person consumes more and more of a product, the marginal utility (extra satisfaction or benefit) falls. Consequently, people are prepared to pay less as their consumption increases with the result that there will be an inverse relationship between the price and quantity demanded.

Total utility is the amount of satisfaction a person derives from the total amount of a product consumed.

Marginal utility is the change in total utility from consuming an extra unit of a product.

The law of diminishing marginal utility states that, as consumption of a product is increased, the consumer's utility increases but at a decreasing or diminishing rate.

The following example shows the utility gained from consuming apples.

Number of apples	Total utility	Marginal utility
1	20	20
2	34	14
3	44	10
4	50	6
5	52	2

The table shows that as a person consumes more and more apples to satisfy her hunger, total utility increases but the marginal utility gained from consuming each extra apple decreases. If monetary values were assigned to marginal utility then it is clear that a rational consumer would be prepared to pay less for each additional apple. This principle provides the basis for the quantity demanded increasing as price falls.

Revision activity

Suppose an increase in the size of the population causes an increase in the demand for soya. Construct a new demand curve on your previous graph based on the following information:

Price per kilo ($)	Quantity of soya demanded per week (kilos)	New quantity of soya demanded per week (kilos)
10	100000	120000
9	120000	140000
8	140000	160000
7	160000	180000
6	180000	200000
5	200000	220000

Now test yourself

TESTED

1 (a) Define the term 'demand'.
(b) What would be the effect of the following on the demand for houses in the UK?
(i) an increase in immigration into the UK
(ii) a decrease in real incomes
(iii) an increase in the price of rented accommodation
(iv) a rise in mortgage interest rates

Answers on p. 216

Price elasticity of demand (PED)

Price elasticity of demand is a measure of the responsiveness of quantity demanded for a product to a change in its price.

Price elasticity of demand measures the sensitivity of the quantity demanded of a product to a change in its own price.

Measurement price elasticity of demand

REVISED

$$\text{PED} = \frac{\text{percentage change in quantity demanded}}{\text{percentage change in price}}$$

Typical mistake

Calculating PED using absolute changes rather than percentage changes.

Exam tip

To calculate a percentage change in, say, quantity demanded, it is necessary to divide the change in quantity demanded by the original quantity demanded and multiply the result by 100.

Calculations of PED and interpretation of results

REVISED

PED will always have a negative value because price and quantity move in opposite directions (since the demand curve is downward sloping).

Examples

Price inelastic demand

Suppose a 100% increase in the price of oil led to a 20% fall in quantity demanded, then PED would be:

$$\frac{-20}{+100} = -0.2$$

Demand is said to be price inelastic (or relatively price inelastic) because a change in price has led to a smaller percentage change in quantity demanded.

When demand is price inelastic, the value of PED will be between 0 and –1.

Price elastic demand

Suppose a 5% decrease in the price of a package holiday to Florida led to a 20% increase in quantity demanded, then PED would be:

$$\frac{+20}{-5} = -4.0$$

Demand is said to be price elastic (or relatively price elastic) because a change in price has led to a larger percentage change in quantity demanded.

When demand is price elastic, the value of PED will be greater than –1.

Exam tip

When considering whether demand is price elastic or price inelastic, compare the percentage changes in price and quantity. If the percentage change in quantity demanded is larger than the percentage price change, then demand is price elastic.

Figures 2.3a and 2.3b illustrate an inelastic and an elastic segment of a demand curve:

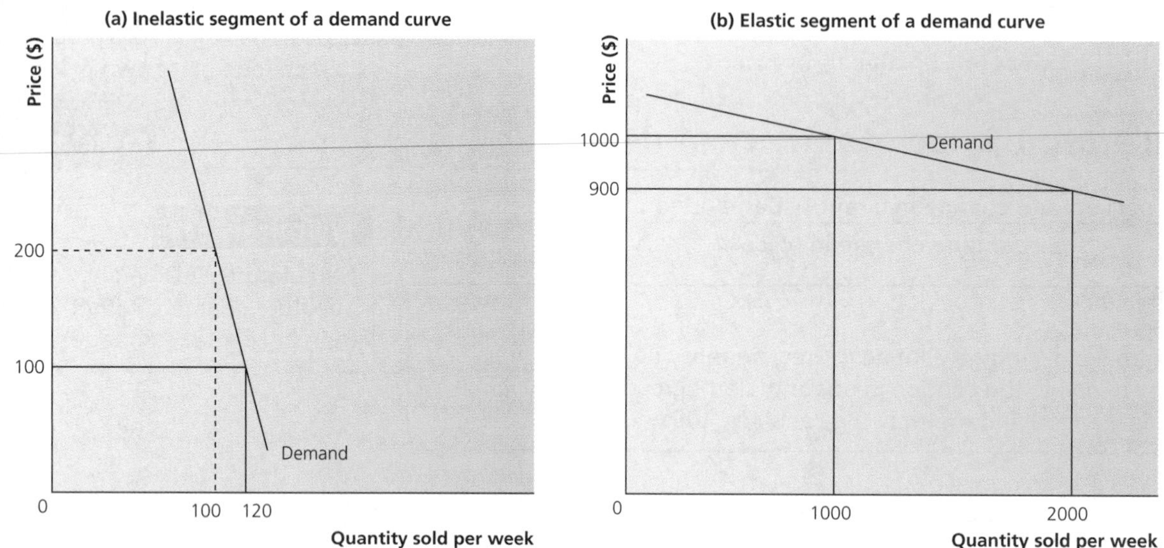

Figure 2.3 An inelastic and an elastic segment of a demand curve

Unit elastic demand

Suppose a 15% decrease in the price of a digital camera led to a 15% increase in quantity demanded, then PED would be:

$$\frac{+15}{-15} = -1.0$$

Demand is said to be unit elastic because a change in price has led to the same percentage change in quantity demanded.

When demand is unit elastic, the value of PED will be equal to –1 and the demand curve will be a rectangular hyperbola (see Figure 2.4).

Perfectly inelastic demand

Suppose a 10% increase in the price of salt led to no change in the quantity demanded, then PED would be:

$$\frac{0}{10} = 0.0$$

Demand is said to be perfectly price inelastic because a change in price has had no effect on quantity demanded.

When demand is perfectly price inelastic, the value of PED will be 0 and the demand curve will be vertical (see Figure 2.4).

Perfectly elastic demand

Suppose a small increase in the price of a product causes the quantity demanded to fall to zero, then demand is said to be perfectly elastic.

When demand is perfectly elastic, the value of PED would be minus infinity and the demand curve will be horizontal (see Figure 2.4).

> **Exam tip**
>
> Think of perfectly inelastic demand as a set amount demanded whatever the price. The demand curve must therefore be vertical.

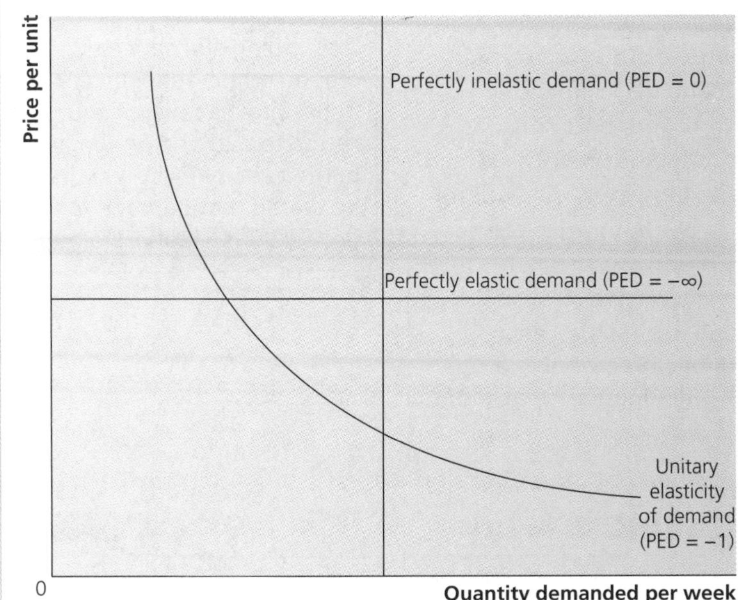

Figure 2.4 Demand curves showing unitary elasticity, perfectly inelastic and perfectly elastic demand

Now test yourself

TESTED

2 Calculate price elasticity of demand in the following examples and comment on your results:
 (a) A rise in the price of electricity from 25 pence to 30 pence per unit causes the quantity demanded to fall from 10 000 kilos to 9000 kilos.
 (b) A rise in the price of gold watches from $1000 to $1100 causes demand to fall from 200 to 170 per week.
 (c) A 6% reduction in the price of tomatoes causes a 6% increase in quantity demanded.

Answers on p. 216

Factors influencing price elasticity of demand

REVISED

Factors which influence the price elasticity of demand include:

- **Availability of substitutes:** if substitutes are available there will be a strong incentive to shift consumption to them when the price of the product rises. The existence of substitutes will therefore tend to make demand for the product elastic.
- **Proportion of income spent on a product:** if only a small percentage of income is spent on a product such as salt then demand will tend to be inelastic, whereas if a high percentage of income is spent on the product then demand will tend to be elastic, e.g. exotic holidays and works of art by famous artists.
- **Nature of the product**: if the product is addictive, e.g. alcohol and tobacco, then demand will tend to be inelastic.
- **Durability of the product:** if the product is long-lasting and hard-wearing, e.g. furniture and cars, then demand will be fairly elastic since it is possible to postpone purchases. However, demand for non-durable goods, e.g. milk and petrol, will tend to be inelastic because these must be replaced regularly.

- **Length of time under consideration:** it usually takes time for consumers to adjust their expenditure patterns following a price change. For example, it will take time for motorists to switch from fuel-greedy to more fuel-efficient cars. Consequently, demand is usually more price elastic in the long run than in the short run.
- **Breadth of definition of a product:** if a product is broadly defined, e.g. fruit, demand is likely to be price inelastic. However, demand for particular types of fruit, e.g. apples, is likely to be more price elastic.

Exam tip

It is not helpful to use the idea of luxuries and necessities as a factor influencing price elasticity of demand because what is a necessity or a luxury changes over time. This distinction is far too imprecise to have any value.

Typical mistake

Describing a product as elastic or inelastic: this is imprecise because it could relate to demand or supply. In the case of PED, it should be stated that demand for product X is elastic/inelastic.

Price elasticity of demand and total revenue

REVISED

There are key relationships between price elasticity of demand and **total revenue** (TR):

- When **demand is inelastic**, a price change causes total revenue to change in the **same direction**.
- When **demand is elastic**, a price change causes total revenue to change in the **opposite direction**.
- When **demand is unit elastic**, a price change causes total revenue to **remain unchanged**.
- When **demand is perfectly inelastic**, a price change causes total revenue to change in the **same direction by the same proportion**.
- When **demand is perfectly elastic**, a price rise causes total revenue to **fall to zero**.

Total revenue is the value of goods sold by a firm and is calculated by multiplying price times quantity sold.

Typical mistake

To conclude that if a price change has no effect on total revenue, the demand is perfectly inelastic. This is incorrect: for total revenue to remain constant following a price change, there must have been an exactly proportionate change in quantity demanded. In other words, demand is unit elastic.

Revision activity

The PED varies along a straight-line demand curve. You can check this yourself by completing the following table:

Price per unit (£)	Quantity demanded per week (kilos)	Total revenue	PED
10	10		
9	20		
8	30		
7	40		
6	50		
5	60		
4	70		
3	80		
2	90		
1	100		

Significance of PED for firms

REVISED

If firms know that demand for their product is price inelastic then they know that they can increase total revenue by increasing price.

However, if firms know that demand is price elastic, then they can increase total revenue by reducing price. For example, if there are a lot of restaurants in a high street then one of these might have special offers on certain days, knowing that this will increase its revenue.

Significance of PED for the government

REVISED

If the government wishes to maximise its tax revenue then it will place indirect taxes on those products whose demand is price inelastic, e.g. goods such as alcohol, petrol and tobacco. However, in this case the consumer will bear most of the tax burden.

The government may therefore also tax products and services whose demand is price elastic, in which case the producers will bear a higher proportion of the tax burden.

Now test yourself

TESTED

3 If the demand for petrol is price inelastic, what will happen to the total revenue of a garage selling petrol following an increase in price?
4 If a rise in the price of gold jewellery leads to a fall in the total revenue of shops selling this type of jewellery, what can be deduced about price elasticity of demand?
5 An increase in the price of iPads has no effect on total revenue. What can be inferred about the price elasticity of demand?
6 Why is demand for a particular brand of rice likely to be price elastic?
7 Would you expect demand for coffee to be price elastic or inelastic?
8 Why might demand for milk be price inelastic?

Answers on p. 216

Cross elasticity of demand (XED)

The meaning of cross elasticity of demand (XED)

REVISED

Cross elasticity of demand is a measure of the responsiveness of quantity demanded for one product (Y) to a change in the price of another product (X).

Cross elasticity of demand is the sensitivity of demand for one product to a change in the price of another product.

Measuring cross elasticity of demand

REVISED

$$\text{XED} = \frac{\text{percentage change in quantity demanded of product Y}}{\text{percentage change in price of product X}}$$

Interpreting results

Again for XED, the sign is very significant.

- A **positive sign** indicates that the products are **substitutes**, e.g. a rise in the price of one product will cause an increase in demand for another product.
- A **negative sign** indicates that the products are complements, e.g. a rise in the price of one product will cause a decrease in demand for another product.

Exam tip

If the cross elasticity of demand is close to zero then it implies that the products are not closely related.

Typical mistake

Misinterpreting the result of a calculation of XED. The key point is that if the result is positive, then the goods are substitutes and if negative then the goods are complements.

Value to businesses

REVISED

A knowledge of cross elasticity of demand is helpful to businesses in setting prices for their products. For example, if the firm is selling a product with a close substitute then it would expect demand for its product to fall considerably if it decided to increase its price.

Firms also know that complementary goods can command high prices. For example, printers are often relatively cheap but the ink cartridges required for them are relatively expensive because a certain type is required for each particular printer.

Income elasticity of demand (YED)

Income elasticity of demand is a measure of the responsiveness of quantity demanded for a product to a change in real income.

Income elasticity of demand is the sensitivity of demand for a product to a change in real income. Note: real income discounts the effects of inflation.

Measuring income elasticity of demand

REVISED

$$\text{YED} = \frac{\text{percentage change in quantity demanded}}{\text{percentage change in real income}}$$

Interpreting results

For YED, the sign is very significant. A **positive sign** indicates that the product is a **normal good**, i.e. a rise (fall) in real income will cause an increase (decrease) in demand.

Examples

Income elastic demand

If a 5% increase in real income leads to a 25% increase in demand then

$$\text{YED} = \frac{25}{5} = +5$$

Demand is income elastic because the change in real income has led to a more than proportionate change in demand. Whenever YED is greater than +1, demand is income elastic.

Income inelastic demand

If a 10% increase in income causes a 3% increase in demand then

$$\text{YED} = \frac{3}{10} = +0.3$$

Demand is income inelastic because the change in real income has led to a less than proportionate change in demand. Whenever YED is between 0 and +1, demand is income inelastic.

Inferior goods

A **negative sign** indicates that the product is an **inferior good**, e.g. a rise in real income leads to a fall in demand for the product.

If a 6% increase in real income resulted in a 3% fall in demand then YED would be negative:

$$\text{YED} = \frac{-3}{+6} = -0.5$$

As the name suggests, inferior goods are those for which consumption will decline as real incomes increase because consumers can now afford better, higher-quality alternatives.

Typical mistake

Misinterpreting the result of a calculation of YED. The key point is that if the result is positive, then it is a normal good but if the result is negative then the good is an inferior good.

Exam tip

Inferior goods (those with a negative YED) are usually low-quality goods with more expensive substitutes.

The relationship between demand and income may be illustrated diagrammatically. For a normal good there is a positive relationship between income and demand but for an inferior good the relationship is negative as shown in Figures 2.5a and 2.5b.

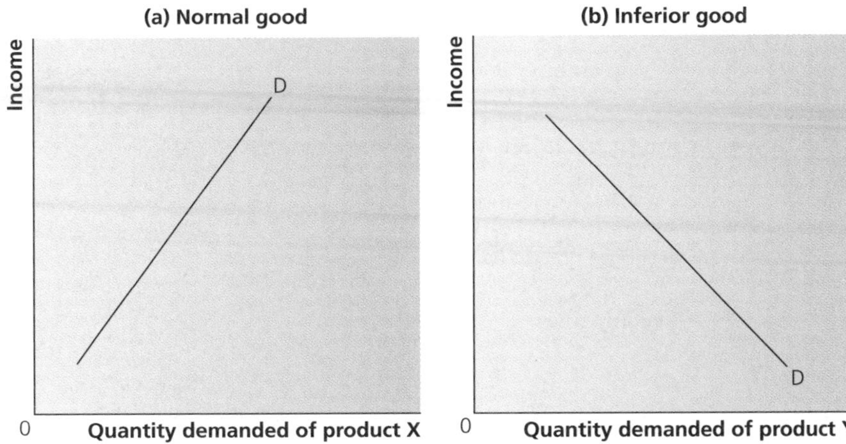

Figure 2.5 The relationship between demand and income

Exam tip

Note that to illustrate normal and inferior goods, income must be on the vertical axis.

Significance of YED for firms

REVISED

If firms know that demand for their product is income inelastic then they know that demand and total revenue will increase significantly during periods of rapid economic growth but fall significantly during recessions. Consequently, knowledge of income elasticity of demand may be important for firms when making investment decisions.

Significance of YED for the government

REVISED

If the government wishes to maximise its tax revenue during an economic boom it will place indirect taxes on those products whose demand is income elastic. Knowledge of income elasticity of demand might also help the government in estimating tax revenues from indirect taxes on particular goods and services.

Now test yourself

TESTED

9 (a) For each of the following calculate the cross elasticity of demand and comment on your answer:
   (i) A 10% increase in the price of tea causes a 15% rise in the demand for coffee.
   (ii) A 5% increase in the price of product Y causes a 10% decrease in the demand for product X.
  (b) If a 7% increase in the price of good X causes a 7% increase in the demand for good Y then:
   A Goods X and Y are complements.
   B The price elasticity of demand for good X is 1.
   C Goods X and Y and substitutes.
   D Cross elasticity of demand is –1.

10 For each of the following, calculate the income elasticity of demand and comment on your answer:
   (a) A 3% decrease in real incomes causes a 9% fall in the demand for new cars.
   (b) A 5% increase in real incomes causes a 2% fall in demand for soya.
   (c) A 10% increase in real incomes causes a 2% increase in the demand for oranges.

Answers on p. 216

Supply

Supply refers to the amount supplied by producers at given prices over a certain period of time. As with demand, it is important to include a reference to prices and to the time period in the definition.

Supply refers to how much is supplied at each price over a certain period of time.

Shape of the supply curve

REVISED

Figure 2.6 shows that the supply curve is upward sloping from left to right, indicating that more will be supplied as price increases.

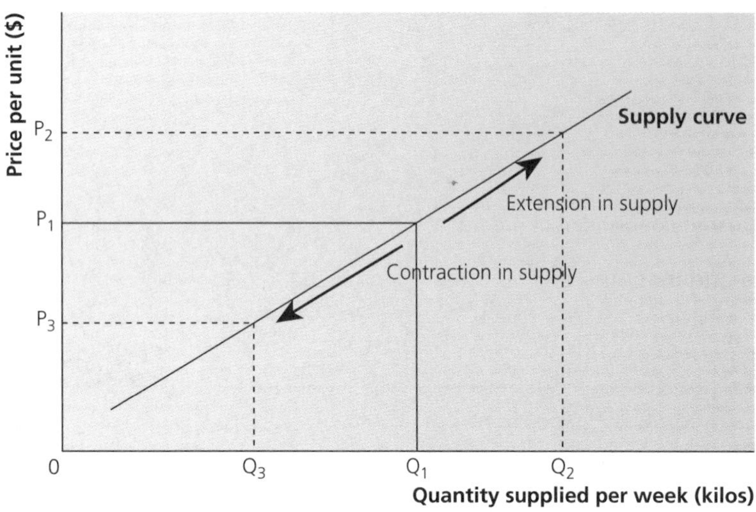

Figure 2.6 Movements along a supply curve

When the price rises it becomes more profitable for producers to supply a product and so they have an incentive to increase production. In contrast, when there is a fall in price it becomes less profitable to supply a product and so firms will reduce output and/or exit the market.

Therefore:

- a rise in price will cause an increase in the quantity supplied (or an extension in supply) and
- a fall in price will cause a decrease in quantity supplied (or contraction in supply)

Revision activity

Construct a supply curve on graph paper based on the following information:

Price per kilo ($)	Quantity of soya supplied per week (kilos)
10	200000
9	180000
8	160000
7	140000
6	120000
5	100000

Movements along the supply curve

REVISED

It may be seen from Figure 2.6 that movements along a supply curve are caused by price changes. Given that the supply curve has a positive slope, then a rise in price will cause a rise in quantity supplied and a fall in price will cause a fall in quantity supplied.

Shifts in the supply curve

REVISED

Various factors will cause a shift in the whole supply curve. These include changes in:

- **Costs of production.** These include wages, raw materials, energy and rent. An increase in costs of production, such as electricity prices, will cause the whole supply curve to shift to the left.
- **Productivity of the workforce.** Labour productivity refers to the output per worker per hour worked. If there is a rise in productivity then the whole supply curve will shift to the right.
- **Indirect taxes.** An indirect tax raises the cost of supply and so causes the supply curve to shift to the left. A rise in VAT will cause the supply curve to become steeper because it is a percentage of the price of a product, whereas a rise in a specific tax, e.g. 20p per unit, will cause a parallel leftward shift in the supply curve.
- **Subsidies.** These are grants to producers from the government which effectively lead to a reduction in costs of production so causing a rightward shift in the supply curve.
- **Technology.** New invention and new technology usually result in an increase in productivity so causing the supply curve to shift to the right.
- **Discoveries of new reserves of a raw material.** If, for example, a country discovers new oil reserves then the supply curve will shift to the right.

Figure 2.7 illustrates that an increase in supply will cause the whole supply curve to shift to the right, whereas a decrease in supply will cause the whole supply curve to shift to the left.

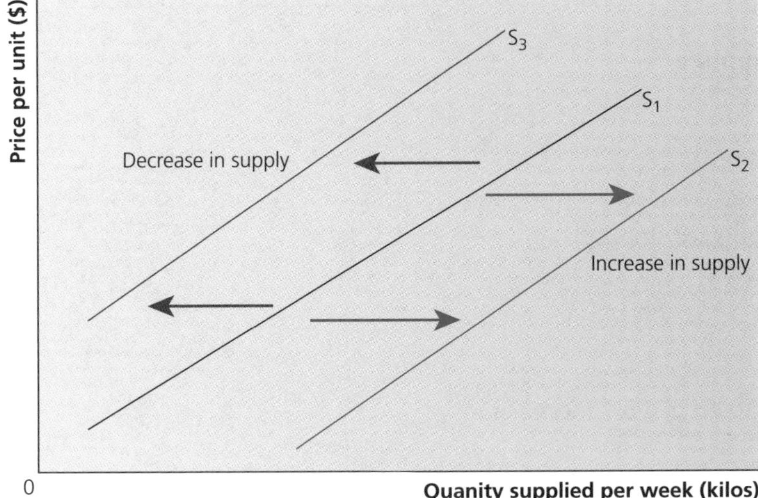

Figure 2.7 Shifts of a supply curve

Exam tip

It is only when there is a change in the conditions of supply that the whole supply curve shifts. Price changes cause a movement along an existing supply curve.

Revision activity

Assume there is a good soya harvest. Construct a new supply curve on graph paper based on the following information:

Price per kilo ($)	Quantity of soya supplied per week (kilos)	New quantity of soya supplied per week (kilos)
10	200000	220000
9	180000	200000
8	160000	180000
7	140000	160000
6	120000	140000
5	100000	120000

Typical mistake

Showing an increase in supply as an upward (leftward) shift. Remember that an increase in supply will cause the supply curve to shift to the right.

Now test yourself

TESTED

11 Define the term 'supply'.

12 What would be the effect of the following on the supply of tea?

(a) a subsidy to tea producers

(b) an increase in wages of tea plantation workers

(c) an increase in productivity of tea workers

(d) a drought in tea growing regions

Answers on p. 216

Price elasticity of supply (PES)

Price elasticity of supply is a measure of the responsiveness of quantity supplied for a product to a change in its price.

Price elasticity of supply is the sensitivity of supply of a product to a change in its price.

Measuring price elasticity of supply

REVISED

$$\text{PES} = \frac{\text{percentage change in quantity supplied}}{\text{percentage change in price}}$$

Interpreting results

PES will always have a positive value because price and quantity move in the same direction (since the supply curve is upward sloping).

Examples

Price inelastic supply

Suppose a 10% increase in the price of wheat led to a 5% increase in quantity supplied, then PES would be:

$$\frac{5}{10} = 0.5$$

Supply is said to be price inelastic (or relatively price inelastic) because a change in price has led to a smaller percentage change in quantity supplied. When supply is price inelastic, the value of PES will be between 0 and 1 (see Figure 2.8).

Price elastic supply

Suppose a 2% decrease in the price of PCs led to 12% decrease in quantity supplied, then PES would be:

$$\frac{12}{2} = 6.0$$

Supply is said to be price elastic (or relatively price elastic) because a change in price has led to a larger percentage change in quantity supplied. When supply is price elastic, the value of PES will be greater than 1 (see Figure 2.8).

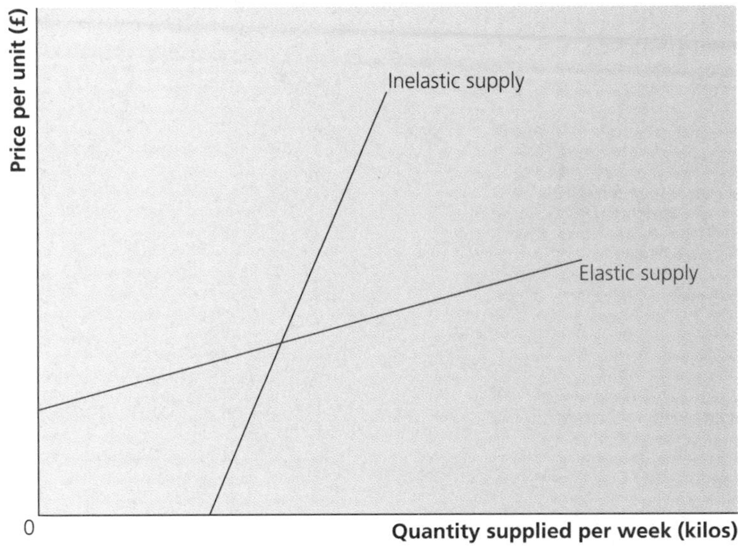

Figure 2.8 Inelastic and elastic supply

Unit elasticity of supply

Suppose a 7% increase in the price of bread led to a 7% increase in quantity supplied, then PES would be:

$$\frac{7}{7} = 1.0$$

Supply is said to be unit elastic because a change in price has led to the same percentage change in quantity supplied. When supply is unit elastic, the value of PES will be equal to 1 and the supply curve will be a straight line drawn through the origin as shown in Figure 2.9.

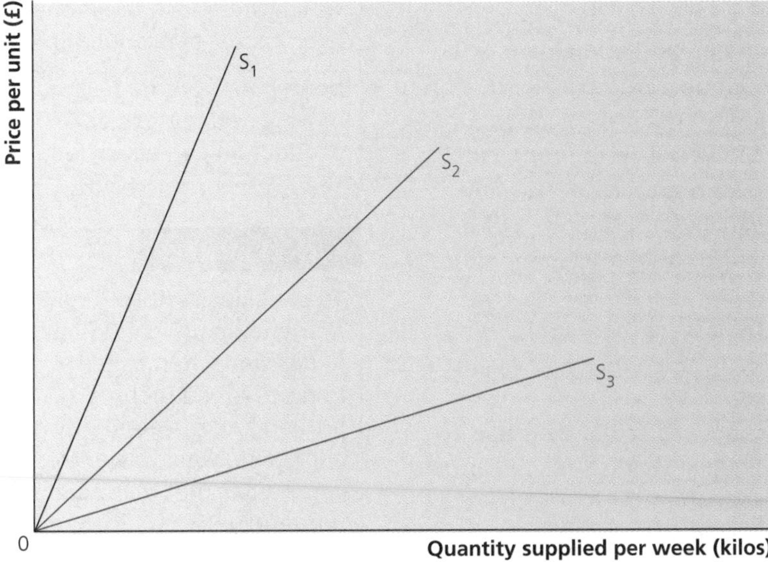

Figure 2.9 Unitary elasticity of supply

Perfectly inelastic and perfectly elastic supply

Suppose a 10% increase in the price of a product led to no change in the quantity supplied, then PES would be

$$\frac{0}{10} = 0.0$$

Supply is said to be perfectly price inelastic because a change in price has had no effect on quantity supplied. When supply is perfectly price inelastic, the value of PES will be 0 and the supply curve will be vertical (see Figure 2.10). On the other hand, if an infinite amount could be supplied at a certain price, then supply is said to be perfectly elastic. When supply is perfectly elastic, the value of PES would be infinity and the supply curve will be horizontal.

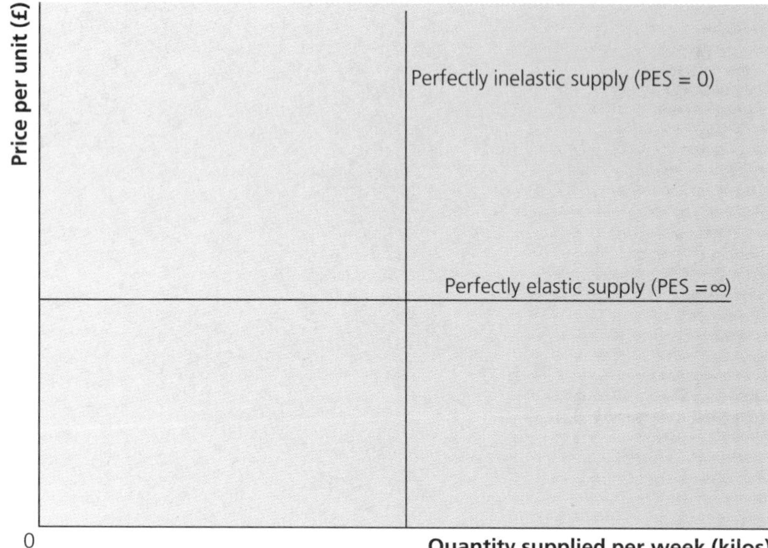

Figure 2.10 Elasticity of supply

Exam tip

A simple rule that applies to all elasticity calculations is that quantity is always the top of the calculation.

Factors influencing price elasticity of supply

REVISED

Factors which influence the price elasticity of supply include:

- **Time.** Elasticity of supply is very likely to vary over time. In economics, the **short run** is defined as that period of time in which at least one factor of production is fixed, whereas the long run is the period of time in which all factors of production are variable. It is often difficult to change supply quickly in response to a price change in the short run, making supply very inelastic. However, in the **long run**, supply is likely to be more elastic because all resources are variable.
- **Stocks.** If stocks of finished goods are available, the supply will be relatively elastic because manufacturers will be able to respond quickly to a price change.
- **Spare capacity**. If a firm has under-utilised machinery and under-employed workers or if it is possible to introduce a new shift or workers, then supply is likely to be elastic.
- **Availability and cost of switching resources from one use to another.** If resources, such as labour, have specific skills or machinery is highly specific, or it is expensive to reallocate resources from one use to another, then supply will be relatively inelastic.

Short run is a time period in which there is at least one fixed factor of production.

Long run is a time period in which all factors of production can be varied.

Typical mistake

To consider factors influencing price elasticity of *demand* when asked to discuss the factors influencing the elasticity of *supply*. To avoid this error, remember that the factors influencing elasticity of supply are those affecting businesses, not consumers.

Now test yourself

TESTED

13 For each of the following calculate the elasticity of supply and comment on your answer:
 (a) A 20% increase in the price of lemons leads to a 2% increase in quantity supplied.
 (b) A 5% fall in the price leads to a 15% reduction in the quantity supplied.
14 Why might you expect the supply of tomatoes to be inelastic?
15 Under what circumstances might the supply of butter be elastic?

Answers on p. 216

Price determination

The **equilibrium** price and output are determined by the interaction of supply and demand (see Figure 2.11).

When the quantity supplied is equal to the quantity demanded of a particular product, equilibrium is said to exist. The equilibrium price and output will not change unless one of the conditions of supply or conditions of demand change.

Equilibrium (price and quantity) is determined by the interaction of the supply and demand curves. The equilibrium price and quantity would not change unless there was a change in the conditions of demand or supply.

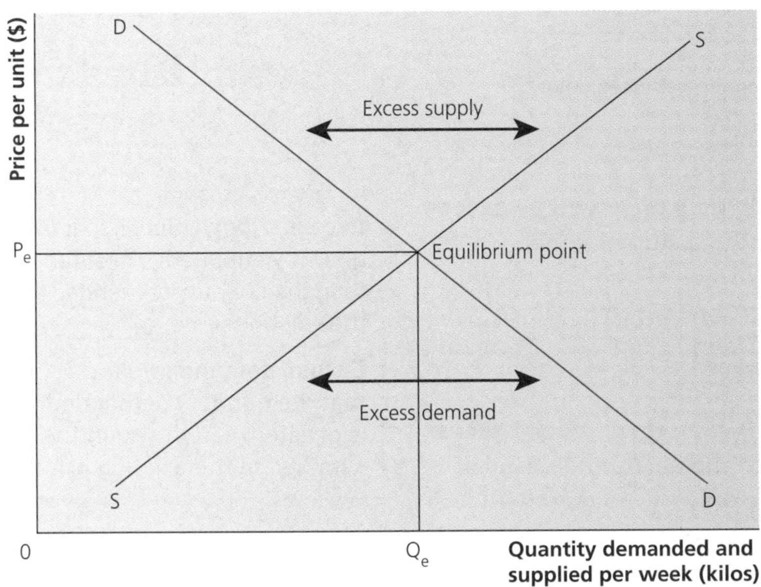

Figure 2.11 Equilibrium price and quantity

Typical mistake

Mislabelling the supply and demand curves. The revision activity should help you to remember that the demand curve is downward sloping from left to right while the supply curve is upward sloping from left to right.

Revision activity

Construct a demand curve and a supply curve on graph paper based on the following information:

Price per kilo ($)	Quantity of soya demanded per week (kilos)	Quantity of soya supplied per week (kilos)
10	100 000	200 000
9	120 000	180 000
8	140 000	160 000
7	160 000	140 000
6	180 000	120 000
5	200 000	100 000

Find the equilibrium point and show the equilibrium price and quantity on your diagram.

Exam tip

Before considering any change in equilibrium price and quantity, you should always begin with a diagram showing the initial equilibrium price and output.

Excess demand and excess supply

REVISED

Figure 2.12 illustrates what happens if the price is not currently at its equilibrium level.

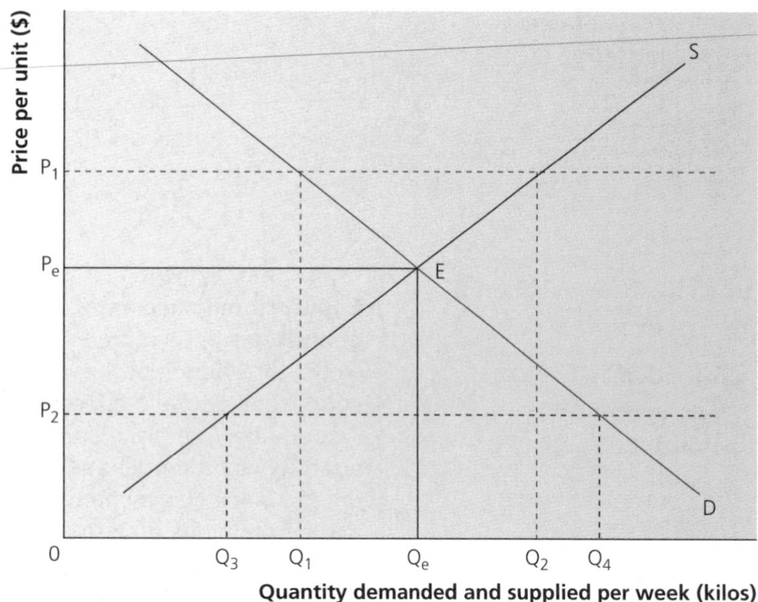

Figure 2.12 Excess demand and excess supply

If the price is above the equilibrium price of P_e then there will be **excess supply**. For example, if the price is at P_1 then the quantity demanded will be only Q_1, while the quantity supplied will be Q_2, so there will be a surplus of Q_1Q_2. Market forces will cause price to fall to P_e which will lead to an extension of demand and a contraction in supply so eliminating the excess supply.

If the price is below the equilibrium price of P_e then there will be **excess demand**. For example, if the price is at P_2 then the quantity demanded will be Q_4 while the quantity supplied will be only Q_3, so there will be a shortage of Q_3Q_4. Market forces will cause price to rise to P_e which will lead to an extension of supply and a contraction in demand so eliminating the excess demand.

Excess supply implies that the quantity supplied is greater than the quantity demanded at the existing price.

Excess demand implies that the quantity demanded is greater than the quantity supplied at the existing price.

Now test yourself

TESTED

16 If the current price is above the free market price, identify whether there is excess supply or excess demand.

17 If the existing market price is above the equilibrium price, explain how equilibrium is restored?

Answers on p. 216

Changes in the equilibrium price

REVISED

A change in the equilibrium price can be caused by:

- a change in the conditions of demand (which would cause the demand curve to shift) or
- a change in the conditions of supply (which would cause the supply curve to shift)

An increase in demand

This would cause a rightward shift in the demand curve, a rise in price and an increase in the quantity as shown Figure 2.13.

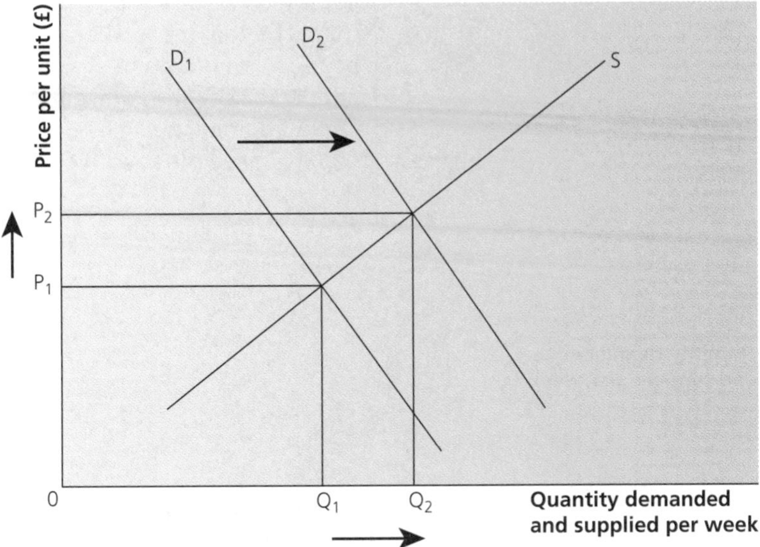

Figure 2.13 An increase in demand

A decrease in demand

This would cause a leftward shift in the demand curve, a fall in price and a decrease in the quantity as shown in Figure 2.14.

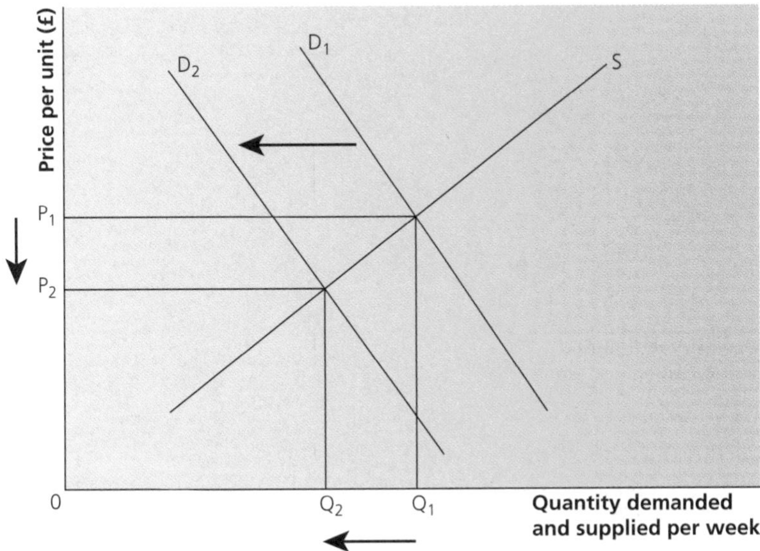

Figure 2.14 A decrease in demand

An increase in supply

This would cause a rightward shift in the supply curve, a fall in price and an increase in the quantity as shown in Figure 2.15.

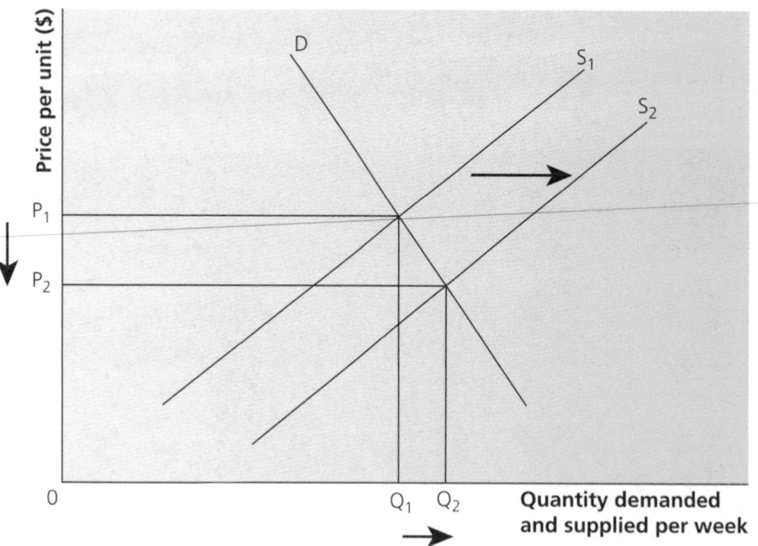

Figure 2.15 An increase in supply

Typical mistake

Assuming that an increase in supply would shift the supply curve upwards (to the left). This is incorrect because an increase in supply means that more is supplied at each price so the supply curve must shift to the right.

A decrease in supply

This would cause a leftward shift in the supply curve, a rise in price and a decrease in the quantity as shown in Figure 2.16.

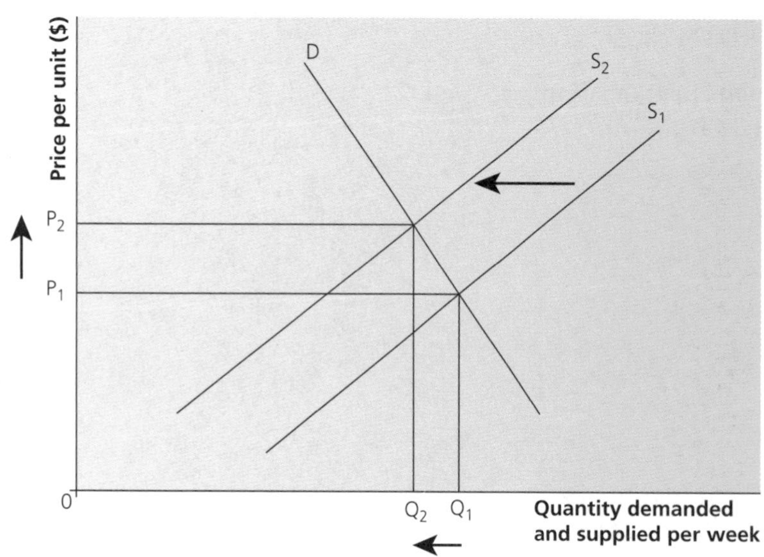

Figure 2.16 A decrease in supply

Typical mistake

Assuming that a decrease in supply would shift the supply curve downwards. This is incorrect because a decrease in supply means that less is supplied at each price so the supply curve must shift to the left.

Now test yourself

TESTED

18 For each of the following explain what happens to the equilibrium price and quantity (you might find it helpful to sketch supply and demand diagrams):

(a) the effect on the price of beef of a rise in the cost of animal feed
(b) a change in tastes in favour of blueberries
(c) the impact on rice of an increase in the productivity of workers harvesting rice
(d) a health scare relating to bananas

Answers on p. 216

The price mechanism

The key functions of the price mechanism in a free market economy may be summarised as follows:

- As a **rationing device** — market forces will ensure that the amount demanded is exactly equal to the amount supplied.
- As an **incentive** — the prospect of making a profit acts as an incentive to firms to produce goods and services.
- As a **signalling device** to producers to increase or decrease the amount supplied.
- To determine **changes in wants** — a change in demand will be reflected in a change in price.

Typical mistake

Assuming that the function of a free market economy is to keep prices stable. While it is true that the forces of supply and demand (market forces) help to determine the equilibrium price, any change in the conditions of supply and demand will cause the equilibrium price to change.

The price mechanism in different types of markets

REVISED

A market refers to all those buyers and sellers of a product or service involved in making exchanges with each other and who help to determine its price. Consequently, markets take on many different forms and do not necessarily operate in one geographical location. They may be local, national or global. For instance, farm shops could be an example of a **local market** since the produce is grown and sold locally. On the other hand, there are **national and/or international markets** for certain goods such as wheat, rice, or certain types of labour, e.g. nurses and teachers. The internet has enabled markets for some goods and services to become much wider because it has made it easier to bring buyers and sellers together.

Consumer and producer surplus

Consumer surplus

REVISED

This refers to the difference between how much a person is willing to pay and how much they actually pay, i.e. the market price. Diagrammatically, the **consumer surplus** is the area under the demand curve and above the market price.

Producer surplus

REVISED

This refers to the difference between how much firms are willing to supply at each price and the market price. Diagrammatically, the **producer surplus** is the area between the supply curve and the market price.

Figure 2.17 illustrates both consumer surplus and producer surplus.

Consumer surplus is the difference between how much consumers are willing to pay and what they actually pay for a product.

Producer surplus is the difference between the cost of supply and the price received by the producer for the product.

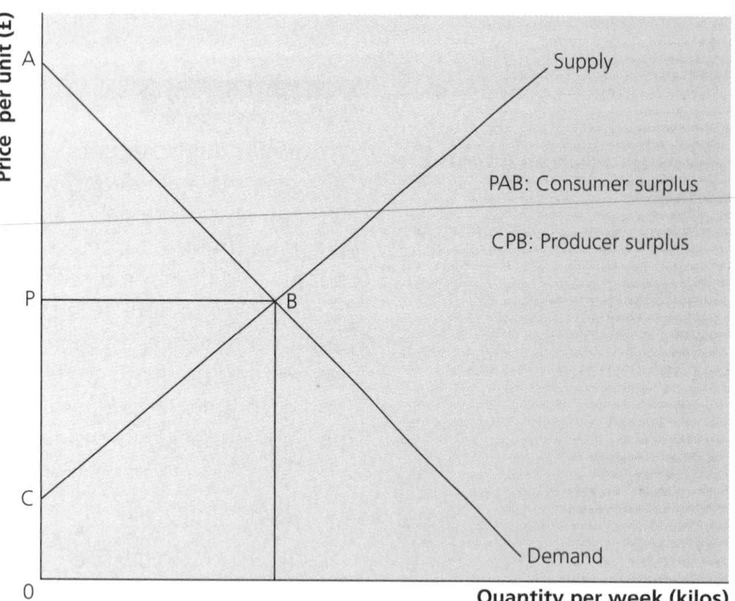

Figure 2.17 Consumer and producer surplus

Typical mistake

Confusing consumer surplus with producer surplus on a diagram. A simple way of avoiding this is to think that producer surplus relates to suppliers and so is the area above the supply curve and below the equilibrium price.

Factors affecting consumer surplus

REVISED

- The gradient of the demand curve: the steeper it is the greater the consumer surplus will be.
- Changes in the conditions of demand. For example, an increase in demand will increase the amount of consumer surplus

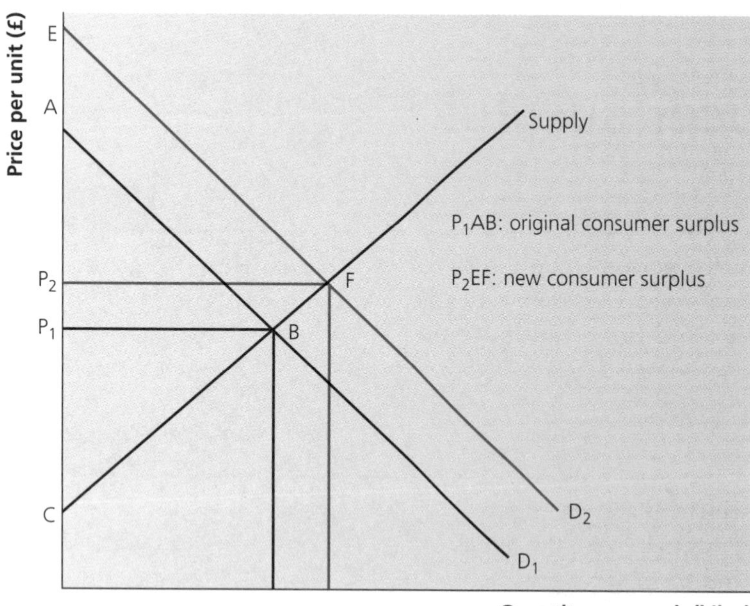

Figure 2.18 Effect of an increase in demand on consumer surplus

Factors affecting producer surplus

REVISED

- The gradient of the supply curve: the steeper it is, the greater the producer surplus will be.
- Changes in the conditions of supply. For example, an increase in supply will increase the amount of producer surplus. This is illustrated Figure 2.19.

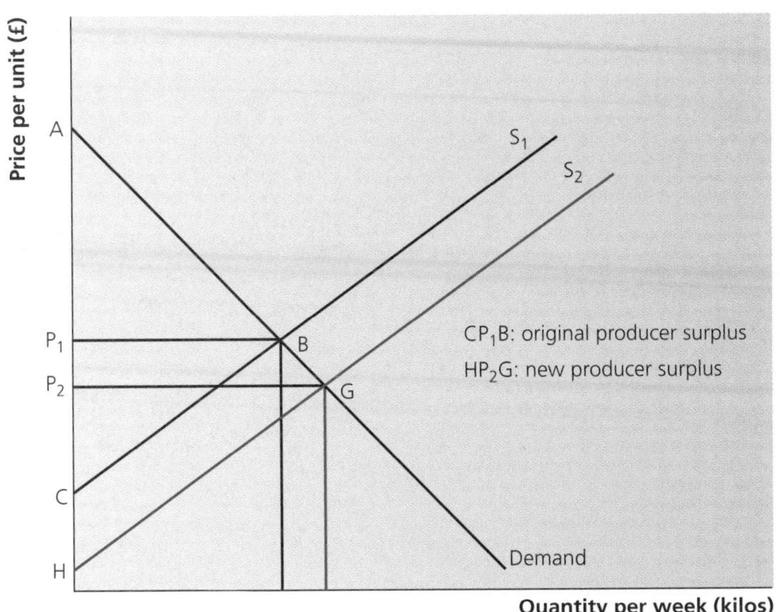

Figure 2.19 Effect of an increase in supply on producer surplus

Indirect taxes and subsidies

Indirect taxes

REVISED

Indirect taxes are taxes on expenditure and include taxes such as Value Added Tax (VAT), excise taxes and taxes on gambling. Such taxes cause an increase in the cost of supply and so cause the supply curve to shift to the left.

There are two types of **indirect taxes**: *ad valorem* and specific.

Indirect taxes are taxes on expenditure.

Ad valorem taxes

REVISED

***Ad valorem* taxes** are a percentage of the price of a product or service and so will cause the supply curve to shift to the left and become steeper than the original supply curve. An example of an *ad valorem* tax is VAT which is currently levied at 20% in the UK.

***Ad valorem* taxes** are a percentage of the *price* of the product.

Specific taxes

REVISED

In contrast, a **specific tax** or flat rate tax is a set amount of tax on each unit consumed. Therefore, the effect of a specific tax is to cause the supply curve to shift to the left, parallel to the original supply curve.

Figure 2.20 illustrates the impact of a specific tax when demand is inelastic.

P_1 is the initial equilibrium price and Q_1 is the initial equilibrium output. An indirect tax will cause the supply curve to shift to the left from S_1 to S_2. In turn, this causes the price to increase to P_2 and the quantity to fall to Q_2. It can be seen that when demand is inelastic the consumer bears a much larger proportion of the tax burden (P_1P_2AB), whereas the producer bears a much smaller part of the tax burden (EP_1BC). This distribution of the tax burden is called the **incidence of tax**. The total tax revenue to the government is, therefore, EP_2AC.

Specific taxes are a set amount per unit of the product.

Incidence of tax relates to how the burden of a tax is distributed between different groups e.g. producers and consumers.

Typical mistake

Assuming that an indirect tax causes the demand curve to shift to the left.

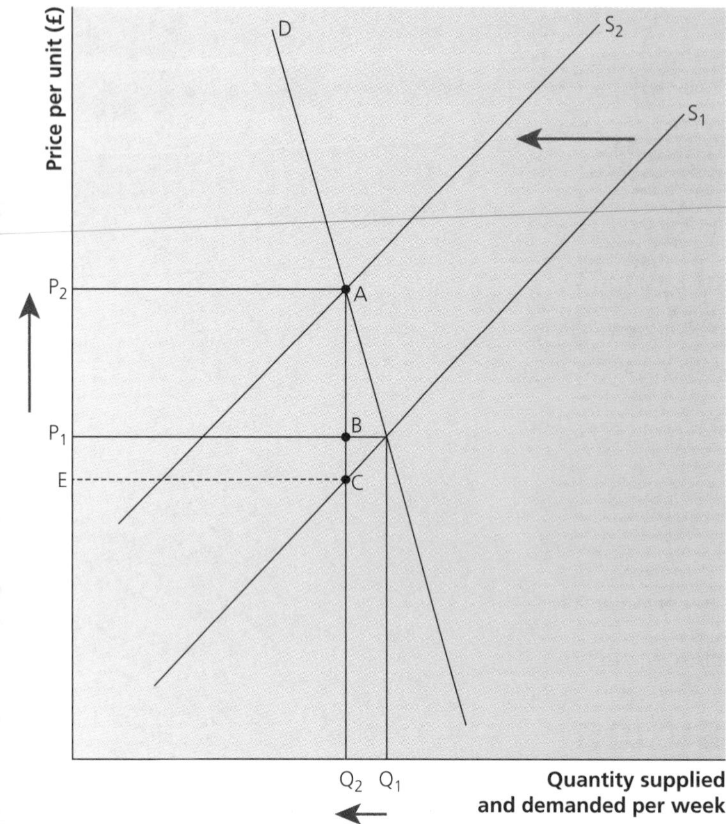

Figure 2.20 Indirect tax when demand is inelastic

In contrast, Figure 2.21 illustrates the impact of a specific tax when demand is elastic.

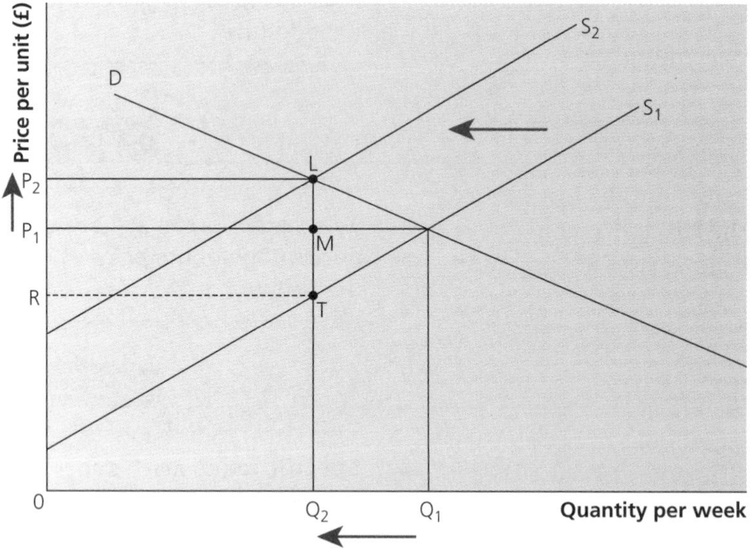

Figure 2.21 Indirect tax when demand is elastic

P_1 is the initial equilibrium price and Q_1 is the initial equilibrium output. An indirect tax will cause the supply curve to shift to the left from S_1 to S_2. In turn, this causes the price to increase to P_2 and the quantity to fall to Q_2. It can be seen that when demand is elastic the producer bears a much larger proportion of the tax burden (RP_1MT), whereas the consumer bears a much smaller part of the tax burden (P_1P_2LM), i.e. the incidence of the tax falls mainly on the producer. The total tax revenue to the government is, therefore, RP_2LT.

Subsidies

REVISED

A **subsidy** is a grant from the government. These grants have the effect of reducing costs of production. Consequently, subsidies will cause the supply curve to shift to the right. Figure 2.22 illustrates the impact of a subsidy.

A **subsidy** is a grant from the government which has the effect of reducing costs of production.

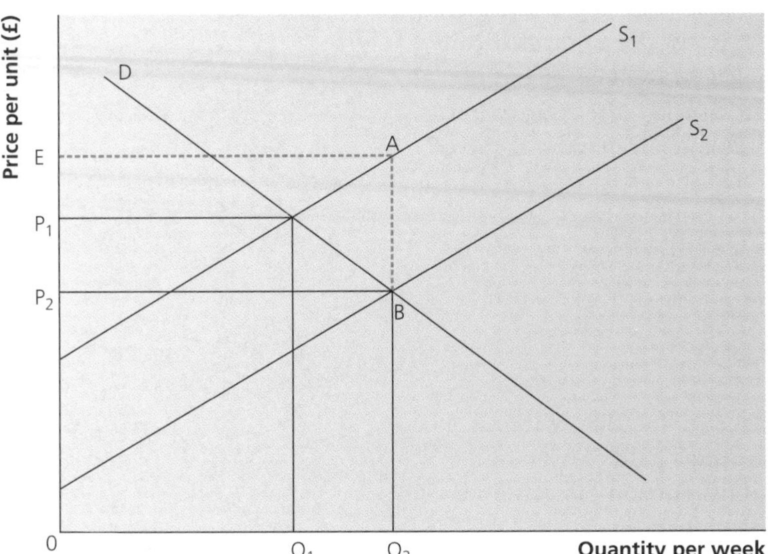

Figure 2.22 The effect of a subsidy

The initial equilibrium price and quantity are P_1 and Q_1 but after the subsidy is granted by the government to producers, the new equilibrium price falls to P_2 and the quantity rises to Q_2. AB represents the subsidy per unit and the total cost of the subsidy to the government is P_2EAB, i.e. the subsidy per unit multiplied by the quantity.

Typical mistake

Shifting the demand curve to right to illustrate the effect of a subsidy. A subsidy affects suppliers and so affects the *supply* curve, not the demand curve.

Now test yourself

TESTED

19 In 2011, VAT was increased from 17.5% to 20% in the UK. How would this have affected the supply curve for restaurant meals?

Answer on p. 216

Alternative views of consumer behaviour

As indicated at the beginning of this chapter, standard economic analysis makes the assumption that people act rationally and aim to maximise utility. In practice, this assumption may be unrealistic because people's behaviour is subject to a range of influences and motives. **Behavioural economics** applies psychological insights into human behaviour to explain economic decision-making.

Behavioural economics is a method of economic analysis that applies psychological insights into human behaviour to explain economic decision-making.

Reasons why consumers may not behave rationally

REVISED

- **Consideration of the influence of other people's behaviour:** much of a person's behaviour is affected and influenced by that of others. Indeed, it is argued that a person subconsciously learns from the behaviour of others as a guide to their own behaviour — a process known as 'social learning'. Examples of how our behaviour is dependent on others might include the clothes and smartphones we buy or the food we eat.

- **The importance of habitual behaviour:** the frequency of our past behaviour influences our current behaviour. Consequently, such behaviour involves little or no thought — it is just done automatically. Habits are difficult to change if they are repeated frequently and if they are associated with rewards which arise quickly after the action. Incentives (which may be financial or non-financial) may be required to change such habits. For example, charging for plastic bags has had a major impact in countries such as Ireland and South Africa.
- **Inertia:** consumers might not make an active effort to change their behaviour for several reasons including:
  - information overload
  - the complexity of the information available
  - too much choice available

  Inertia might arise because people are loss averse, i.e. they will put more effort into preventing a loss than winning a gain. This could explain, for example, why a relatively small proportion of consumers switch their bank accounts or their energy suppliers.
- **Consumer weakness at computation:** people tend to pay more attention to recent events than to distant events when they make decisions. Linked with this, consumers find considerable difficulty in calculating the probability of something happening. They are also influenced by how a choice is presented.

Implications of behavioural economics

REVISED

The points outlined above mean that standard mathematical analysis based on the neoclassical principles of rationality will not accurately describe human behaviour. Consequently, they might have perverse and unintended results when used to formulate policy.

A key implication of this approach therefore is that policymakers need to focus more on the psychology of behaviour when devising policy.

Exam practice

1 (a) A rational consumer will:
- A minimise current consumption
- B maximise satisfaction
- C minimise profits
- D maximise costs of making a decision [1]

(b) What factors might influence a consumer's decision to buy a product? [3]

2 (a) The law of diminishing marginal utility implies that, as more of a product is consumed by a person:
- A total utility will increase at an increasing rate
- B marginal utility will increase
- C total utility will always be negative
- D marginal utility will decrease [1]

(b) How does the law of diminishing returns help to explain the shape of the demand curve? [3]

3 (a) The demand curve for iPads will shift to the right if there is:
- A an increase in costs of production
- B a rise in VAT on iPads

C an increase in the productivity of workers producing iPads
D an increase in real incomes of consumers [1]

(b) Identify three reasons why demand for iPads might increase in the future. [3]

4 (a) How might the shape of the supply curve be explained? [3]

(b) The supply curve of potatoes will shift to the left if:
A the cost of fertiliser increases
B there is an increase in advertising of potatoes
C new machinery enables more potatoes to be produced per acre
D the price of rice, a substitute for potatoes, increases in price [1]

5 A baker sells 100 cakes at $5 each on a particular day. When he reduces the price to $4 on the following day, his sales rise to 140 cakes.

(a) Calculate the change in total revenue resulting from the price reduction. [1]

(b) What may be inferred about the price elasticity of demand for cakes? [2]

6 Total expenditure on product X falls as price falls, but demand increases as income falls. Which of the following can be concluded from this information?

	Price elasticity of demand	Income elasticity of demand
A	elastic	negative
B	elastic	positive
C	inelastic	positive
D	inelastic	negative

[1]

7 (a) Product Y has a price elasticity of supply of 0.5. Calculate the change in quantity supplied following a price rise of 30%. [3]

(b) Which of the following could account for this low price elasticity of supply?
A There are no close substitutes for product Y.
B Product Y is addictive.
C Product Y is a heavily advertised brand of coffee.
D The specialist machinery required for product Y is fully utilised. [1]

8 (a) 100 000 jars of jam are demanded per day at £2 a jar. If the price elasticity of demand for these jars is –3 and the price is raised by 10%, the number of jars demanded per day would fall to:
A 60 000
B 70 000
C 80 000
D 90 000 [1]

(b) Explain three factors which might influence the price elasticity of demand for strawberries. [3]

9

Between July 2014 and January 2015 crude oil prices fell from $107 a barrel to $45 a barrel. This was caused by a slowdown in economic growth in rapidly growing economies such as China, very slow growth in the Eurozone and increasing supplies resulting from the shale gas revolution especially in North America.

Lower oil prices have also been accompanied by significant falls in the price of commodities including wheat whose price fell from $330 per tonne in May 2014 to $235 per tonne in February 2015. Oil prices have an impact on wheat prices because oil is required for transport and is an important source of energy in food production. Wheat prices have also fallen due to:

- countries such as China and Brazil having huge stocks
- larger harvests in Argentina, Russia and the rest of Europe
- fall in demand for wheat for animal feed because corn is now much cheaper following record harvests

Low wheat prices have led to less planting of wheat which might force prices higher by 2016.

(a) Under what circumstances might the short-run supply curve for wheat be price elastic? [4]

(b) Explain the reasons for the fall in the price of crude oil. Illustrate your answer with a supply and demand diagram. [6]

(c) Calculate the percentage change in the price of wheat from the information given in the article. [5]

(d) Assess the impact of a decrease in the price of oil on the market for wheat. [10]
(e) Discuss the factors influencing the income elasticity of demand for oil and wheat. [15]
EITHER
(f) Evaluate minimum guaranteed price schemes as means of reducing price fluctuations in commodities such as wheat. [20]
OR
(g) Evaluate the effect of falling wheat prices on consumers and producers. [20]

Answers and quick quiz 2 online

ONLINE

Summary

You should have an understanding of:

- The assumption of rationality and the reasons why consumers may not behave rationally in practice.
- How a price change causes a movement along a demand curve.
- How changes in the conditions of demand cause shifts in the demand curve.
- How a price change causes a movement along a supply curve.
- How changes in the conditions of supply cause shifts in the demand curve.
- How the equilibrium price and output is determined.
- The causes of changes in the equilibrium price and quantity.
- How market forces will eliminate excess demand and excess supply.
- Price elasticity of demand: how it is calculated and how to interpret the results.
- The factors influencing price elasticity of demand.
- The relationship between price elasticity of demand and total revenue.
- Income elasticity of demand: how it is calculated and how to interpret the results.
- The distinction between normal goods and inferior goods.
- Cross elasticity of demand: how it is calculated and how to interpret the results.
- The distinction between complements and substitutes.
- Price elasticity of supply: how it is calculated and how to interpret the results.
- The factors influencing price elasticity of supply.
- The functions of the price mechanism.
- Consumer surplus and producer surplus and the factors influencing each of these concepts.
- The effect of indirect taxes and subsidies using supply and demand analysis.

3 Market failure

Types of market failure

The meaning of market failure

REVISED

Market failure refers to the failure of the market system to allocate resources efficiently. It arises because the price mechanism has not taken into account all the costs and/or benefits in the production or consumption of the product or service.

Market failure occurs when the forces of supply and demand (market forces) do not result in the efficient allocation of resources.

Types of market failure

REVISED

There are various reasons why the free market system may fail including:

- externalities: negative externalities and positive externalities
- public goods
- information gaps

These market failures are considered in detail later in this chapter.

Exam tip

Ensure that you know that there are several forms of market failure. The above list is not complete. For example, other forms of market failure include labour immobility, monopoly and inequality but these are not required for the AS specification. These are, however, examined in Themes 3 and 4.

Reasons for market failure

REVISED

For resources to be allocated efficiently, it is necessary for social marginal costs (SMC) to be equal to social marginal benefits (SMB). In practice, some costs and/or benefits may not be included because they may not be known or difficult to quantify. Social marginal cost refers to the addition to total cost of producing an extra unit of output, whereas social marginal benefit refers to the addition to total benefits of consuming an extra unit.

Now test yourself

TESTED

1 What is market failure?
2 Identity three types of market failure.
3 What condition must be met for resources to be allocated efficiently when there are externalities?

Answers on p. 216

Externalities

The meaning of externalities

REVISED

These are costs and benefits to third parties who are not directly part of a transaction between producers and consumers. They are, in effect, spillover effects arising from the production or consumption of a product or service which are not taken into account by the price mechanism. **Externalities** are therefore a form of market failure because market forces will not result in an efficient allocation of resources.

Externalities affect parties that are not directly involved in a transaction and may be either costs or benefits.

Types of externality

REVISED

Two types of externality may be distinguished:

- external costs (negative externalities) and
- external benefits (positive externalities)

Exam tip

Think of externalities as effects on stakeholders, e.g. consumers, firms, workers, the government, who are not part of a transaction between others.

Private costs

REVISED

Private costs are those costs paid directly by the producer and consumer in a transaction:

- Private costs of a producer: typically these will include, wages, rent, raw materials, energy.
- Private costs for a consumer: the cost to the consumer is usually the price paid for the product/service.

Private costs are the direct costs to producers and consumers for producing and consuming a product.

External costs (negative externalities)

REVISED

External costs are costs to third parties, i.e. other than to the producer or consumer directly involved in the transaction. They are spillover costs from the production or consumption which the market fails to take into account.

Examples of **external costs of production** include:

- air pollution, e.g. noxious gases from a factory
- noise pollution, e.g. from building work associated with a new factory or from machinery used in the production process
- pollution arising from the destruction of the rain forest to grow crops

Examples of **external costs of consumption** include:

- passive smoking, i.e. a non-smoker might suffer from adverse health effects if he/she is in the presence of a smoker over a period of time
- overeating by individuals: obesity might result in significant costs for the National Health Service and, in turn, taxpayers

External costs are the costs in excess of private costs that affect third parties who are not part of the transaction.

Social costs

REVISED

Social costs are simply the sum of private costs and external costs. So:

social costs = private costs + external costs

Therefore:

external costs = social costs – private costs

Social costs are the sum of private costs and external costs.

Exam tip

Diagrammatic analysis of the external costs of production is required for the examination but not of the external costs of consumption.

Analysis of external costs of production

REVISED

Figure 3.1 illustrates the welfare loss occurring from the production of a good, which results in external costs to third parties.

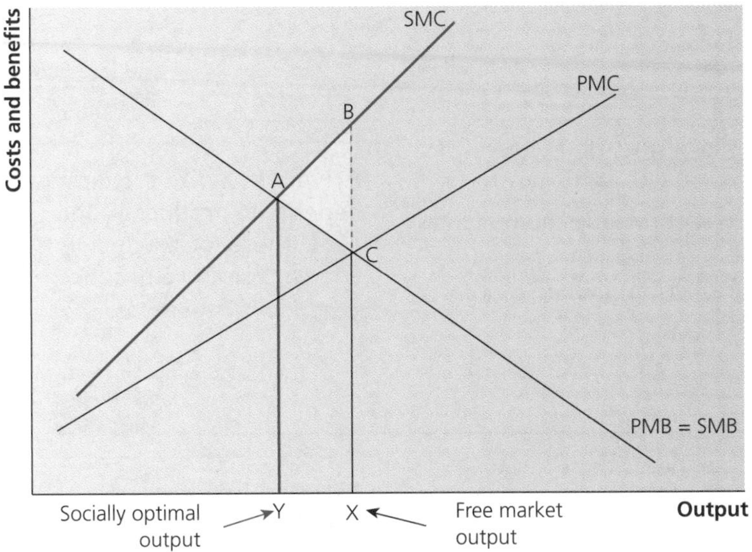

Figure 3.1 External costs of production

- In Figure 3.1, the private marginal benefit curve (PMB) is the demand curve and indicates that private benefits to the consumer decrease as consumption increases. In this case, it is assumed that there are no external benefits so the PMB will be the same as the social marginal benefit (SMB) curve.
- The private marginal cost (PMC) curve is the supply curve and indicates that private costs of providing the product rise as output rises.
- In a free market economy, therefore, the equilibrium will be determined from the equilibrium point at which PMB = PMC, which will be output 0X.
- However, 0X would not be the socially optimal level of output because no account has been taken of the external costs of production.
- The social marginal cost (SMC) curve includes both the private costs and external costs and is, therefore, drawn to the left of the PMC curve.
- The socially optimal level of output is determined from the equilibrium point at which SMC = SMB which will be 0Y.

Welfare loss

- It can be seen that in a free market economy there is over-production and over-consumption of XY.
- This results in a welfare loss, shown as ABC in Figure 3.1.

Typical mistake

Drawing a basic supply and demand curve when considering externalities.

Exam tip

External costs are an extra cost, so this means that the social marginal cost curve must be to the left of the private marginal cost.

Typical mistake

Welfare loss area identified incorrectly. To avoid this error, remember that at the free market output, the social marginal cost is greater than the social marginal benefit — use this information to determine the welfare loss.

Now test yourself

TESTED

4 A firm producing chemicals pays another firm for its raw materials and pays an average wage of £35 000 to its workers. It discharges its waste into a river adjacent to the factory, which causes the fish to die. Fishermen downstream suffer from a loss of income. Farmers pay the chemical company £100 per kilo for the fertiliser produced by the chemical company.
In the above extract, which are private costs and which are external costs?

Answers on p. 216

Private benefits

REVISED

Private benefits are those benefits that are received directly by the producer and consumer in a transaction.

- Private benefits to a producer: typically these will include the revenues received from the sale of the product/service.
- Private benefits to a consumer: the utility(satisfaction) gained by the consumer from the consumption of the product/service.

Private benefits are direct benefits to producers and consumers for producing and consuming a product.

External benefits

REVISED

External benefits are benefits to third parties, i.e. other than to the producer or consumer directly involved in the transaction. They are spillover benefits from the production or consumption which the market fails to take into account.

Examples of **external benefits of consumption** include:

- Individuals deciding to have vaccinations preventing the spread of disease to others.
- Households with well-kept gardens increasing the market value of neighbouring properties.

Examples of **external benefits of production** include:

- A farmer who keeps bees to make honey. The bees will benefit surrounding farmers by pollinating their crops.
- A firm trains workers in computing skills. Other firms that do not train workers might benefit from employing workers from this firm.

External benefits are benefits in excess of private benefits which affect third parties who are not part of the transaction.

Social benefits

REVISED

Social benefits are simply the sum of private benefits and external benefits. So:

social benefits = private benefits + external benefits.

Therefore:

external benefits = social benefits – private benefits

Social benefits are the sum of private benefits and external benefits.

Analysis of external benefits of consumption

REVISED

Figure 3.2 illustrates the welfare loss that occurs due to the consumption of a good, which results in external benefits to third parties.

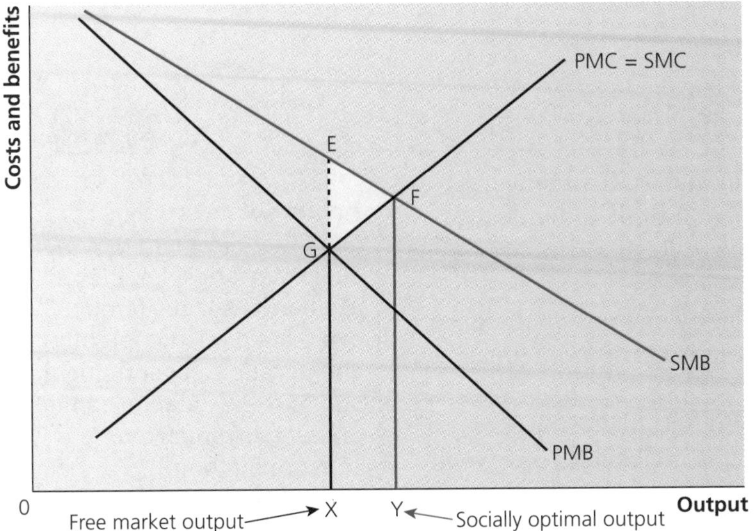

Figure 3.2 External benefits of consumption

- In Figure 3.2, the private marginal benefit curve (PMB) is the demand curve and indicates that private benefits to the consumer decrease as consumption increases.
- The private marginal cost (PMC) curve is the supply curve. In this case, it is assumed that there are no external costs, so the PMC will be the same as the social marginal cost (SMC) curve.
- In a free market economy, therefore, the equilibrium will be determined from the equilibrium point at which PMB = PMC which will be output 0X.
- However, 0X would not be the socially optimal level of output because no account has been taken of the external benefits of production.
- The social marginal benefit (SMB) curve includes both the private benefits and external benefits and is, therefore, drawn to the right of the PMB curve.
- The socially optimal level of output is determined from the equilibrium point at which SMC = SMB which will be 0Y.

Welfare gain

- It can be seen that in a free market economy there is under-production and under-consumption of XY.
- If the socially optimum output is produced, then there will be a welfare gain, shown as EFG in Figure 3.2.

Typical mistake

Welfare gain area identified incorrectly. To avoid this error, remember that at the free market output, the social marginal benefit is greater than the social marginal cost — use this information to determine the welfare loss.

Now test yourself

TESTED

5 It has been estimated that an economics graduate can earn significantly more than a student with two A-levels. Research suggests that graduates secure more interesting and satisfying jobs than non-graduates. A highly skilled workforce might attract more foreign direct investment. Further, graduates learn transferable skills that can help to increase productivity. Both these factors, therefore, help to increase economic growth of the country.
In the above extract, which are private benefits and which are external benefits?

Answers on p. 217

Public goods

The difference between public and private goods

REVISED

The characteristic which makes **public goods** unique is that the benefit that they provide affects many people rather than just one individual. Pure public goods have two special characteristics which distinguish them from private goods:

- **Non-rivalrous:** this means that consumption by one person does not limit consumption by others, i.e. the benefit to others is not reduced by one person's consumption.
- **Non-excludability:** this means that if a good is available for one person, then it is available for everyone, i.e. it is impossible to prevent or exclude anyone from using it.

This is in contrast to **private goods** which are rival and excludable, i.e. consumption by one person means that it cannot be consumed by anyone else and that it is not available to anyone else.

Public goods are those good that have two key characteristics, i.e. they are non-rivalrous (amount available does not fall after one person's consumption) and non-excludable (cannot prevent anyone from consuming them).

Examples of public goods

REVISED

It is arguable whether there are any examples of pure public goods displaying the characteristics of those described above, but examples commonly used include:

- street lighting
- nuclear defence systems
- national parks

The free rider problem

REVISED

These characteristics mean that when a public good is provided by someone, other people will be able to benefit from it without paying — in other words, they get a '**free ride**'. This is a problem because in such circumstances the market will fail: an insufficient number of people will be willing to pay for the product and it will not be profitable for a business to provide it.

Free rider problem is the problem that once a product is provided it is impossible to prevent people from using it and, therefore, impossible to charge for it.

Typical mistake

Assuming that all goods provided by the state, such as health and education, are public goods. This is not necessarily true because health and education are also provided by the private sector.

Now test yourself

TESTED

6 How do private goods differ from public goods?
7 Why does the free rider problem occur?
8 If a person buys a television, it is not possible the prevent him using it whether or not he has a television licence. How do the authorities try to make this an 'excludable' service?

Answers on p. 217

Information gaps

Symmetric and asymmetric information

REVISED

The free market system is based on the assumption that consumers and producers make rational choices and decisions based on perfect and equal market knowledge. In practice, this assumption may be unrealistic. For example, producers may have more information than consumers about a product or service, or consumers may simply not have sufficient information to make a rational decision. As a result of this **asymmetric information**, resources may be allocated inefficiently resulting in market failure.

Symmetric information is where both parties in a transaction have the same information.

Asymmetric information is where one party in a transaction has more or superior information compared to another.

Examples of asymmetric information

REVISED

The following provide some examples of markets in which asymmetric information is possible:

- **Housing market:** estate agents may know more about the potential problems of a house than the potential buyer.
- **Life insurance:** the consumer may not reveal all aspects of his health profile to the insurance company, making it difficult for the firm to assess the risk.
- **Second-hand car sales:** the car salesperson will know more about the car than a potential buyer.
- **Financial services:** a bank may be unaware of the likelihood of a default by the borrower.
- **High-tech products:** consumers are unlikely to have as much information as producers about products such as smart phones and pharmaceuticals.

Exam tip

Remember that asymmetric information and incomplete information are a form of market failure because they restrict the ability of consumers and producers to make rational choices.

Now test yourself

TESTED

9 What information gaps might exist between a dentist and her patient?

Answer on p. 217

Exam practice

1 An oil freighter runs aground not far from a seaside resort. Damage to the freighter causes a major oil spillage which ruins the beaches of the resort. This deters tourists many of whom cancel their bookings at local hotels.

(a) Using examples from the above extract, distinguish between the private costs and external costs. [3]

(b) The above example illustrates that:

A Social costs are less than external costs.
B Private costs are greater than social costs.
C External costs are less than private costs.
D Social costs are greater than private costs. [1]

2 (a) Public goods are:
  A provided without any opportunity cost
  B only used by producers
  C under-provided by the private sector
  D only provided to those on low incomes [1]

(b) National defence and street lights are usually provided by the state and financed from tax revenues.
Explain the characteristics of public goods and how they differ from private goods. [3]

3

It has been estimated that an economics graduate can earn significantly more than a student with two A-levels. Research suggests that graduates secure more interesting and satisfying jobs than non-graduates. A highly skilled workforce might attract more foreign direct investment. Further, graduates learn transferable skills which can help to increase productivity. Both these factors, therefore, help to increase economic growth of the country.

Tuition fees were increased from £3375 in 2011 to £9000 in 2012. This resulted in a 10% fall in applications to English universities. The government argued that private benefits of going to university are significant, so the increase in fees is justified. Free market economists suggest that government subsidies to universities encourage inefficiency and a lack of responsiveness to market demand. Further, many courses may have no benefits to the economy.

(a) What might be the opportunity cost to the government of funding universities? [4]
(b) Explain why university education is not a public good. [5]
(c) Giving examples, explain the private costs for an individual student of a university education. [6]
(d) Assess the private and external benefits of university education. [15]
(e) From the information provided, calculate the price elasticity of demand for university education. Critically examine your result. [10]

EITHER

(f) Evaluate the economic arguments for an increase in university tuition fees. [20]

OR

(g) Evaluate the extent to which information gaps make it difficult for a student to decide whether to go to university. [20]

Answers and quick quiz 3 online

ONLINE

Summary

You should have an understanding of:

- The meaning of market failure.
- Three types of market failure: externalities, public goods and information gaps.
- External costs and external benefits.
- Diagrams depicting external costs of production and external benefits of consumption.
- Public goods: key characteristics non-rivalrous and non-excludability; the free rider problem.
- Information gaps: meaning and significance.

4 Government intervention

Government intervention in markets

Indirect taxes

REVISED

Indirect taxes are taxes on expenditure and include taxes such as Value Added Tax (VAT), excise taxes and taxes on gambling. Such taxes cause an increase in the cost of supply and so cause the supply curve to shift to the left. As outlined in chapter 2 page 45, there are two types of indirect taxes: ***ad valorem*** and **specific**.

Governments intervene in a variety of ways, one of the most common of which is through indirect taxes, which are taxes on expenditure. This method may be used to deal with external costs such as pollution. The aim of indirect taxes is to **internalise the externality** by taxing the product so that output and consumption will be at the level at which SMB = SMC. This is illustrated in Figure 4.1.

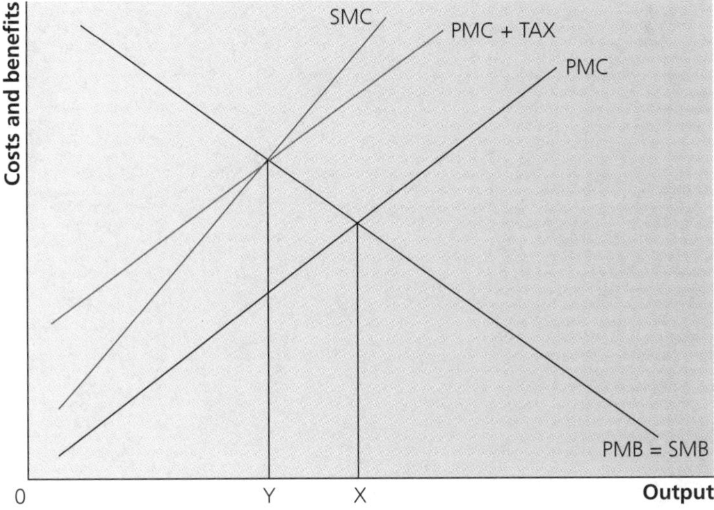

Figure 4.1 The taxing of a firm producing external costs

It can be seen that the tax will cause a leftward shift in the supply curve. If judged correctly, the tax will cause consumption and output to fall to 0Y, the socially optimum level.

Advantages

- incentive to reduce pollution
- source of revenue for the government and few costs administering this method

Disadvantages

- ineffective in reducing pollution if demand is price inelastic
- difficulty of setting an appropriate tax because of the problem of quantifying the external cost

Exam tip

Indirect taxes affect the costs of production and so cause shifts in the *supply* curve and not the demand curve.

Now test yourself

TESTED

1 How does an internal tax on a producer causing pollution 'internalise the externality'?
2 Why is it difficult to determine how much tax to place on a company whose production causes external costs?
3 Nitrogen from diesel fumes is widely believed to cause undesirable health effects. Draw a supply and demand diagram to illustrate the impact of an increase in VAT on diesel. Show the area of tax borne by:
(a) the consumer and
(b) the producer

Answers on p. 217

Subsidies

REVISED

The government might provide grants to producers to lower production costs so that the product or service can be provided at a lower price. This method may be used to deal with the issue of external benefits. In turn, this should encourage consumption so that it reaches the socially optimal level.

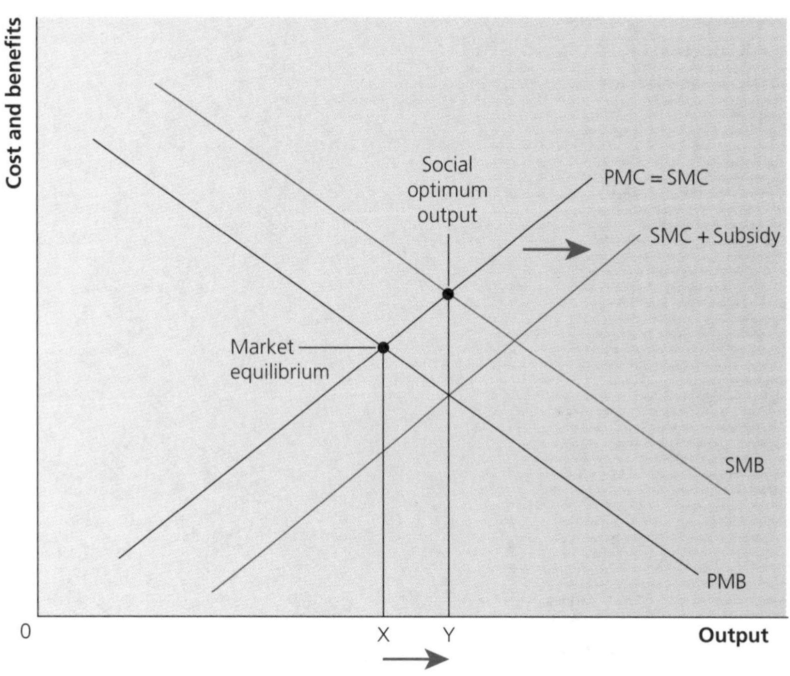

Figure 4.2 A subsidy to encourage consumption of a product which has external benefits

It can be seen that the **subsidy** will cause a rightward shift in the supply curve. If judged correctly, the subsidy will cause consumption and output to rise from 0X to 0Y, the socially optimum level.

Subsidies are government grants to businesses that reduce production costs causing a rightward shift in the supply curve.

Advantages

- reduction in cost of production enabling suppliers to reduce the price
- incentive for people to increase consumption

Disadvantages

- cost to the taxpayer of providing subsidies
- ineffective in increasing consumption if demand is inelastic
- difficulty of setting an appropriate subsidy because of the problem of quantifying the external benefit

Now test yourself

TESTED

4 Explain the effect of a decrease in the subsidy for wind farms.

Answer on p. 217

Maximum prices

REVISED

Maximum price controls or price ceilings have been used by governments in a variety of contexts, e.g on rented accommodation, for wages of rugby league players and for items of food.

A **maximum price** is a price, usually set by the government, which makes it illegal for firms to charge more than a certain price for a given quantity of a product.

Figure 4.3 illustrates the effects of a maximum price scheme.

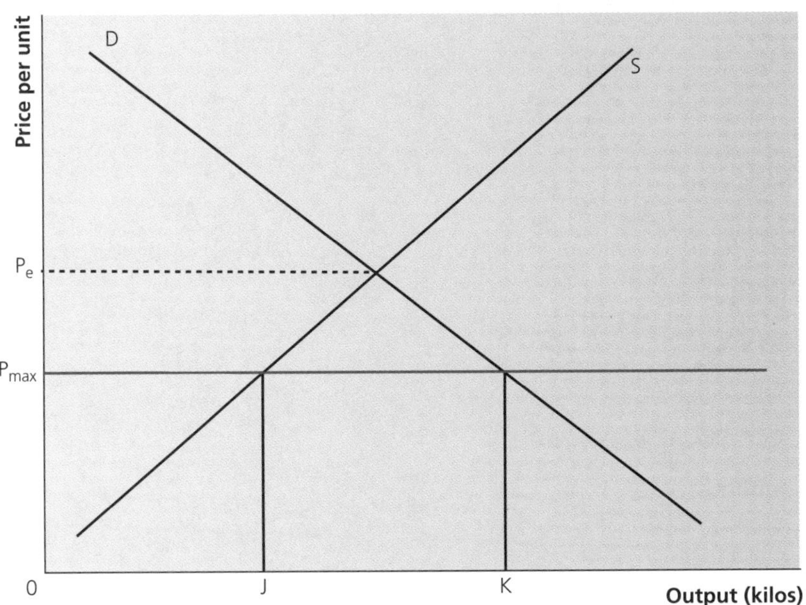

Figure 4.3 A maximum price set below the equilibrium price

- The equilibrium price is P_e.
- Suppose the government sets a maximum price (P_{max}) below the equilibrium price. This will result in a shortage of JK kilos.

The shortage could result in a black market in which those with supplies of the product sell it illegally at a price significantly higher than the maximum price.

Advantages

- They enable consumers on low incomes to be able to afford to buy a product.
- They help to prevent an increase in the country's rate of inflation.

Disadvantages

- There is a danger that shortages mean that some consumers are unable to find supplies of the product.
- Producers may exit the market in order to use their resources to produce goods that are more profitable.
- If the government subsidises producers to encourage them to maintain output, then there will be a significant cost to the taxpayer.

Minimum prices

REVISED

Minimum prices may be used in a variety of ways. For example, many countries have a national minimum wage. In terms of commodities and food, a government may set a **minimum guaranteed price** (MGP) for a particular commodity. This means that producers know in advance that they will receive a certain price per kilo no matter how much is produced. This is designed to ensure greater certainty and, therefore, act as an incentive to producers to supply sufficient quantities of the commodity.

Minimum guaranteed price is a price, usually set by the government, which is guaranteed to producers.

Figure 4.4 illustrates the effects of a guaranteed minimum price scheme.

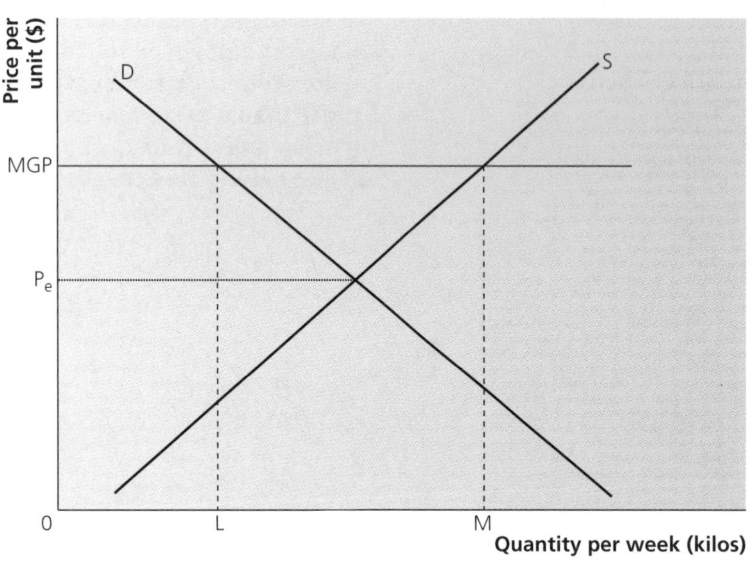

Figure 4.4 A minimum guaranteed price scheme

- The equilibrium price is P_e.
- Suppose the government sets a minimum guaranteed price (MGP) above the equilibrium price. This will result in a surplus of LM kilos.
- The government will buy this surplus and store it for times in which there is a shortage.

Advantages

The advantages of minimum guaranteed price include:

- Producers know in advance the price they will receive for their product.
- This greater certainty enables producers to plan investment and output.

Disadvantages

The problems associated with minimum guaranteed prices are similar to those of buffer stock schemes:

- If the minimum guaranteed price is set too high, then there will be surpluses each year.
- These schemes involve costs of storage which must be borne by taxpayers.
- These schemes encourage over-production and may, therefore, result in an inefficient allocation of resources.

Minimum prices might also be set for some products sold by retailers in order to deter consumption. For example, Scotland plans to impose a minimum retail price for alcohol which is designed to make it less affordable and so reduce consumption.

Now test yourself

TESTED

5 What is the main purpose of a guaranteed minimum price for a product such as wheat?
6 Explain the effect on quantity demanded and quantity supplied of a guaranteed minimum price that is set above the free market price.

Answers on p. 217

Tradable pollution permits

REVISED

Tradable pollutions permits is another method used to reduce external costs. Permits are issued by the government to firms that allow them to pollute up to a certain limit. Any pollution above this limit is subject to fines. The key to this system is that the permits may be traded between firms so that firms that are 'clean' can sell their surplus permits to firms which are more polluting.

Tradable pollution permits (according to the OECD) are rights to sell and buy actual or potential pollution in artificially created markets.

Advantages

- These schemes work through the market mechanism.
- They are an incentive for firms to reduce pollution.
- The costs of administering these schemes are low relative to those associated with systems of regulation.

Disadvantages

- Pollution will continue, albeit at a lower level than previously.
- Large, efficient firms might buy up the permits and continue to pollute.

State provision of public goods

REVISED

The usual policy response to the lack of provision of public goods by the free market is for the government to provide them financed through taxation. The most obvious benefit is that this ensures that the product or service is provided.

However, a disadvantage of this approach is that ultimately politicians will determine the amount of resources allocated to these public goods without direct reference to the electorate.

Alternative methods of providing some public goods are via agencies appointed by the government (contracting-out) or by charities and voluntary organisations.

Provision of information

REVISED

Information gaps may be closed by publications in the media, on the internet and written publications which are designed to inform consumers about issues concerning products and services. Examples include information:

- for parents aimed at encouraging them to have their children vaccinated against measles
- about the health risks associated with smoking
- about opportunities for apprenticeships and courses available in higher education

Obviously there is a cost associated with this and there is no guarantee that the policy will be effective.

Regulation

REVISED

Legal regulations can be imposed on the activities of consumers and producers. Such measures include:

- A complete ban on the production of the good or provision of the service.
- Regulations which place limits on the production process or on the amount of pollution allowed.
- Regulations relating to the consumption of a product, e.g. the prohibition of smoking in public places or the age limit on buying cigarettes.

In theory, this should restrict the activity to the required level but without enforcement firms may not meet the legal requirements.

Advantages

- Regulation can limit the extent of the activity.
- It might act as an incentive to producers to develop new technologies that avoid the activity.

Disadvantages

- The cost of enforcement of laws/regulations, e.g. inspectors may have to be employed to ensure that producers and/or consumers abide by the rules.
- Problems of determining the socially efficient levels of the production process or activity.

Property rights

REVISED

Another form of regulation, which can be used to deal with external costs, is the extension of **property rights**. This involves assigning ownership (property) rights to those who might be affected by external costs. This means that owners are given the right to claim damages against those causing the external cost.

Property rights are the exclusive authority to determine how a resource is used, whether that resource is owned by government, collective bodies, or by individuals. In other words, property rights are ownership rights.

Advantages

- Property rights act as an incentive for firms to take into account both the private costs and the external costs.
- The opportunity to fine firms caught polluting and use the money to compensate those damaged.
- The administration costs of these schemes are low relative to other forms of regulation.

Disadvantages

- There is the initial problem of assigning property rights.
- If a breach of property rights has occurred, there may be an expensive legal procedure to determine how much compensation should be paid and to whom.
- It may be difficult to agree on the monetary value of the external cost.

Now test yourself

TESTED

7 How can a system of tradable permits be used to reduce pollution?
8 Why might laws passed to reduce pollution fail to meet their objective?

Answers on p. 217

Government failure

Government failure arises as a result of government intervention in a market in an attempt to correct a market failure which causes output and consumption to move further away from the socially efficient output. In other words, government failure is a situation in which government intervention would result in a more inefficient allocation of resources and would, therefore, lead to a net welfare loss.

Government failure is when government intervention results in a net welfare loss.

Typical mistake

Confusing government failure with market failure.

Causes of government failure

REVISED

Distortion of price signals

Government intervention often involves manipulation of prices, for example, by maximum or minimum price controls. However, such measures would undermine the key functions of the price mechanism such as signalling, rationing and incentives. Ultimately, this would mean that resources are not allocated efficiently.

Unintended consequences

Some types of government intervention may have an impact which was not predicted by policymakers. For example, high taxes imposed on spirits in the UK designed to raise tax revenues as well as preventing an increase in consumption actually resulted in a decrease in tax revenues. Similarly, very high taxes on cigarettes in the UK have resulted in a significant increase in cigarette smuggling from which the government gains no tax revenue.

Excessive administrative costs

Although government intervention might seem to be desirable, the costs may be considerable. For example, the cost of administering means-tested benefits may be very large.

Information gaps

When a government intervenes in a market it is unlikely to have all the information required. Consequently, the intervention could move output further away from the socially optimal level.

Now test yourself

TESTED

9 Would government failure result in a movement closer to or further away from the socially efficient level of output?
10 How could government failure occur in the EU's system of fishing quotas?

Answers on p. 217

Government failure in various markets

REVISED

Government intervention in a market may have unforeseen and undesirable consequences. The following are examples where government failure might be observed:

- **Indirect taxes:** very high indirect taxes might result in smuggling as a means of avoiding the tax. Further, if the indirect tax is set too high it might result in a movement further away from the socially optimum level of output.
- **Agricultural stabilisation schemes**, e.g. minimum guaranteed prices. As explained previously, these schemes could result in massive surpluses which would involve huge storage costs. Further, such surpluses imply that resources may not be allocated efficiently. For example, in the case of wheat, it might suggest that land should be used for alternative crops.
- **Housing policies:** state provision of housing at low rents might be thought to be desirable for those on low incomes. However, housing subsidies prevent the market from working efficiently. For example, there will be little incentive for people to move even if their incomes rise so limiting the geographical mobility of labour.
- **Environmental policies:** subsidies have been given for the establishment of wind farms but many argue that the energy produced from them is relatively expensive and that they cause an environmental eyesore. A further example of government failure in this context was the payment by the government of £2.8 million to wind farm owners on one day in August 2014 to stop producing electricity because the electricity network was unable to cope with the amount of electricity being generated from this source.

These are just a few examples but there are many other examples including government intervention in the fishing industry which may result in the depletion of fish stocks; and high taxes on alcohol and tobacco which might encourage smuggling to such an extent that a further tax rise on these products could result in a fall in tax revenues.

Exam practice

1 (a) When a government increased the tax on whisky the tax revenue fell despite an increase in sales because there was increased tax evasion. This illustrates an example of:
   - A an inferior good
   - B asymmetric information
   - C external benefits
   - D government failure [1]

   (b) Identify three possible sources of government failure. [3]

2 (a) If a government provides a subsidy to producers of wind power, it will cause
   - A a decrease in consumer surplus
   - B an increase in producer surplus
   - C a decrease in profits of producers
   - D an increase in external costs [1]

   (b) In 2014, subsidies to wind farm owners were estimated to be £1.8 billion. The industry employs 15 500 workers.
   - (i) Calculate the subsidy per worker to the wind farm industry in 2014. [1]
   - (ii) Explain one reason why subsidies are given to wind farm operators. [2]

3

The price of raw sugar fell from 29 cents per pound in January 2011 to just 15 cents per pound in March 2015 following bumper crops and weak sales. Sugar has been associated with obesity, tooth decay and various health diseases such as diabetes. Consequently there has been pressure on manufacturers to reduce the amount of sugar in processed foods such as breakfast cereals and yoghurts. Meanwhile, consumers have increasingly been turning to sugar-free versions of products such as soft drinks. Such products are often sweetened with artificial sweeteners. However, for many people sugar is addictive: for example, they may be unable to drink tea or coffee without sugar and need frequent sugar boosts from biscuits, cakes and soft drinks. It has been estimated that a 10% rise in the price of sugar would only result in a 0.1% fall in the quantity demanded in the European Union.

Given the adverse health effects of excessive sugar consumption some scientists have proposed a tax of up to 100% on soft drinks and confectionery.

Sugar production often involves undesirable consequences. In Australia, for example, the expansion of sugar cane production has caused a number of problems such as drainage issues and disruption of habitats for wildlife. Further, production is increasingly dependent on the use of chemical fertilisers which has caused loss of fish, land erosion and a deterioration in the quality of the land.

Some local authorities in England pay for 3 free months' membership of a fitness club for people with high blood pressure and who are obese. If the person loses 10% of their body weight the free membership is extended for a further 3 months. The benefits of losing weight include lower blood pressure and a reduced risk of contracting other diseases such as diabetes. There are also benefits to the wider community, for example, higher productivity and less absenteeism by workers and lower costs incurred by the National Health Service.

(a) Calculate the price elasticity of demand for sugar from the information provided. Comment on your result. [4]
(b) What might be inferred about the cross elasticity of demand between sugar and artificial sweeteners? [5]
(c) Explain how producer surplus might be affected following the fall in demand for sugar. [6]
(d) Assess the reasons for the fall in the price of sugar. Illustrate your answer with a diagram. [10]
(e) Discuss whether a government decision to ban sugar production in the UK might result in government failure. [15]

EITHER

(f) Evaluate the case for a 100% tax on soft drinks and confectionery. [20]

OR

(g) Evaluate the private costs and external costs of sugar production. [20]

Answers and quick quiz 4 online

ONLINE

Summary

You should have an understanding of:

- Methods of providing public goods.
- Asymmetric information: meaning and significance.
- Ways of dealing with asymmetric information.
- Government failure: meaning and causes.
- Examples of government failure in different markets.

5 Measures of economic performance

Economic growth

Measuring growth

REVISED

Economic growth is a measure of an increase in **real** gross domestic product (GDP). GDP is the total value of goods and services produced in a country in one year, or the total amount spent, or the total amount earned.

Potential economic growth is a measure of the increase in capacity in an economy. It can be shown by a movement outwards of the PPF curve (see chapter 1, page 14). It is a measure of how efficient the economy is in using its resources.

If an economy has two consecutive quarters (3 months, starting January, April, July or October) of negative economic growth then it is in a ***recession***. The UK went into recession in 2008, and after a brief period, another slowdown, but not technically a recession, in 2012. A recession means that there is less spending, income and output in the economy. It is likely to lead to firms closing, increased unemployment and a resulting fall in living standards.

Real means that inflation has been taken into account. Real values are sometimes referred to as 'constant prices'. If inflation is left in the figures they are known as 'nominal' or 'current'.

Recession — if an economy has two consecutive quarters of negative economic growth then it is in a recession. A quarter is 3 months, starting January, April, July or October.

Now test yourself

TESTED

1 What are the characteristics of a recession?

Answer on p. 217

Changing living standards

REVISED

An increase in GDP is likely to cause an increase in **standards of living**, which means that people can afford more goods and services, or feel that their lives are better because they do not need to work as hard to achieve their requirements in life.

However, a rising income does not necessarily make standards of living rise. It depends on how the extra money is distributed, whether inflation is being taken into account (real versus nominal), the amount spent on investment and long-term socially beneficial projects and population change. When the total population has changed (if there are more people then the increased income has to be spread out over the greater number) it is better to look at **GDP per capita**.

Now test yourself

TESTED

2 Does a higher growth rate mean a country is enjoying higher living standards?

Answer on p. 217

Standard of living is a measure of the quality of life. The measure can include physical assets and consumption, and less easily measured variables such as happiness, lack of stress, length of hours worked, lack of pollution, capacity of houses.

GDP per capita (per head) is total GDP divided by the population. Total population figures cannot be assumed to be constant when looking at GDP, so GDP per capita gives a better indicator of incomes.

Growth in different countries

REVISED

An increase in GDP in one country of 10% does not mean that the country is increasing living standards more quickly than a country with an increase of 5%. It depends on:

- how much of the output is self-consumed so does not appear as GDP
- methods of calculation and reliability of data
- relative exchange rates — do they represent the purchasing power of the local currency?
- type of spending by government — is money spent on warfare, or on **quality of life** issues such as education and health?
- what size of economy you start with. For example, after a recession an economy grows faster, but it might not reach its former GDP for some years.

Quality of life is a measure of living standards that takes into account more than just income (or GDP).

Volume versus value

REVISED

An increase in the volume of output does not always mean that there is an increase in the value of output. Volume of output measures the number of items produced, but if these are falling in price (perhaps because lots of countries are producing the same thing) then value might fall even when volume rises.

Exam tip

Look out for 'falling growth levels'. If growth rates are falling but still above zero then *levels* of income are still rising, although at a slower rate.

Typical mistake

Economic growth is a change in the level of real GDP, not GDP itself. Do not give GDP figures on their own — show a percentage change.

Understanding purchasing power parities

REVISED

Purchasing power parities (PPPs) are used to compare GDP in different countries, and take into account the cost of a 'basket of goods' that could be bought in each of the countries being compared. The PPP exchange rate is the rate where the same basket of goods costs the same in each country.

Example

A Coldplay album costs £10 in the UK and $10 in the US. The exchange rate on the currency markets is £1 = $1.50 but the PPP rate is £1 = $1.

This means the pound is overvalued (too strong) on the currency markets, and you would expect the official exchange rate of the UK economy to give values for incomes that are over-inflated in terms of purchasing power parity.

Purchasing power parities — when values of income are expressed at PPP it means that the exchange rate used is the one where the same basket of goods in the country could be bought in the USA at this rate of currency exchange.

Gross national income (GNI)

REVISED

Gross national income (GNI) measures income received by a country both domestically (gross domestic product) and net incomes from overseas.

GNI and GNP measure output from the workers and companies of a particular nation, regardless of the country the income earners are based in.

Exam tip

GNP may be much less than GDP if much of the income from a country's production flows to foreign people or firms. But, if the people or firms of a country hold large amounts of the stocks and bonds of firms or governments of other countries and receive income from them, GNP may be greater than GDP.

National happiness

REVISED

An alternative way to measure standards of living in a country is to use 'national happiness' which is a measure of national **wellbeing**. Surveys attempt to measure **subjective happiness**, such as security and social interactions, alongside the traditional measures such as real incomes.

Subjective happiness is a measure of how people feel about themselves.

Now test yourself

TESTED

3 Assess one way in which happiness is considered more important than economic growth as an objective of government policy.

Answer on p. 217

Exam tip

Subjective happiness on any one day is an unreliable indicator, as our moods change with the weather, short-term health issues (such as headaches) or events in the news. So, for example, people might not be able to tell you accurately how they felt about life yesterday but if you keep on asking over several years they might be able to give you a good overall view.

Inflation

Inflation is a *sustained* rise in the *general* price level. It is a weighted average of spending of all households in a country (that is, general spending). Changes in the **consumer price index** (CPI) are used as the measure of inflation used for inflation targeting in the UK. The CPI does not include housing costs such as rent payments and mortgage interest repayments. Changes in the **retail price index** (RPI) (also known as the headline rate), include housing costs, and may be used in data for comparison with CPI.

Consumer price index is the measure of inflation used for inflation targeting in the UK. It does not include housing costs such as mortgage interest repayments or rent.

Retail price index is a measure of inflation. It is also known as the headline rate, and includes housing costs. The RPI is used for setting the state pension and for price capping (e.g. for stopping rail fares rising too quickly) so the RPI is an important measure. If housing costs rise faster than other components of inflation the RPI will be higher than the CPI.

Exam tip

Deflation is a fall in the general level of prices. **Disinflation** is a fall in the rate of inflation, so prices are *rising more slowly*.

Deflation is a fall in the general price level. It is a sign of stagnation in an economy. In recent years Italy has suffered from deflation.

Disinflation occurs when prices rise more slowly than they have done in the past. For example, inflation might fall from 3% to 2%, meaning that prices are rising but rising less quickly than they were. In 2015, falls in oil prices in the UK brought about disinflation, as inflation fell to 0.3% and beyond.

Exam tip

Look out for falling inflation levels. If inflation rates are falling but still above zero then *levels* of prices are still rising, although at a slower rate.

Now test yourself

TESTED

4 If oil prices go up sharply is this inflation?

Answer on p. 218

Calculating the rate of inflation

REVISED

Inflation is a measure of the increase in the average price level. The price level is measured by the consumer price index, which is a weighted average of things on which people spend their money. Key points to note:

- Inflation is measured in the UK by *changes* in the CPI.
- The CPI is given as an **index number**. This means that it is a number shown as a percentage relative to the **base year**, which is given the value 100.
- Inflation is usually shown on a year-to-year basis, so you need to calculate the change over the original × 100.

An **index number** is a number shown relative to another number in percentage terms, so the actual figures are removed and just the relative difference is shown.

A **base year** is used for comparison between price levels in different time periods. It is given the number 100.

Typical mistake

What is inflation if the consumer price index changes from 125 to 130? This is an increase of (5/125) times 100 which is an inflation rate of 4% not 5%. Most people divide by 100 rather than the 'original', which is 125.

Households spend different amounts on various items. It is important to incorporate this in the calculation of inflation so that price changes will be fully reflected in the cost of living. In order to find a rate of inflation that represents the changes in costs of living that households experience:

- **Weights** are assigned to each item that is bought by the average household.
- The *Living Costs and Food Survey* collects information from a sample of nearly 7000 households in the UK using self-reported diaries of all purchases.
- The weights show the proportion of income spent on each item.
- A price survey is undertaken by civil servants who collect data once a month about changes in the price of the 650 most commonly used goods and services in a variety of retail outlets.

The price changes are multiplied by the weights to give a price index; you can measure inflation from this by calculating the percentage change in this index over consecutive years.

Weights show the proportion of income spent on items and are used to ensure that the percentage change in price reflects the impact on the average family in terms of their spending.

Exam tip

Many students think that the CPI or RPI is inflation. But it is *changes* in these price levels that show inflation.

Now test yourself

TESTED

5 Does the price survey involve looking at just 650 items? If more, why is this?

Answer on p. 218

The causes of inflation

REVISED

There are three main explanations of why inflation can occur:

- **Demand-pull inflation**. This occurs when aggregate demand (total demand) in the economy increases. It might be because interest rates have fallen, the level of confidence has risen, governments might be spending more, or because exports are rising relative to imports. All of these changes will have multiplier effects (see page 93) which can cause upward pressure on prices.

- **Cost-push inflation.** This occurs when aggregate supply decreases, i.e. the total costs of production increase. This may be because oil prices have risen, the exchange rate has fallen (making imports more expensive) or because the minimum wage has risen in real terms.
- **Growth in the money supply.** Some economists (***monetarists***) argue that inflation is mainly caused by increases in the money supply.

Exam tip

A fall in the value of a currency can cause cost-push inflation (as imports become expensive) or cause demand-pull inflation (as exports become more attractive and imports become less attractive), so there is more total spending (aggregate demand) in the economy.

Demand-pull inflation is caused by increases in **aggregate demand**. This means that spending is rising above sustainable levels. An example is that interest rates might be cut so that people want to spend more in the shops. More people wanting to buy the same amount of goods means that prices will rise.

Cost-push inflation is inflation caused by decreases in **aggregate supply**. This means that costs of production are rising or firms are willing and able to produce less at any price level. For example, an increase in food prices will cause more general rises in costs in an economy.

Monetarism is the school of economics based on the belief that inflation tends to be a problem of too much money in the economy.

The effects of inflation

REVISED

Inflation is an important measure of the success of an economy, and inflation rates that are too high or too low are a sign that the economy is experiencing problems.

In the UK there is an **inflation target** (currently this is a 2% rise in CPI with a range allowed of + or –1%). This means that a rise in the average level of prices of 2% is the desired level.

If UK inflation is 2% then the average cost of living will rise by 2%. If earnings rise on average by 2%, then on average no one is worse off. But the measure of inflation might not be a true representation of the changes in living costs. It does not include housing costs, which are a significant item of expenditure for most households in the UK. Some people do not have representative spending patterns and so might experience cost of living rises of more or less than the average shown by the CPI.

Inflation is damaging to an economy for reasons including the following:

- Inflation above 3% may significantly damage **international competitiveness**, i.e. it makes exports relatively expensive in foreign markets and imports from abroad seem cheap. This tends to worsen the balance of payments.
- It is damaging for people on **fixed incomes**. If people find their incomes do not rise in **real terms** then they will get progressively worse off, even if in **nominal terms** they are earning the same amount or more.
- Inflation is damaging to workers if the rate of inflation is higher than their nominal wage rises. In this case, their real income is falling. However, if wages rise faster than inflation then real incomes rise.
- High inflation rates might make the Monetary Policy Committee decide on a rise in interest rates. This is known as **tight monetary policy**

Inflation target — in the UK the government tasks the Monetary Policy Committee with the objective of 2% inflation, within a range of tolerance of plus or minus 1%.

International competitiveness is the degree to which a country's goods and services can be sold on international markets.

Fixed incomes — many groups of people, such as university students and pensioners, do not usually enjoy wage increases in line with inflation. This means that they suffer when the cost of living rises.

Real terms are figures where inflation has been taken into account.

Tight monetary policy is when the interest rates are kept high because of inflationary fears.

and can have damaging effects, for example on investment by firms (it falls because investment costs more), or for people paying off debts.

- Inflation can be damaging to the government because it makes it look as if it is unable to control the economy. But inflation is also good for governments if there are high levels of national debt. Debt does not change in its nominal value when there is inflation, so in real terms it is cheaper to finance and to pay back.

Revision activity

Ask an older person who has had a mortgage whether the payments seemed to get smaller as they got older. If they found that it became easier to repay their mortgage this is because inflation eroded the real cost of financing it. It is the same benefit an indebted government gets when there is inflation.

Now test yourself

TESTED

6 How does a high inflation rate damage other parts of the economy?
7 Give two reasons why the CPI measure might be inaccurate as a measure of the average cost of living in the UK.
8 Cherry gets a 1% pay rise from her employer, but the rate of inflation is 4%. What, to the nearest whole number, happens to her real wage?

Answers on p. 218

Revision activity

Calculate your own rate of inflation, and that of the people with whom you live. Type 'inflation calculator' into a search engine, then type in the amount you spend on various items. The BBC and the statistics.gov.uk websites have very clear guidelines for this task.

If you find your personal inflation rate is higher than average you might like to negotiate higher levels of pocket money.

Employment and unemployment

Employment

REVISED

Employment can be measured as a level (number of people in work) or as a percentage (number of people in work divided by the total number of people who are **economically active** multiplied by 100).

Those people who are not available to work, such as students or people caring for other people as unpaid activity and those who are unable to work are referred to as **economically inactive**.

Economically active — those people who are at work or who are willing to work. Also called the workforce, the term includes unemployed people.

Economically inactive — those people who are not available to work, such as students or people caring for other people as unpaid activity and those who are unable to work.

Typical mistake

Confusing economic activity with employment. This is incorrect, because people who are willing to work but cannot find employment are still economically active.

Unemployment

REVISED

Unemployment can be measured as a level (number of people looking for work but unable to find it) or as a percentage (number of people out of work divided by the total number of people who are economically active, multiplied by 100).

Types (or causes) of unemployment

- **Cyclical** (or demand-deficient) — where lack of spending in the economy/recession means that people are out of work. In a recession you expect this type of unemployment.
- **Structural** — where industries are in decline and workers' skills are becoming obsolete (out of date).
- **Frictional** — where people are between jobs.
- **Seasonal** — where people are out of work for some periods of the year, for example ski instructors in the summer and surf instructors in the winter.
- **Classical or real wage inflexibility** — where there are problems with the supply side of labour, e.g. the minimum wage is too high. This might be because the national minimum wage is set above the equilibrium wage. Some economists (classical approach) argue that this is the cause of persistent unemployment in some countries, and that the economy cannot be in equilibrium with demand deficiency.

Costs of unemployment

- Costs to the person without an income.
- Non-income costs to the unemployed person. Skills become obsolete, and people can lose confidence.
- Costs to firms — people don't spend as much in the shops.
- Costs to governments. Governments have to spend more on **jobseeker's allowance** (JSA) and they receive less in income tax and other taxes.

Jobseeker's allowance (JSA) is a payment made to people who are willing and able to work but are not currently in employment. When an economy grows, JSA is likely to fall as more people who are willing to work do manage to find work.

Now test yourself

TESTED

9 If you add together the percentage of the population employed with the percentage unemployed you will only get to around 80% of the population in the UK. What is the other 20% doing?

Answer on p. 218

Measures of unemployment

The two measures of unemployment used in the UK are:

- The **ILO measure** (conducted by the Labour Force Survey): this uses a questionnaire to ask people aged 16–65 whether they have been out of work over the last 4 weeks and are ready to start within 2 weeks.
- The **claimant count:** this records people who are successfully claiming jobseeker's allowance.

Now test yourself

TESTED

10 Why might the ILO measure be higher than the claimant count measure?
11 Why might the claimant count rise relative to the ILO measure of unemployment?

Answers on p. 218

The distinction between unemployment and underemployment

REVISED

Unemployed people don't have a job. But many people have jobs which don't offer them enough hours. These **underemployed** people are not taken into account in the unemployment figures, so the unemployment figures may under-represent the problem of joblessness. The Office for National Statistics (ONS) publishes figures for underemployment, and the estimate is just over 10%. As an evaluation point you might consider that many people are also overqualified for the work they do, as well as wishing to work more hours or on a stable contract. For example, people on zero hours contracts might be able to take on more work if they could be sure it would be offered.

Significance of increased employment

REVISED

The benefits of increased employment might include:

- **Increased incomes** — with rises in standards of living for households.
- **Improved skills** (**human capital**) of workers.
- **Multiplier effects** — as increased incomes lead to increased spending, so firms might see increased profits.
- **Higher government taxation revenue** as more people pay tax, and people spend more (VAT and corporation tax also tend to rise when employment rises).

Human capital is the education and skills that a workforce possesses. Investment in people has a value.

Significance of decreased unemployment and inactivity

REVISED

Many of the benefits are the same as the benefits of rising employment, but to these we can add:

- Falling government spending on JSA and other out-of-work benefits.
- Decreased unemployment can have exponential benefits because people who are out of the job market for a long period become increasingly unemployable.
- The job market becomes more flexible (there are more workers for employers to choose from).
- Decreased dependency ratios (the number of inactive people that active and employed people are supporting, directly or indirectly).

Revision activity

Using the reverse of the arguments for increasing employment, explain the costs of decreasing employment. Are these the same as the costs of increasing unemployment?

Migration and employment/unemployment

REVISED

Migration may occur when people:

- are searching for work or better-paid work
- study abroad
- escape from social or political problems in original country
- accompany family members
- disagree with tax structures
- wish to 'get away from' or 'get to' people or places

The economic implications for employment and unemployment depend largely on the reasons for both **immigration** and **emigration**.

- If immigrants come into a country to fill vacancies, then immigration leads to an increase in employment.
- But if immigrants are looking for work and either do not find it or displace other people from work, then employment may be unchanged and unemployment might increase.

Migration is a general term that looks at both immigration, emigration and the overall balance between the two in a country (net migration).

Immigration is when people enter a country for long-term stay.

Emigration is when people exit a country for long-term stay.

Revision activity

Think of one reason why each of the causes of migration might increase both employment and unemployment. For example, people looking for work might find jobs that people in the UK cannot fill (increased employment of, say, doctors) and might increase unemployment (immigrants finding work might displace people currently working in the UK).

Typical mistake

Don't assume that migration means there is an overall cost to the government. Remember that employed immigrants pay tax to the UK government, increasing government revenue.

Now test yourself

TESTED

12 If immigrants come into the UK for full-time study, what will happen to the level of employment and unemployment?

Answer on p. 218

Balance of payments

The balance of payments is a record of international payments over the course of a year.

The current account

REVISED

The current account records payments for transactions between countries in the present year (other than investments or speculation) and comprises:

- trade in goods
- trade in services
- investment income (interest, profit and dividends)
- transfers, e.g. tax payments to foreign governments

Typical mistake

Thinking that investment income on the current account is the flow of investment funds, which are not featured on the current account. Investment income is the *reward* for investment, which is paid in the current period.

Exam tip

Capital account and financial account accounts relate to other parts of the balance of payments (investment and speculation) that you do not need to know for the AS exam, but you will see in the full A-level Economics GCE. Be careful not to include anything other than the current account of the balance of payments in your AS revision notes.

Typical mistake

Thinking that imports are flow *in* rather than a flow *out* of money from a country. If you go on holiday in a foreign country then your spending is recorded as an import, because money is flowing out of the UK.

Current account deficit

REVISED

Causes of a **current account deficit** might include:

- the currency is too strong relative to other countries, e.g. if the pound buys many euros then people holding euros will not want to buy goods

and services from the UK and people in the UK will be keen to buy things from the euro area
- high rates of inflation relative to other countries
- high wage costs relative to other countries
- high level of growth in a country, meaning people with higher incomes tend to buy more imports from abroad

A **current account deficit** of the balance of payments occurs when more money is flowing out of the country than is flowing in.

Current account surplus

REVISED

Causes of a **current account surplus** might include:

- the currency is too weak relative to other countries, e.g. if the Chinese renminbi buys few US dollars then people in China will find it difficult to buy things from outside China
- low rates of inflation relative to other countries
- low wage costs relative to other countries
- low level of growth in a country, making it difficult to buy imports from abroad and creating a strong incentive for firms in the country to export

A **current account surplus** on the balance of payments occurs when more money is flowing into the country than is flowing out.

The interconnectedness of economies through international trade

REVISED

International trade means that countries become interdependent, i.e. they rely on each other:

- for income (exports are part of a country's aggregate demand)
- for resources and goods and services (imports are necessary for production and consumption of goods in all countries)

Some people argue that interdependence is beneficial because it makes countries cooperate with each other, but it can also cause trade blocs to become powerful, which can leave some developing countries unable to trade fairly.

Revision activity

From the information given above, note down the causes of a current account surplus.

Now test yourself

TESTED

13 You go to Spain for a holiday. Is this an export or an import on the UK's balance of payments?

Answer on p. 218

Revision activity

Visit the BBC news website and find 'economy tracker'. Look at the measures of success of the UK economy according to these measures. Make a note of key figures such as the employment and unemployment rates, which you might refer to in your exam.

Exam practice

Changes to the composition of the basket of goods

Apple iPads and Samsung Galaxy tablets have been added to the basket of goods used to measure how quickly consumer prices are rising, as have teen novels, baby wipes and chicken and chips takeaways from fast-food outlets, according to the government body that compiles official inflation rates. The growing popularity of tablet devices made them suitable for addition in their own right for 2012. 'Chicken and chips' was being added because that type of product was under-represented, perhaps because cash-strapped Britons are consuming more cheap and easy meals at a time of high food prices.

The removal of prices for processing colour film reflects the growing use of digital cameras.

Source: adapted from The Office for National Statistics (ONS).

1 With reference to the article, explain why items get added and removed from the 'basket'. [5]
2 Examine the issue of what is in the 'basket' and the proportion spent on each item. [10]
3 Very few pensioners currently use tablet-device computers. Explain why this might cause a problem for a government in the process of setting the annual change in pension allowance. [6]

Answers and quick quiz 5 online

ONLINE

Summary

- Economic growth measures increases in real GDP or increases in potential capacity in an economy. It can lead to an increase in living standards, but this is not guaranteed, and many other factors are also required for an improvement in welfare.
- Controlling inflation is another of the main objectives of governments. In the UK there is a target for CPI changes of 2% (+ or −1%). The task of controlling inflation is the responsibility of the Monetary Policy Committee in the UK. It raises interest rates to try to cut inflation, and cuts interest rates if inflation is low to allow other areas of the economy to improve.
- Employment and unemployment are not opposites, but different ways of looking at efficiency in the use of the country's workforce. Inactivity helps to explain this. Underemployment is a good way of evaluating the measure of unemployment.
- The balance of payments is another way to judge the health of an economy, by looking at flows of money in and out of the country. Exports bring money flows into a country, and imports see money flowing out.

6 Aggregate demand (AD)

The characteristics of AD

Aggregate demand is made up of the following components (which are each explained in detail below):

> **consumption (C) + investment (I) + government expenditure (G) + net trade (exports (X) − imports (M))**

AD is the total amount of planned spending on goods and services at any price level in an economy.

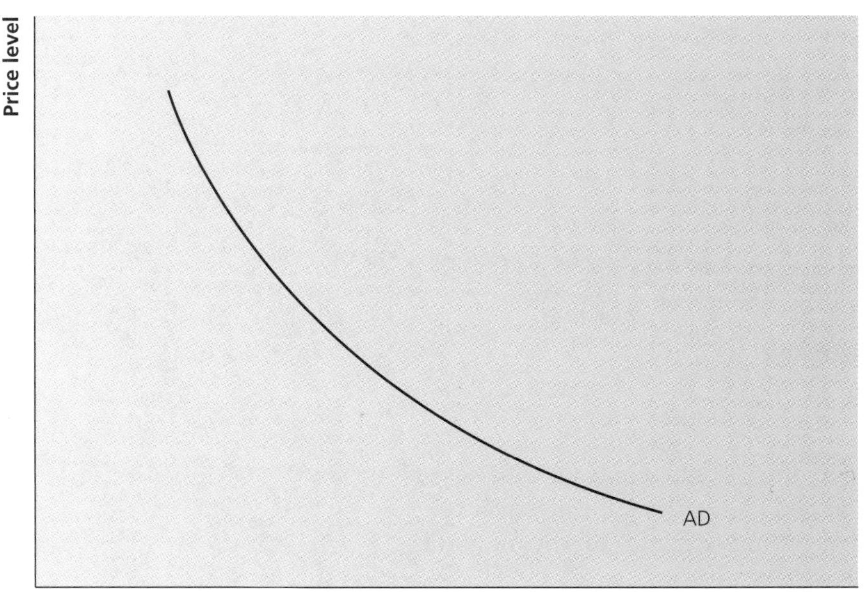

Figure 6.1 An aggregate demand curve

Important features about the aggregate demand curve:

- This diagram (see Figure 6.1) can be drawn as a straight line or a curve.
- Total expenditure by the economy remains much the same along the AD curve and this is called the **real balance effect**. This means that when prices fall, people still spend approximately the same amount in total but they buy a larger amount of items.
- Similarly, higher prices cannot be avoided by buying cheaper alternatives (which is the microeconomic analysis) so the total area under the AD curve remains approximately the same whatever the price level.

Revision activity

Give a reason why the AD curve is downward sloping. Remember that just saying 'prices are lower so we buy more' is not correct.

Exam tip

It does not make any difference to your mark whether you draw AD as a straight line or a curve. Choose the method that you feel most comfortable with.

The AD curve

REVISED

A movement along the AD curve

- This occurs when there is a change in the price level caused by factors that are not related to aggregate demand, i.e. changes in aggregate supply.
- For example, a fall in oil prices (causing a decrease in the cost of production for all firms) would result in a expansion in AD and a fall in the price level, as shown in Figure 6.2.

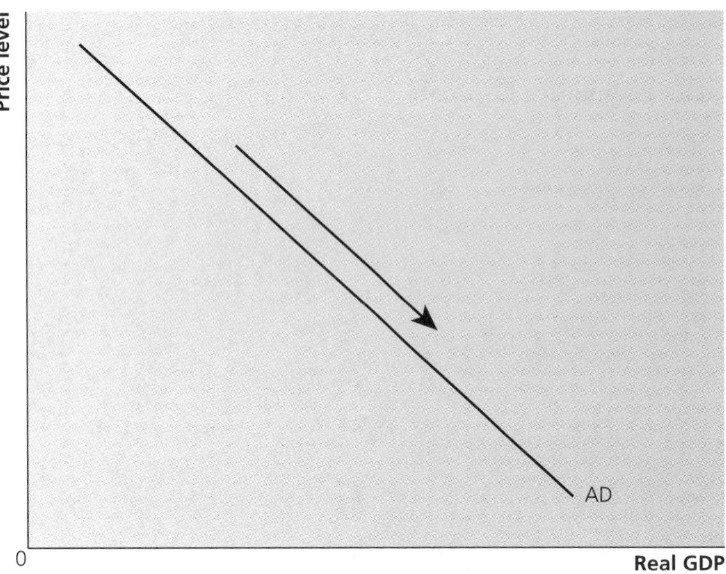

Figure 6.2 Expansion in aggregate demand

Shifts of the AD curve

Aggregate demand shifts when any one of the components C + I + G + (X – M) changes (see Figures 6.3 and 6.4). The analysis above explains why they might change. The size of the change depends on the multiplier effect (see page 93).

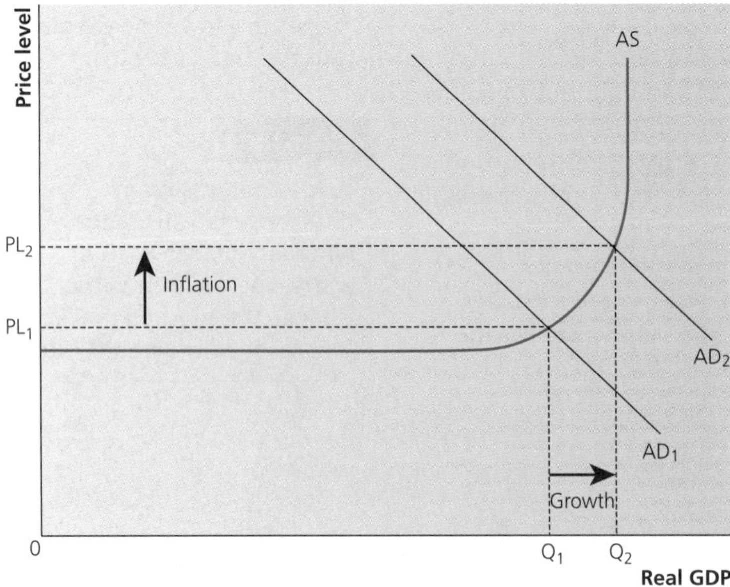

Figure 6.3 An increase in aggregate demand

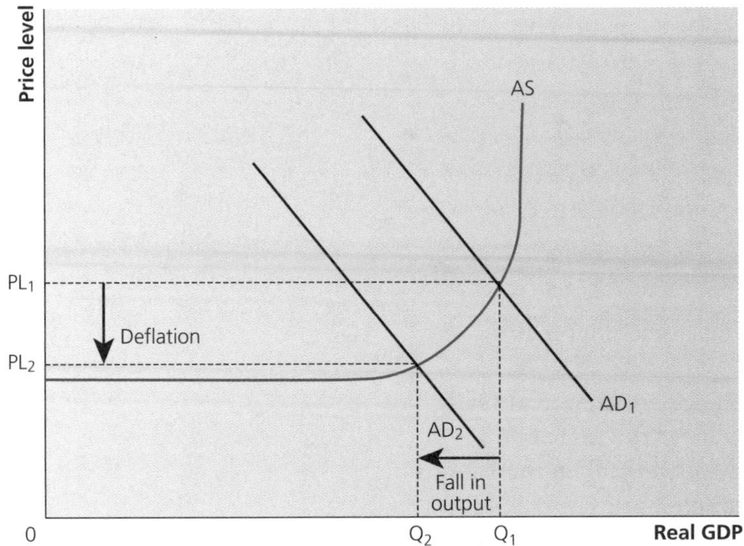

Figure 6.4 A decrease in aggregate demand

When aggregate demand shifts there will be changes in the price level and equilibrium real output.

- If aggregate demand increases, we expect the average level of prices to rise (inflation) and real output to increase (economic growth).
- If aggregate demand decreases, we expect the average level of prices to fall (deflation or falling prices) and real output to decrease (slowdown or recession).

Exam tip

Remember to put the average price level or price level on the vertical axis of your diagrams. You will not gain the marks if you simply label it 'price' because this will look like a micro diagram. You should also avoid putting inflation on the vertical axis as this alters the analysis. On the horizontal axis never use 'Q' — use 'Real GDP' (or 'real national income') or another macro label such as this.

Now test yourself

TESTED

1 What is the difference between a movement along the AD curve and a shift?

Answer on p. 218

Consumption (C)

Consumption is spending by households on goods and services, and is the main component of AD (about 65%). For example, it records how much you spend on food and clothes. The main determinants of consumption are:

- **Interest rate (the cost of credit).** If **interest rates** rise, then it costs us more to borrow if we are going to spend on credit and it increases the opportunity cost of spending (i.e. saving); higher interest rates mean that more money can be earned by leaving money in the bank.
- **Consumer confidence.** If householders feel secure in their jobs and future prospects for the economy, then they are more likely to buy big-ticket items such as new cars or expensive electrical goods. Because of this, what people think is going to happen to the economy has a big influence on what actually does happen.
- **Wealth effects.** An increase in share or house prices means that households are willing and able to spend more. For example, if my house is worth more I might take out a larger loan on my house, and if my shares go up in value I might be more willing to book a foreign holiday, even if I do not in fact sell my house or my shares.
- **The level of employment.** The higher the level of employment the more will be spent in a country (which might lead to even higher employment).

The **interest rate** is the cost of credit (borrowing) or the reward for saving.

The **wealth effect** is the effect on spending or incomes when asset prices change.

Now test yourself

TESTED

2 If interest rates fall what will happen to consumption?

Answer on p. 218

Investment (I)

Investment is defined as an increase in the capital stock. The main influences are:

- **The rate of economic growth.** If there is an increase in real GDP then firms will need more capital in order to meet the increased demand. So an increase in real GDP causes I to rise, and an increase in I causes real GDP to rise. This is a virtuous circle (unless it happens in reverse).
- **Confidence levels.** If firms think that they will sell more in the future (business confidence is high) they are more likely to invest today.
- **Interest rates.** If interest rates rise, investment tends to fall because it costs more to borrow the money in order to invest.
- **Animal spirits.** This is a term used by Keynes. Sometimes consumers and firms are not totally rational, and they act on gut instinct. According to Keynes, investment does not happen automatically — an additional boost might be needed by government. Firms might look at evidence that suggests that investment is worthwhile, but may need more than this to spur them into action. Consumers might decide they can afford to spend more but may need something to trigger the spending. Similarly, when prices and investment rise too quickly the government might need to intervene to calm down inflationary bubbles.
- **Risk.** The higher the level of risk, the lower the level of investment.
- **Access to credit.** Low interest rates do not necessarily mean that all firms can borrow cheaply. Banks might not be willing to take risks in their lending (even if the new financial controls allowed them to lend). In the aftermath of the credit crisis, firms often found it difficult to borrow even if they wanted to.
- **Government decisions.** Changes in government decisions and rules have a significant impact on capital spending, especially if firms have to face fines if they do not react. Government policy might mean changes in tax rates which directly affect firms. For example, if the government decides to cut **corporation tax** (a tax on profit) then firms are more likely to invest.
- **Government bureaucracy.** If the government relaxes planning restrictions — as they have done recently with buildings in the UK — firms are more likely to invest in building projects.

Gross investment is the total amount of investment, before any account is taken of depreciation of assets. Capital loses value as it wears out or becomes less efficient. Much investment in technology is quickly outdated, for example computer equipment.

Net investment takes account of the fall in value of capital assets. It is more useful as a sign of improvements in the prospects for the economy. It is the increase in capital less depreciation.

Corporation tax is a tax on profits that firms make. This tax affects the level of investment that firms make (aggregate demand) and it also affects the amount that firms are willing to supply at any price level, i.e. aggregate supply.

Government bureaucracy is the level of government regulations and paperwork that is required to make any business decisions.

Exam tip

Do not confuse interest rates with inflation. Interest rates may be used to control inflation, but otherwise they are very different concepts.

Government expenditure (G)

Governments can choose to some extent how much they spend and deliberately manipulate total spending in the economy by changing their own level of spending. This is called **discretionary fiscal policy**.

Fiscal policy is the government's position or set of decisions on government spending and taxation.

Points to note about government expenditure include:

- The government does not have to 'balance its books' in the short run, meaning that it can spend more or less than it earns in taxation.
- If the government spends *more* than it earns, this is known as a **fiscal or budget deficit**; this will increase the flow of income, or aggregate demand.
- If the government spends *less* than it earns, this is known as a **fiscal or budget surplus** and leads to a contraction of aggregate demand.
- The government automatically spends more in a recession as government spending increases on out-of-work benefits and taxation receipts fall as workers and firms earn less
- The government automatically spends less in a boom as government spending decreases and taxation receipts rise as wages and employment rise.

Many governments deliberately change taxes and benefits in order to influence the level of aggregate demand. For more on fiscal policy see chapter 10.

Exam tip

Examiners tend to use the words 'budget' or 'fiscal' to mean the same thing, so do not be alarmed if you are asked to explain a budget or fiscal deficit — your answer will be the same. It means that the government is spending more than it is receiving in taxation.

Net trade (X – M)

Net trade (exports minus imports) is the last component of aggregate demand. In the UK this is a negative figure, meaning that the outflow of money for foreign goods and services is greater than the inflow that the UK receives from its exports.

The causes of changes in **net exports** are:

- **Real income.** If incomes rise within an economy, then there is a reduced incentive for domestic firms to export, because they can sell their goods and services in the domestic economy.
- **Change in exchange rate.** If the **exchange rate** rises, net exports are likely to fall as exports become less competitive abroad and imports become more competitive in the domestic economy. However, in the short run a strong exchange rate might increase the value of exports and decrease the value of imports, as spending patterns do not adjust quickly to price changes. This is known as low price elasticity of demand for exports and imports. It causes the opposite reaction to AD than the one normally expected, as people take time to adjust their spending.
- **Changes in the state of the world economy.** The value of UK exports is heavily dependent on growth rates around the world. The slowdown in the Eurozone has caused UK exports to fall, especially to Spain. The crisis in the Eurozone has meant that spending on Chinese imports has been dramatically reduced, causing Chinese growth rates to fall because China is heavily dependent on exports to the Eurozone.
- **The degree of protectionism.** If there are high tariffs, quotas or other restrictions on trade, then firms will find it difficult to export to certain countries.
- **Non-price factors.** Demand for exports and imports is determined by many things apart from price, such as quality of engineering, reliability of after-sales service, tariffs and transport costs.

Net exports — the export of goods and products means that money flows into a country; when the value of the money flowing out of the country (as imports) is deducted, a figure for net exports is the result.

The **exchange rate** is the price of one currency in terms of another.

Exam tip

If our currency gets stronger, it means we can buy more of a foreign currency, so our imports are cheaper and exports cost more to people abroad. To remember this, use the mnemonic SPICED — 'strong pound, imports cheap, exports dear (expensive)'.

Now test yourself

TESTED

3 Does a fall in the currency value increase or decrease aggregate demand?

Answer on p. 218

Exam practice

1 Which of the following is the best explanation of the shape of the AD curve?
  - A When prices are lower people buy more.
  - B When costs rise firms will raise prices.
  - C When prices are lower the country is more likely to export and less likely to import.
  - D When prices are higher the country is more likely to export and less likely to import. [1]

2 If interest rates rise, what is likely to happen to AD? Consider the impact on three components of AD. [6]

Answers and quick quiz 6 online

ONLINE

Summary

- Aggregate demand is the total amount of planned spending on goods and services at any price level in an economy. It is made up of C + I + G + (X – M).
- The largest component of AD in the UK, around two-thirds of AD, is consumption (C).
- Investment can be considered before it depreciates (gross investment) or after (net investment).
- Government spending is determined by the trade cycle. It is also determined by deliberate decisions of the government, set out in its fiscal policy or *budget*.
- Net trade is money received from exports (X) less money from imports (M). The overall impact is a major determinant of growth. In times of global recession, net trade will fall, meaning that the crisis in other countries (such as the south Eurozone area) will impact upon the UK.

7 Aggregate supply (AS)

The characteristics of AS

Aggregate supply is the amount that all firms in the economy are willing to supply at various price levels.

- It is based on the costs of production and incorporates rent, wages, interest and profits.
- As prices rise, firms are generally willing to supply more but there comes a point where firms reach maximum capacity which we will call full employment (at Y_f on Figure 7.1).
- You can draw AS as a straight line sloping upwards to indicate that there are rising costs as firms try to produce more.
- Or you can show AS with a horizontal section where there is spare capacity, an upward sloping part where there are bottlenecks in the economy, and a vertical part at full employment.

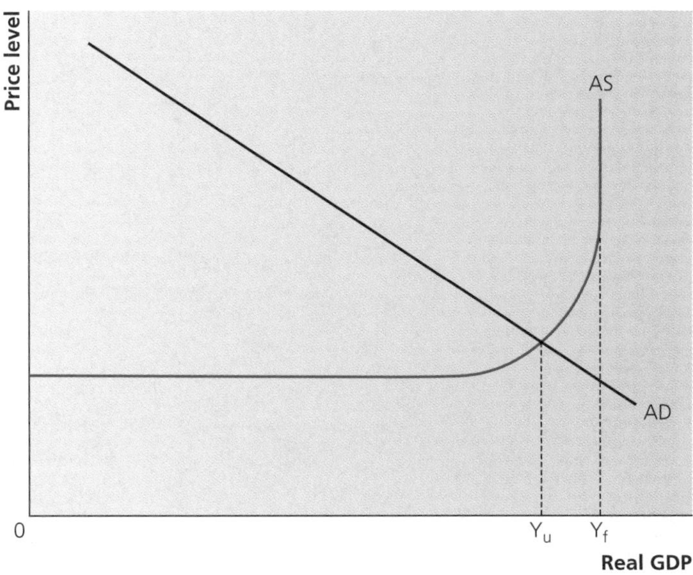

Figure 7.1 Aggregate supply

If the costs of production rise, the aggregate supply shifts left/upwards or *decreases*. For example:

- If the price of oil rises, firms will not be willing to supply unless they can receive more money for the same output.
- If investment falls, for example because interest rates have risen, then again aggregate supply decreases.
- If there is a shortage of certain factors of production, for example skilled labour, then this will raise costs for firms.

Exam tip

Note that visually the shift is up/left, but when we say 'up' it confuses us with an *increase*, which is in fact the opposite.

If an economy can increase output without significant increase in costs (that is, the aggregate supply is not vertical), we say there is **spare capacity** (or an output gap, see page 98). In this case, there are unused resources in the economy, meaning some unemployment (at Y_u in Figure 7.1).

- The Keynesian view is that there can be equilibrium in an economy and also spare capacity.
- The argument is that you cannot leave unemployment and recession to disappear by themselves as market forces push prices down and make the resources more employable.

Spare capacity is where there are unemployed resources in an economy.

Approaches to aggregate supply

REVISED

The **Keynesian approach** to aggregate supply reflects the belief that an economy can be at equilibrium when there is spare capacity.

The **classical approach** to aggregate supply reflects the view that if there is spare capacity in the economy it cannot be said to be at equilibrium, and eventually the spare capacity will disappear, i.e. the aggregate supply is vertical in the long run.

Movements along the aggregate supply curve occur when aggregate demand shifts and the price level changes (see Figures 7.2 and 7.3).

- If there is an increase in aggregate demand, aggregate supply will expand and firms will produce more (Keynesian AS).
- If there is a decrease in aggregate demand, aggregate supply will contract and firms will produce less (Keynesian AS).

The **Keynesian approach** is the view that there can be equilibrium unemployment, and governments can take action to stimulate aggregate demand to achieve long-term growth and employment.

The **classical approach** is the view that markets work best if left to themselves. If there is unemployment, then labour markets should be left to themselves. Wages will fall until people can find work.

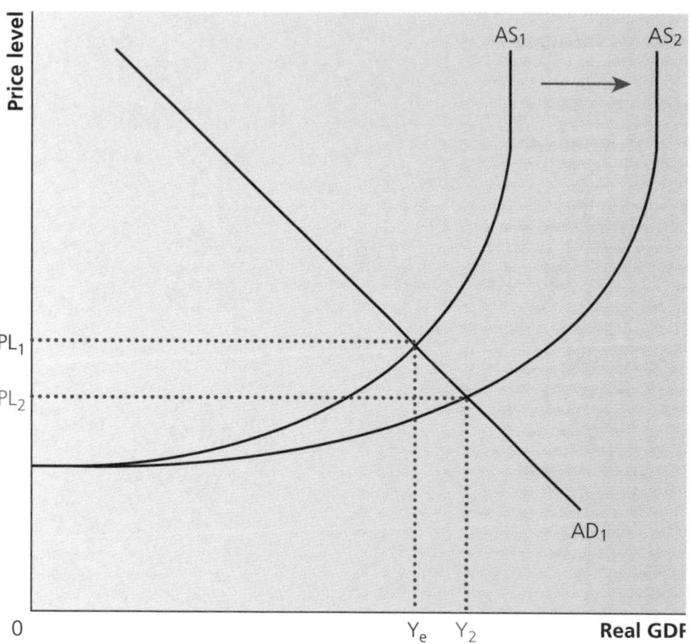

Figure 7.2 An increase in aggregate supply

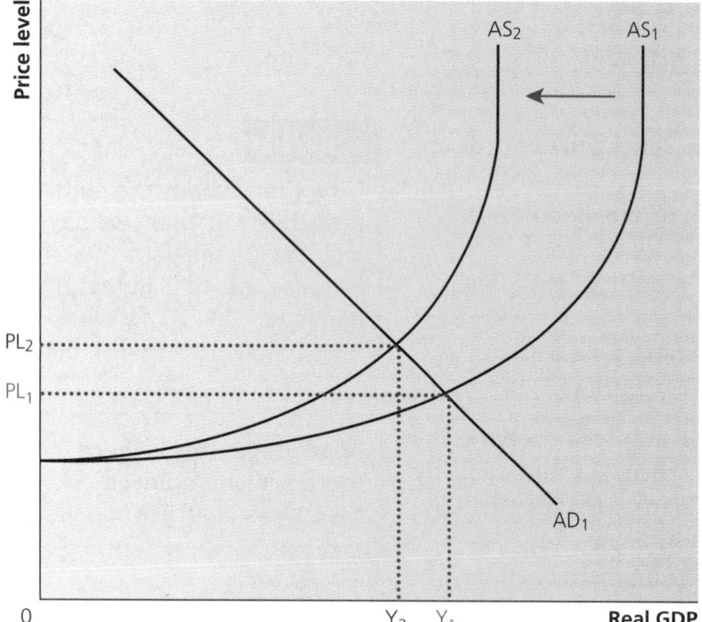

Figure 7.3 A decrease in aggregate supply

Exam tip

It is probably worth drawing the AS curve as a curve rather than a straight line. This will make it easier for you to talk about output gaps and other Keynesian analysis. It will also make it easier for you to evaluate, as you can discuss where the AD crosses the AS and the differing impact of the price level on real output that results.

Now test yourself

TESTED

1 Why do AS curves sometimes get drawn as a backwards-facing L-shape?

Answer on p. 218

Why does aggregate supply shift?

REVISED

There are many changes that might make firms willing to supply more or less at any given price level. If costs to firms decrease, we say that there is an increase in aggregate supply, and if costs to firms increase, we say that there is a decrease in aggregate supply.

Short-run AS

The following factors might cause a shift in aggregate supply in the **short run**:

- **Change in costs of raw materials.** If the cost of oil rises, the cost of production of almost everything will rise, meaning that aggregate supply decreases (shifts to the left or upwards).
- **Change in the level of international trade.** If, for example, trade is inhibited by a new tax on imports (a tariff), costs for domestic firms tend to rise as they cannot enjoy low production costs using cheap raw materials, and AS decreases (shifts upwards).
- **Change in exchange rates.** If the pound gets stronger, imports become cheaper and aggregate supply increases (shifts downwards).
- **Change in tax rates.** If there is a cut in an indirect tax such as VAT you would expect AS to increase (downwards).

These changes mean that firms have a change in their costs of production, but no change in the total amount they are able and willing to make, i.e. their productive capacity remains the same.

Long-run AS

The following factors might cause a shift in aggregate supply in the **long run**.

- **Technological advances.** New computer-aided technology, for example, can reduce costs for a broad range of firms.
- **Relative productivity changes.** Productivity is defined as output per unit of input. If there is an improvement in the division and workflow becomes more efficient, then AS shifts down or to the right.
- **Education and skills changes.** If more people are well educated then aggregate supply increases.
- **Demographic changes and migration.** Demographic changes are the changes in the way the population is made up, e.g. when people live longer and the birth rate also falls we will see an ageing population. Demographic changes have a direct effect on the supply, skills and cost of labour, and therefore impact on aggregate supply as a whole. Migration has a specific demographic effect in that many migrants are of working age or are students, so increases in migration in the short run cause the aggregate supply to increase, but if migrants stay in the country and have children or become dependent in their old age, the effect on aggregate supply might stagnate.

- **Competition policy and regulation changes.** If firms are forced to compete with each other rather than act as monopolies, they have to cut prices or improve their quality. Effective policing of competition makes the aggregate supply increase (shift right or downwards). If the government makes new laws to make it easier to set up and run businesses, then aggregate supply increases. This is sometimes called a cut in red tape or cut in bureaucracy. Some regulations add to firms' costs (a decrease in AS).
- **Changes in the minimum wage.** Increases in the minimum wage can increase costs for firms meaning that aggregate supply falls. However, there is evidence that increasing minimum wages can increase productivity of workers, which might mean that aggregate supply increases.
- **Changes in the tax and benefit system.** A cut in taxes on firms might increase aggregate supply. A cut in benefits might make people more desperate to keep their jobs or to find work, meaning productivity increases — although it might mean that people are less healthy, or less able to concentrate at work, or cause living standards to worsen.

These changes mean there is a change in the productive capacity of an economy, or that the economy can produce more at any given price level.

Exam tip

When you are trying to decide whether there will be a change in AD or AS, remember that AS is the firms' perspective. Think about costs of production.

Typical mistake

Shifting AS the wrong way. Remember than an increase in AS makes it shift right or down. This sounds a bit odd. But it is because when there is an increase, it is the *output* increasing at any particular price level.

Now test yourself

TESTED

2 Will an increase in the interest rate cause aggregate supply to increase or decrease?

Answer on p. 218

Exam practice

1 Explain the difference between production and productivity. [2]

2 Using a Keynesian long-run AS curve, annotate the diagram below to show the effect of a **decrease** in productive capacity on an economy where there is a negative output gap. [2]

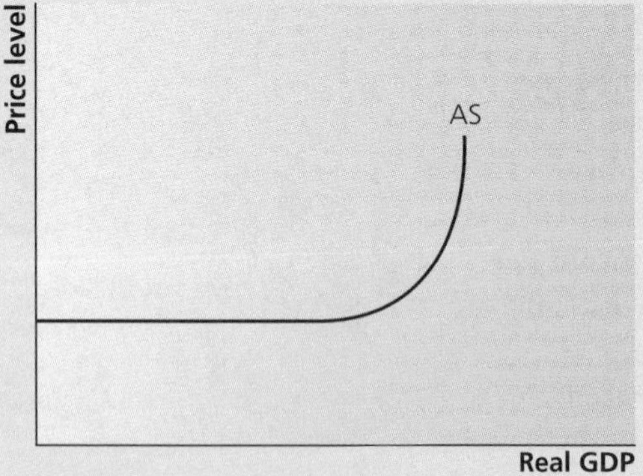

3 There is a rise in exchange rates. This means that aggregate supply will:

A increase in the short run (shift downwards/right) but not change in the long run
B increase in the short run (shift downwards/right) and may increase in the long run
C decrease in the short run (shift downwards/right) but not change in the long run
D not change in the short run (shift downwards/right) but decrease in the long run [1]

Answers and quick quiz 7 online

ONLINE

Summary

- Aggregate supply is the amount that all firms in the economy are willing to supply at various price levels.
- When the price level changes there is a movement along the AS curve. This occurs because there has been a change in aggregate demand. AS expands when AD increases, and contracts when AD decreases.
- Aggregate supply shifts when costs that firms face change, or the amount they can produce at any particular price changes.
- Short-run changes in aggregate supply occur when costs change. Examples are changes in oil prices, exchange rates or taxes.
- Long-run changes in aggregate supply occur when output capacity changes. Examples are changes in the quality of factors of production or improved competition.

8 National income

The concept

National income is the amount received by various agents in an economy, by households, firms and government.

- It is the same as gross domestic product (GDP) measured by households, firms and government.
- It is the same as total spending by households, firms and government.
- It is the same as gross domestic income, which is all the income earned in the economy.
- This assumes that **leakages** (savings, tax and imports) and injections (investment, government spending and exports) have been taken into account.

National income is a flow of money, i.e. a movement of money from one person to another, rather than a stock of money such as savings in a bank, physical **assets** such as buildings or shares. The stock of assets in an economy is called **wealth**.

Leakages (also known as 'withdrawal') are an exit from the circular flow of money. These comprise saving, taxation and the money spent on imports.

An **asset** is an accumulation of wealth; factors which can be used to provide income in the future.

Wealth is a stock of assets, e.g. factories or land.

Income and wealth

REVISED

There is a strong **correlation** between **income** and wealth. The ownership of wealth in itself can mean that there are interest payments or rent. When wealth changes in value, e.g. house prices rise or fall, there is an impact on people's spending and therefore incomes. For example, if my house is worth more than I paid for it, I might feel more confident about buying a new car and the bank manager might lend me the money because he is confident that my house can act as **collateral**.

Income is a flow of money, e.g. wages.

Collateral assets are used as security for a loan.

Injections and withdrawals

Injections

REVISED

Changes to the flow of income (see Figure 8.1) occur when there is a change in one of the three **injections** into the circular flow of income.

Injections are an input into the circular flow of money. These inputs comprise investment, government spending and export income.

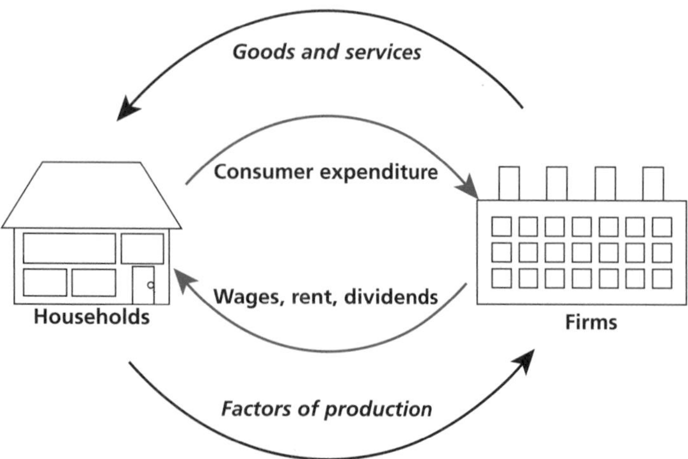

Figure 8.1 The circular flow of income (income is shown in red)

The injections are:

- **Investment (I):** an increase in the capital stock (assets).
- **Government spending (G):** where the government buys goods and services such as health care in the NHS.
- **Exports (X):** where people from abroad buy domestically produced goods and services.

Investment is an increase in spending when capital assets are bought as well as consumer items. So, for example, if a firm buys a new machine, there is more spending in the economy because the machine has to be made, which in turn means a greater number of incomes.

Typical mistake

Confusing saving with investment. In fact, they are complete opposites. Saving represents a decrease in the amount of spending in the economy as we forgo current spending for future spending.

Withdrawals

REVISED

Withdrawals are leakages out of the circular flow of income. If money is not re-spent within the economy, then it is being withdrawn or pulled out of the circular flow. The three reasons this happens are:

- **Savings (S).** When we decide to spend money later rather than now it means that there is less spending in the current time period.
- **Tax (T).** When the government demands your money you cannot spend it. It is true that in many cases all the money that the government takes in tax is re-spent as government spending (G), but if the government starts to run a budget surplus, then this will not be the case. Try to think of G and T as independent.
- **Imports (M).** When we buy goods and services from abroad, our money or spending flows out of the country. This means less income for the domestic circular flow.

Now test yourself

TESTED

1 If the government decreases its spending on defence, what will happen to the total amount of spending in an economy?

Answer on p. 218

Equilibrium levels of real national output

Equilibrium

REVISED

When aggregate demand meets aggregate supply there is an **equilibrium** point, which tells us the price level and real GDP of a country (see Figure 8.2).

An **equilibrium** is a balancing point where there is no tendency to change.

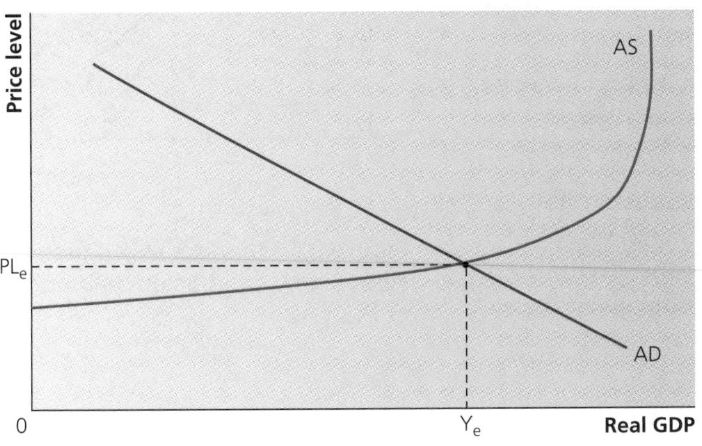

Figure 8.2 Equilibrium

An equilibrium is a balancing point where there is no tendency to change the price level or output level.

- If prices were higher than the balancing point PL_e, there would be a tendency for them to fall because supply would be greater than demand and there would be lots of unsold goods and services.
- If prices were lower than the balancing point, there would be shortages and prices would start to rise in order to make sure that everyone could get what they were prepared to pay for.
- If, for example, a worldwide recession and a fall in aggregate demand occurred, you would expect to see falls in prices (or that prices would not rise very quickly).

The use of AD/AS diagrams to show how shifts in AD or AS cause changes in inflation and growth

REVISED

When AD shifts to the right (expansionary) then we would expect there to be an increase in the equilibrium price level, i.e. inflation, and an increase in growth, i.e. an increase in real national output. This is shown in Figure 8.3.

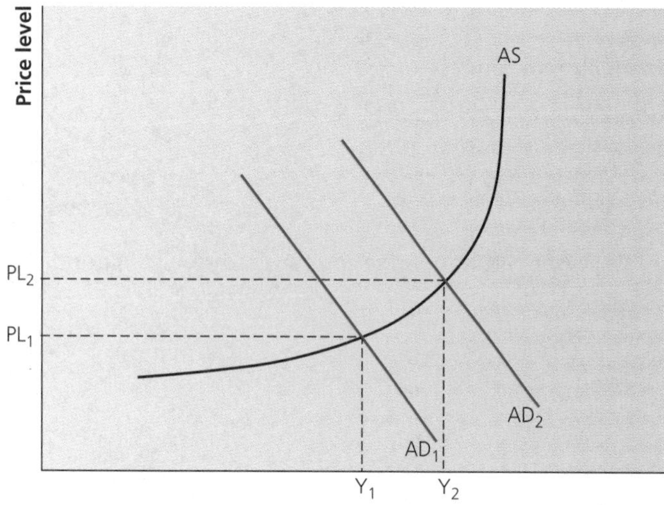

Figure 8.3 When AD shifts to the right a new equilibrium is found at PL_2 Y_2

However, this depends on AS being upward sloping. The more elastic the AS, the more the effect is seen on the growth axis rather than the price level axis. If AS is perfectly inelastic (the classical approach discussed on p. 86), then there will be no effect on output at all, and just an increase in prices.

When AS shifts to the right we would expect there to be a decrease in the equilibrium price level, i.e. deflation, and an increase in growth, i.e. an increase in real national output. See Figure 8.4.

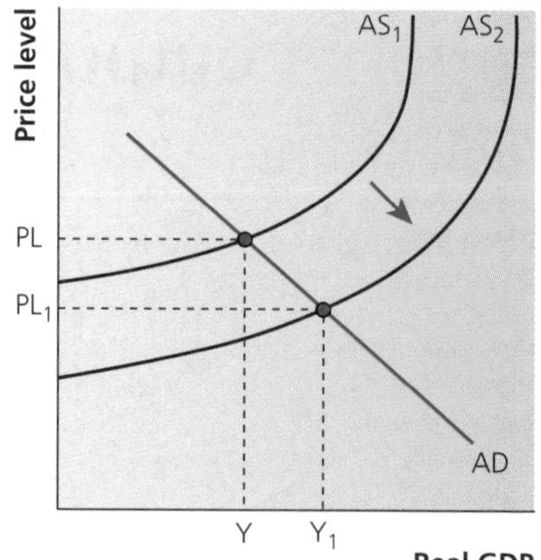

Figure 8.4 When AS shifts to the right a new equilibrium is found at PL_1 Y_1

However, this depends on AD crossing the AS where AS is not perfectly elastic (horizontal). If AS is perfectly elastic (the Keynesian output gap approach discussed on pp. 85–86), then there will be no effect on output or prices at all. The only effect would be an increase in the **output gap**.

Now test yourself

TESTED

2 Is equilibrium a good thing?

Answer on p. 219

The multiplier

The multiplier ratio

REVISED

The multiplier shows the amount by which a change in an injection or leakage causes total spending to change. It is the result of income being re-spent in the economy, having second and successive effects. The multiplier ratio, if written as x:y, shows how much of an impact an initial injection (x) will have on total incomes (y).

If the injections into the circular flow increase, then there will be a larger final change on total spending in the economy. The multiplier times the injection gives the final change to spending.

If the leakages from the circular flow increase, then the multiplier effect will be smaller. For example, when the 2008 recession hit the UK, the saving ratio rose markedly, reducing the multiplier effect.

Understanding marginal propensities (the tendency to do something with any extra money you have)

REVISED

- If I give you £10 and you spend half of it straight away, then you have a marginal propensity to consume (MPC) of 0.5, that is, 50% of any extra injection will be re-spent in the economy in macroeconomic terms. The MPC is 0.5.
- If I give you £10 and you save £1, then your marginal propensity to save (MPS) is 0.1. The more you save, the less you spend, so the lower the multiplier is. This means that an injection has a smaller overall impact on the economy. The multiplier ratio falls when the marginal propensity to save rises.
- If I give you £10 and you buy some cigarettes, which have a specific tax of £3, then the effect on the economy will not be as great as if you spent the money on some locally grown apples (no tax). The higher the marginal propensity to tax (MPT), the lower the multiplier ratio.
- If I give you £10 and you spend the money at Starbucks, the profits will leave the country as an import on the current account (investment income). So, if £1 leaves the country to return to the USA, the marginal propensity to import (MPM) is 0.1, and the effect is to reduce the value of the multiplier compared to buying some milk produced by UK cows.

The multiplier is 1 divided by the sum of the marginal propensities to withdraw. In other words, it is an inverse relation to the amount I end up spending in my own economy, that is 1/(1 – MPC) or 1 divided by what is left when everything else has leaked out of the circular flow of income.

The multiplier process

REVISED

For your exam you need to be able to show the effect of the multiplier numerically. Every time AD shifts or there is a change in an injection into the circular flow you should mention the multiplier. So for example, for any extra £1 that is injected into the circular flow, 0.1 or 10% might be saved (the marginal propensity to save or MPS), 0.4 or 40% might be spent on tax (marginal propensity to tax or MPT), 0.4 or 40% might be spent on imports (marginal propensity to import or MPM). All that is left is 0.1 or 10%, which is the amount that will be re-spent within the economy (the marginal propensity to consume or MPC).

Using these numbers we can say that the multiplier is 1/(MPS + MPT + MPM). This means that the effect on the economy of a new injection will have a magnified impact on the total expenditure in the economy, but this is limited by the amount of money that *leaks out* of the circular flow. Put another way, the multiplier is 1/(1 – MPC) meaning that the increase in total spending depends on how much is left for spending in the economy when all the leakages have been taken out.

Now test yourself

TESTED

3 If there is an injection of £1 million into an economy and the multiplier is 2, what is the total change in spending in the economy?

Answer on p. 219

The effects of the multiplier on the economy

REVISED

The effect of the multiplier is to magnify the impact of **exogenous changes**. If any of the injections change (I, G or X) then the effect on level of real output and the price level will be more than the initial change. The relationship between the initial change and the total overall change is the multiplier effect.

exogenous changes are changes that arise outside the system, for example, a rise in export earnings.

Calculations using the multiplier

REVISED

If the multiplier is given, then you simply multiply the number given with the change in the injection to give the total overall change in national income.

So, for example, if the multiplier is 2 in the UK and there is an increase of £10 billion through exports to Singapore, then the total change in national income is £20 billion. If, however, the multiplier is 2 and there is a fall in national income through a cut in investment of £2 billion, then the total fall in national income is £4 billion.

Sometimes you might be asked to show the change that the injection will trigger, not the overall change. To do this, just take off the initial change in the injection. For example, if the multiplier is 2 in the UK and there is an increase of £10 billion through exports to Singapore, then further change in national income is £10 billion.

Another calculation you might need is to work out the value of the multiplier itself. For example, assume the multiplier is 2. If there is a rise

Exam tip

The multiplier impact can be positive or negative.

in the marginal propensity to save, from 0.1 to 0.2, the multiplier will go from 1/0.5 to 1/0.6 = 1.67. So an increase in saving means that the multiplier falls in value. This means that any change in an injection will have a smaller impact on the overall level of spending.

The significance of the multiplier to shifts in aggregate demand

REVISED

If there is a change in any one of the injections or leakages, the total effect on the economy as a whole will be greater than the original change as long as it is above 1. The multiplier magnifies the impact of changes on the economy as a whole — the larger the multiplier, the greater the impact of any changes in injections or leakages. Every time you shift aggregate demand (AD) you must remember to shift it that bit further because of the multiplier. The bigger the multiplier ratio, the larger the overall AD shift. Remember that this can be a magnified increase or a magnified decrease.

Exam practice

1 In 2015 the Bank of England estimated that the marginal propensity to import in the UK rose from 0.2 to 0.3.
   (a) Define the term 'marginal propensity to import'. [1]
   (b) If the value of the multiplier was 1.25 before the change, calculate the new value of the multiplier, if everything else is unchanged. [2]
   (c) Which one of the following is the most likely cause of the rise in the marginal propensity to import?
      A a recession in the UK
      B an increase in underemployment
      C a fall in the interest rate
      D a rise in the exchange rate [1]

2 Discuss the likely impact on aggregate demand when there is an increase in the value of the currency. [20/25]

Exam tip

Note that for an AS exam you choose from two essay titles, and these are worth 20 marks. For the full A-level you choose from two essays worth 25 marks. The content and style are very similar, but you have a few more minutes at A-level.

Answers and quick quiz 8 online

ONLINE

Summary

- The main piece of analysis in macroeconomics, and the building block for most of the conclusions you will need to reach, can be found in aggregate demand and supply analysis.
- **Aggregate demand:** there are forces which determine how much people in an economy are prepared to buy at any price level, and the agents of this demand are consumers, firms, the government and foreign purchasers of our exports. We take off the value of imports and use the formula AD = C + I + G + (X – M).
- **Aggregate supply:** the amount that firms are willing to supply at any price level. The higher the prices that can be charged, the more firms are willing to supply. The curve shifts when there are changes in costs that affect all firms, such as changes in oil prices, taxes or productivity of workers.
- Putting aggregate demand and supply together we get an equilibrium price level and output, which tells us what inflation and growth will be as AS or AD shifts. You will be examined on the causes of these shifts — remember that changes in determinants of aggregate demand are magnified by the working of the multiplier. This is the impact of incomes being re-spent in an economy, so any change in spending has second and subsequent round effects.

9 Economic growth

Causes of growth

Growth occurs when there is an increase in aggregate demand or aggregate supply, meaning that there is a new equilibrium output at a level where more is produced.

- It occurs with multiplier effects when there is a shift in aggregate demand.
- If the aggregate supply curve is vertical then when aggregate demand shifts there will *not* be growth — in other words, actual growth cannot occur beyond full capacity.

Aggregate demand shifts

REVISED

Aggregate demand increases when something causes any of the components to increase. Below is a list of possible causes of increases.

Increase in consumption (C)

- A cut in the interest rate means the opportunity cost of saving falls, and the cost of borrowing to invest falls. It can also lead to falls in the cost of mortgage interest repayments, so people have more money left to spend on other things in the economy.
- Increase in confidence.
- Wealth effects from rising house or share prices.

Typical mistake

Consumption is a measure of the spending on goods and services in an economy. It is neither an injection nor a leakage, but a measure of the flow of income in an economy.

Increase in investment (I)

- Firms invest more when the cost of borrowing falls (interest rate cut).
- Increase in confidence of firms. If firms think there will be growth they are more likely to invest, which in itself is likely to stimulate growth.

Typical mistake

Investment is *not* saving in a bank. Investment is an increase in capital assets, for example buying a machine.

Increase in government spending (G)

Governments can use fiscal policy to stimulate the economy. This means spending on government projects, such as road building and education, when the rest of the economy is lacking in aggregate demand. Note that this is a Keynesian policy and that classical economists argue that it will only cause inflation or debt.

Increase in net exports (X – M)

Economies can be stimulated through export-led growth. China and Germany notably sailed through the last recession by maintaining spending through exports. In order to stimulate exports, the following strategies might be successful:

- Hold the exchange rate down (as in China holding the renminbi down). This makes exports relatively cheap and imports relatively expensive. However, in the UK we have a fully floating exchange rate and no manipulation is possible.

- Reduce tariffs and quotas. Encouraging trade tends to lead to an improvement in exports in the long run, but the initial effect is often an increase in imports, which actually reduces AD.
- Encourage the productivity and efficiency in export markets. The problem is that this is really a supply-side policy but it has an impact on the aggregate demand side.

Exam tip

International trade is very important for economic growth because an increase in exports or fall in imports will make AD shift to the right, with **multiplier effects**. Export-led growth means that the economy can grow without a worsening of the current account of the balance of payments.

Typical mistake

Getting confused about the impact of imports on aggregate demand. Remember that when a country imports goods, money is flowing out, so a rise in imports means that more money is leaving the country. This means there is less spending within this country, so there is a fall in aggregate demand.

Aggregate supply shifts

REVISED

Shifting AS to the right or down comes under the category of supply-side policies. These tend to be long run and involve enabling firms to produce more at lower costs. The policies used to achieve this are covered in the section on supply-side policies in chapter 10, p. 105.

Now test yourself

TESTED

1 What happens to growth if there is an increase in investment?

Answer on p. 219

Economic growth – actual and potential

REVISED

Economists have two very different meanings for the term 'economic growth':

1 **Actual growth** is the measure of changes in **real GDP**, found by adding up all the incomes in the country, or all the spending, or all the output. Although none of these measures is entirely reliable, between them we can get a good indication of the changes of activity in the economy.
2 **Potential growth**, probably a more important measure than actual growth, shows how much the economy could produce if all the resources were being used. It is useful for measuring the success of governments and assessing the likelihood of changes in living standards over time.

Actual growth is the increase in real GDP.

Real GDP is the output of an economy, with the effects of inflation removed.

The difference between the actual and potential growth is the **output gap**, and the bigger the output gap, the more inefficient the economy is in its use of resources. In fact a persistent output gap tends to lead to a fall in potential output.

Sustainable growth is the highest rate of growth which does not compromise the welfare of future generations. For example, if an economy grows very quickly by mining all its resources, it might find it difficult to grow in the future.

Potential growth is the amount by which a country could increase its production if all resources were used efficiently.

The **output gap** is the difference between actual GDP (or growth) and potential GDP (or growth).

Output gaps

Output gaps are a sign that the country is not using its resources efficiently, or at their maximum potential. They are formed for a variety of reasons:

- resources available are not suited to the needs of the economy
- the welfare system pays generously for some people not to work
- the effects of relocation of production to other countries
- increased competitiveness of other countries
- structural changes, meaning the economy no longer produces output that is tailored to the needs of the market, e.g. ship-building when the government decides to cut back on the size of the navy.

A negative output gap exists when actual growth rates are below potential growth rates. This is shown in Figure 9.1 by the distance Y_1 to Y_{FE}. Keynesians believe these can persist in the long run.

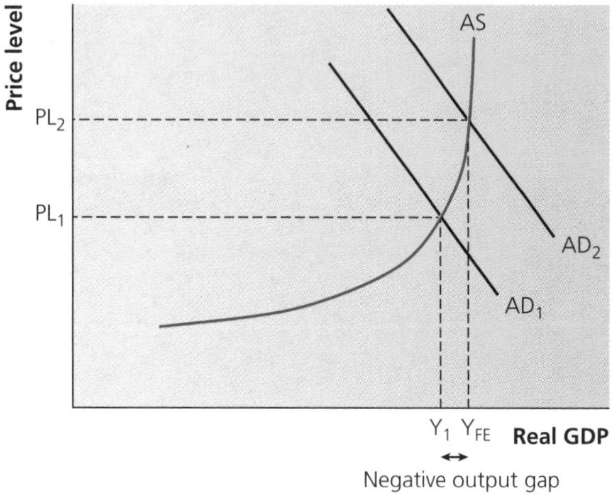

Figure 9.1 Negative output gap using a Keynesian AS curve

A positive output gap is when growth rates are higher than the economy can sustain. This can be shown on a classical AS curve, as a temporary situation where the economy can produce more, but this cannot be sustained in the long run. In the long run, the AS is vertical and the positive output gap disappears. This is shown in Figure 9.2.

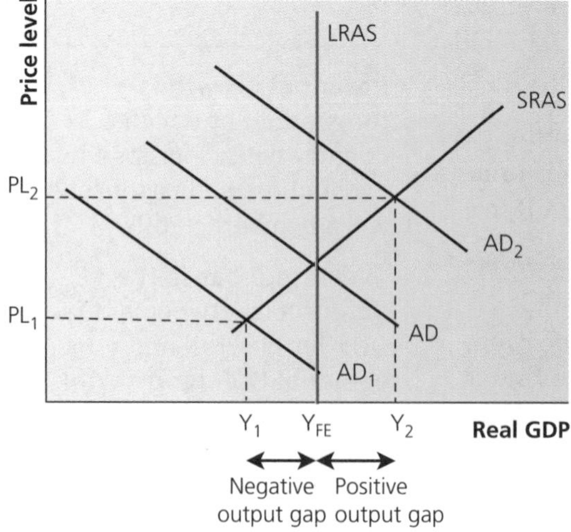

Figure 9.2 Positive and negative output gaps

Revision activity

The Office of Budget Responsibility (OBR) (budgetresponsibility.org.uk) makes a regular estimate of the size of the output gap. Find out what it is today, according to its measure. Does the OBR have any doubts about the reliability of its own measure?

It is difficult to measure both positive and negative output gaps, because we cannot tell what the level of potential output is. All we know is actual output (as measured by real GDP). The potential level depends on spare capacity, and without actually trying to use the spare capacity, we do not know how much the economy can produce.

Typical mistake

Thinking that a falling rate of growth means that real GDP is falling. If the rate of growth is still positive, then a falling rate means that incomes are rising, albeit more slowly.

Now test yourself TESTED

2 If growth rates change from 3.2% to 2.0%, what has happened to the level of real GDP?

Answer on p. 219

Exam tip

There are many ways to draw an output gap on a diagram. Make sure that you are confident in at least one of these ways, e.g. drawing a PPF curve where the point of output is not on the PPF but inside the curve.

Trade (business) cycle

Economic growth changes at different speeds, and there is a pattern that can be observed over time, usually 7 to 10 years. The pattern can involve a **boom** (rapid economic growth) and a **slump** (very slow growth) or even a **recession** (two consecutive quarters of negative economic growth, as in many countries in 2008). Between the boom and the slump there is a slowdown, and between the slump and the boom there is a recovery.

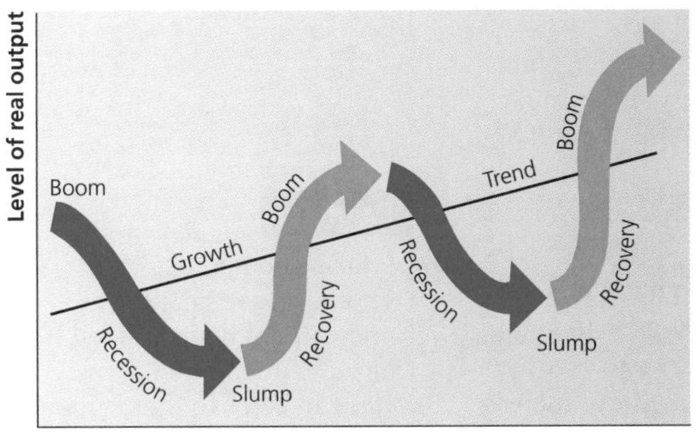

Figure 9.3 The economic cycle

Characteristics of a boom

REVISED

In a boom there is often high employment, increasing living standards, increased investment, but sometimes inflation, widening inequality and increased negative externalities (see The impact of economic growth, overleaf).

Characteristics of a recession

REVISED

In a recession there is often high unemployment or underemployment, lower or not increasing living standards, but sometimes lower inflation, narrowing inequality and decreased negative externalities.

The absence of causes of growth (or constraints on growth) are useful as an evaluation tool when trying to explain a recession. The following are factors which might be used:

- lack of **investment** funds or cash to run businesses
- weak or obstructive governments
- currency instability or a **fixed exchange rate** or too-high exchange rates.

Investment is an increase in the capital stock.

A **fixed exchange rate** is when governments prevent their currencies from moving with market forces. This can be achieved by legislation or through buying and selling currencies to maintain a certain rate.

- lack of human capital
- lack of access to international trade, or a high level of **tariffs** and other forms of protectionism

A **tariff** is a tax on imports that can prevent growth if it means that firms cannot acquire raw materials or capital goods.

Now test yourself TESTED

3 Why can high exchange rates be viewed as a constraint on growth?

Answer on p. 219

The impact of economic growth

Benefits of growth

REVISED

- **Increased incomes and standards of living.** Total income for the country is increasing when there is economic growth, and as long as inflation is not increasing at the same rate at least some people will be better off. However, the distribution of income is likely to change, and while some people might not be any better off, the gap between them and others might increase.
- **Firms are likely to experience increased profits** when there is increased growth. This is likely to mean that they can make more profits and shareholders can enjoy increased returns. However, firms making inferior goods, i.e. where demand falls for these goods when income rises, are likely to suffer. For example, lower-end food suppliers and discount stores such as pound shops tend to do less well in a period of economic growth.
- **Governments benefit in a boom** because more people are working and paying tax and fewer people need benefits such as jobseeker's allowance (JSA), so there is likely to be a fiscal improvement in a boom. However, many governments see a period of economic growth as a time to reduce income inequalities, which become more apparent as top-end incomes tend to rise faster, so rates of benefits such as pensions increase.
- **Current and future living standards.** Growth lifts people out of poverty, and can provide many opportunities for an economy. Developing countries can gain foreign investment, foreign currencies can flow into an economy, and there are likely to be improvements in infrastructure of all types, from airports to mobile phone coverage.

Exam tip

Inferior goods feature in Theme 1 (see chapter 2) and will not be examined directly in Theme 2, but you can refer to them when discussing the impact of growth on some companies where demand falls when consumers have increased income.

Costs of growth

REVISED

Damage to the environment

Damage to the environment can occur, for example, through increased carbon emissions. The by-product of most industrial production is CO_2 and this has an impact on the ozone layer, acid rain and causes health problems such as asthma. Growth also causes a rise in fuel emissions (because a greater number of people are travelling to work or travelling to a holiday destination, possibly further away or more often).

Evaluation: higher incomes can in fact mean that there is more money to clear up environmental damage: catalytic converters can be fitted to cars; firms can be forced to use a certain percentage of bio-fuels or renewable energy; there is money available for investment in new machinery; and firms and governments can be compelled to adopt carbon-offset schemes, or invest in 'green' technology.

Balance of payments problems

Higher incomes mean that people can afford to import more, and the need of firms to export is no longer so pressing as higher profit margins can be made through selling at home rather than abroad. So X falls, M rises and the balance of payments worsens.

Evaluation: if growth is caused by increasing exports however, then an improvement of the balance of payments is expected. For example, in 2015 Germany had the highest rate of growth in the EU, but also a balance of payments surplus.

Exam tip

Remember that an increase in income makes individuals and firms better off, but the country as a whole is worse off if the extra income is used to buy more from abroad.

Widening income distribution

The **distribution of income** is a measure of the difference in incomes between different groups in an economy. These groups can be measured in a variety of ways, but one common way is to compare the highest **decile** or 10% of income earners with the lowest decile.

A **decile** is a 10% chunk of an ordered set of data.

When the economy grows, those who reap the benefits tend to be those who already have a good job. For example, the manager or shareholders of a business will enjoy the increased profits, whereas other employees, e.g. cleaners or factory workers, are not likely to see dividends which relate to profits.

Evaluation: with continued growth, workers may lobby for higher incomes and the rewards may trickle down to those on the lower rungs of the pay scale, especially if there is a shortage of labour and these workers cannot be replaced by machinery. The higher the appropriate skill level of the workers, the more likely they are to benefit.

Exam tip

When a country gets richer overall, there is likely to be a bigger gap between rich and poor.

The opportunity cost to growth

In choosing to achieve economic growth, an economy has to give up other objectives. For example, a country could give more foreign aid, or improve the welfare of pensioners through more generous state aid. These transfer payments are not recorded as growth but may have greater value in terms of improved standards of living.

Evaluation: the opportunity cost of growth is hard to measure, as we cannot know what would have happened if another policy had been used.

Current and future living standards

With increased growth comes increased air and noise pollution, overcrowding, social dislocation and stress. Many people who are made richer by economic growth would say that they would love to return to the simpler life: they would not be happy though if you took away the money they had earned. On this basis, it is arguable how much economic growth improves some people's lives. See p. 70 on national happiness.

Now test yourself

TESTED

4 If economic growth makes someone in the UK's income rise so that she buys a new BMW car from Germany, what are the costs and benefits?

Answer on p. 219

Exam practice

1 The change in national income is measured at 0.4% in real terms for one year. This means that:
   A Price levels are rising.
   B There is a boom.
   C The economy is in a recession.
   D National income is rising slowly. [1]

2 The growth rate in China is shown in Figure 9.4.

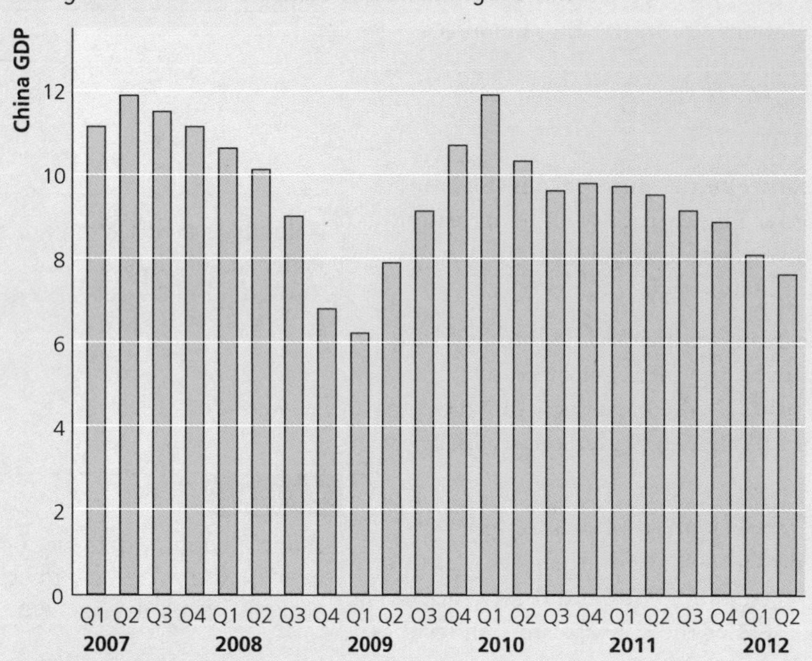

Source: Bloomberg

Figure 9.4 China GDP: quarter compared with previous quarter (annualised % figures)

(a) Explain what was happening to the level of GDP in 2012. [4]
(b) Examine possible reasons for the change in the rate of growth rates. [10]
(c) Discuss the likely benefits of China's growth rate. [25]

Answers and quick quiz 9 online

ONLINE

Summary

- There are two ways to measure growth: actual and potential.
- There are many causes of growth, and to analyse these we usually look at the forces acting on the components of aggregate demand: C + I + G + (X – M).
- The constraints on growth are many, and they depend on which country is being considered. The government might target the constraints on growth as a means of improving welfare in a country, for example by investing in new technological infrastructure.
- The benefits and costs of growth must be weighed against each other in your evaluation. Remember that while there may be benefits, there might be costs in both the short and long term that can cause more damage than the gains from increased income.

10 Macroeconomic objectives and policies

Possible macroeconomic objectives

The seven major objectives

REVISED

There are seven major macroeconomic objectives of governments across the world, but the priority given by each government varies, depending on its political slant. These seven objectives are:

1 Economic growth, i.e. an increase in real incomes or potential output.
2 A reduction in unemployment: the number of people available and willing to work but without employment should be ideally no more than 2%.
3 Control of inflation, i.e. preventing prices from rising too quickly.
4 Restoration of equilibrium in the balance of payments, meaning that there should not be either a persistent and heavy outflow or inflow of income and wealth.
5 Fiscal balance. Over time the government needs to pay its way, so taxation revenues must cover government spending over the course of the economic cycle.
6 Protection of the environment with its consequent impact on the various members of the global community.
7 Making the distribution of income more equal, i.e. ensuring that the top 10% slice (or decile) does not increase much faster than the bottom 10% slice.

Any policies adopted by governments in order to meet any one of these objectives is likely to have an impact on other objectives. Therefore, governments must choose which are its most important policies. Such decisions will determine the opportunity cost in terms of other policies or objectives.

Demand-side policies

There are two types of demand-side policy:

- **Monetary policy:** the manipulation of monetary variables in order to achieve government objectives.
- **Fiscal policy:** the manipulation of government spending and taxation in order to change aggregate demand

Demand-side policies Any deliberate action taken by governments or monetary authorities to shift the aggregate demand curve.

Monetary policy instruments

REVISED

Monetary policy involves the setting of monetary variables, the most important of which are the interest rate (cost of credit or the reward for saving) and quantitative easing or QE (asset purchases to increase the money supply). Until 2008 the main instrument in most countries has been the interest rate, but since then many countries have used both.

Interest rates

If aggregate demand needs to decrease, the interest rate is raised. This means that C, I, and (X – M) will tend to fall. The AD shifts left. There are multiplier effects, increasing the impact of the change.

If aggregate demand needs to increase, the interest rate is cut. This means that C, I, and (X – M) will tend to rise. The AD shifts right. There are multiplier effects, increasing the impact of the change.

The interest rate is set by the Monetary Policy Committee (MPC) of the Bank of England, which meets every month to look at factors that will tend to make prices rise or fall over the coming 18 months or more. The committee takes a vote to determine the interest rate.

Asset purchases

After 2008, many monetary authorities found that interest rates alone could not stimulate aggregate demand. They therefore purchased long-term assets in the money or capital markets. As demand for these assets increased, the price of them rises, which in turn means the dividend yield on them falls. The amount of dividend relative to the price of the bond falls. This is the same impact as cutting interest rates, but has a direct effect on money markets. It means the bonds are more usable in the markets: because people want to buy them, the holders of bonds know they can be sold. It can mean money markets start working again, which is why quantitative easing (QE) is used in a credit crisis. The MPC in the UK spent £375 billion with further spending in 2016 after the 'Brexit' vote. The Federal Reserve in the US spent $3.7 trillion. From this we can see the USA policy response to the global financial crisis has been far greater than in the UK, and many argue that this is why the US economy recovered more quickly than the UK.

Fiscal policy instruments

REVISED

Fiscal policy can involve a government running a government budget or fiscal deficit, where government spending (G) is greater than the amount received in taxation (T). This has an expansionary effect on aggregate demand (AD), with multiplier effects. You can show this by shifting AD on a diagram, for example Figure 8.3 on p. 92.

Fiscal policy can involve a government running a government budget or fiscal surplus, where government spending (G) is less than the amount received in taxation (T). This has a contractionary effect on AD, with multiplier effects.

There are two types of tax: **direct** (on incomes) such as income tax and corporation tax, and **indirect** (on spending) such as VAT. When taxes are changed, the impact depends on which kind of tax is changed. A rise in direct taxes might mean people have reduced incentives to work hard and earn money, whilst if indirect taxes are raised, the cost of living increases, particularly for those on lower incomes because the tax paid will be a higher proportion of income than for those who do not spend all the money they earn.

Strengths of demand-side policies

REVISED

According to Keynesian economics:

- Demand-side policies are the only way to get a country out of demand-deficient unemployment and stagnation, at least in the short run.
- If the multiplier is large, they can have a significant impact on growth.
- If there is spare capacity, the economy can grow quickly.
- If used to control demand-pull inflation, they can act quickly and solve the problem.

Weaknesses of demand-side policies

REVISED

According to both Keynesian and classical economics:

- Expansionary demand-side policies only cause inflation in the long run.
- The multiplier might be so low that they have little effect.
- If there is no spare capacity, then supply-side policies are needed instead in order to achieve economic growth.
- The government can end up running a huge deficit, which adds to national debt, and this can become unsustainable (as in Greece from 2009 onwards).

Supply-side policies

These involve any attempt by the government to shift the aggregate supply (AS) curve to the right. The types of policies that may be used are as follows:

- Cutting corporation taxes (taxes on profits) so that firms have a strong incentive to produce more.
- Removing regulations and other restrictions that are preventing firms from growing, e.g. removing restrictions on mergers to allow these to take place.
- Encouraging investment by forcing banks to lend money, or by easing the credit situation (quantitative easing), or even just cutting the interest rate.
- Increasing competition in markets. Note that this might conflict with deregulation and allowing more monopolies (second point above).
- Privatising or subsidising industries, e.g. the Royal Mail.
- Improving the labour market by increasing educational standards.
- Productivity might increase by spending on the NHS. For example, if waiting lists are shorter, people can get back to work more promptly.
- Improved **incentives** for workers by cutting income tax rates and cutting benefits for out-of-work members of the labour force.
- Improving **infrastructure**, e.g. the transport system and internet coverage.
- Introducing measures to make imports cheaper, such as cutting tariffs, so that for many firms production costs fall. This is especially significant in the UK as the economy relies heavily on imported raw materials.

An **incentive** is a factor that makes the labour resource more effective. It might be higher pay for working harder, or more profits if businesses are run successfully.

Infrastructure is the capital assets that enable resources to move and be moved, for example motorways and internet connections.

Exam tip

Note that cutting interest rates can lead to increases in AD and AS.

Now test yourself

TESTED

1 Why do economists use deciles and quintiles?

Answer on p. 219

Conflicts and trade-offs between objectives and policies

Conflicts between objectives

REVISED

There are many possible conflicts between the seven objectives listed above. Below is a selection of commonly observed **trade-offs**.

Exam tip

Be careful not to confuse conflicts between objectives, e.g. inflation and growth, with conflicts between policies, e.g. fiscal expansion and monetary contraction.

A **trade-off** occurs when one objective is achieved at the expense of another.

Conflict 1: inflation and unemployment

When the government tries to control inflation it is likely to try to dampen aggregate demand.

- Less spending will mean less upward pressure on prices.
- The government might increase taxes or the Monetary Policy Committee (MPC) might increase interest rates.
- The impact of these may prevent inflation but they will also mean less spending in the economy.
- Firms may start laying off workers because they are unable to sell all their goods and services, and as workers are laid off incomes fall and so the cycle continues.
- So, there appears to be a trade-off between the objective of controlling inflation and unemployment because in trying to control inflation, unemployment will rise.

This works in the other direction as well. Here is an example:

- If the government is trying to control unemployment it might start spending more on training workers or subsidising firms to take on more workers.
- This increased spending in the economy is likely to make prices in general rise.
- This is because there is more money chasing the same amount of goods and services.

The trade-off between inflation and unemployment is illustrated in the Phillips curve as shown in Figure 10.1. At point A there is high inflation and low unemployment, but if the government tries to move to point B it only gets rid of inflation at the expense of unemployment.

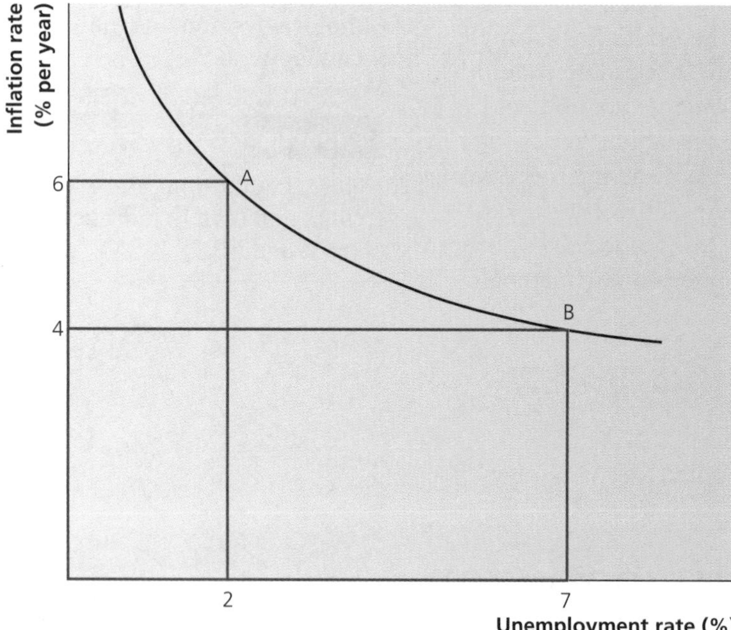

Figure 10.1 The Phillips curve

Now test yourself

TESTED

2 What does the Phillips curve show?

Answer on p. 219

Conflict 2: economic growth and sustainability

When an economy grows, standards of living tend to improve.

- For standards of living to be sustainable, growth must not occur at the expense of future generations.
- There is a conflict between enjoying a resource today and someone else enjoying it in the future.
- This is most important when considering those affected by damage to the environment when we consume resources today.
- So, if our increased use of fuels means that there is more global warming, growth may not be as desirable as it first appears.
- Governments must make a choice, weighing up the welfare of today's generation with that of tomorrow to achieve **sustainable growth**.

Sustainable growth is growth that does not compromise the welfare of future generations.

Conflict 3: inflation and equilibrium on the current account of the balance of payments

Controlling inflation should make a country more competitive internationally and therefore lead to an improvement on the balance of payments.

- Exports become relatively cheap and imports relatively expensive.
- Therefore, controlling inflation should not conflict with dealing with a balance of payments deficit.
- However, the actions required to control inflation can damage the balance of payments. For example, raising interest rates to control inflation might have the effect of raising the exchange rate which in turn makes exports expensive and imports cheap.
- By contrast, contractionary fiscal policy — which might alternatively be used to control inflation — tends to improve the balance of payments because people have less money to purchase foreign goods.

Typical mistake

Confusing the budget with the balance of payments. A budget refers to the government's fiscal position and that the balance of payments is a record of international flows of funds.

Now test yourself

TESTED

3 What is contractionary fiscal policy?

Answer on p. 219

Conflicts between macroeconomic policies

REVISED

Conflict 1: fiscal policy and monetary policy

Changes in the planned levels of spending and taxation by the government (fiscal policy) have a direct impact on the decision-making of the MPC (monetary policy).

- If the MPC believes that fiscal policy is too loose, e.g. government spending is too generous relative to taxation, then the MPC might seek to counterbalance the effect on inflation by raising interest rates.
- If the MPC believes that fiscal policy is too tight, e.g. government spending is not generous relative to taxation, then the MPC might seek to counterbalance the effect on inflation by cutting interest rates.

When fiscal policy means that there is an enormous deficit, this has to be paid for by borrowing. Increased demands in the money markets for funds means that other borrowers, apart from the government, might have to pay more to borrow money. So financing fiscal policy can have an impact on market interest rates.

Now test yourself

TESTED

4 Why does loose fiscal policy affect interest rates?

Answer on p. 219

Conflict 2: monetary policy and supply-side policy

Changes in interest rates and other monetary policy decisions have a direct impact on the costs of firms, therefore shifting the aggregate supply curve.

- If interest rates rise, it will costs firms more to produce, which might mean that firms are willing to produce less at any particular price level.
- If interest rates fall, it will costs firms less to produce, which might mean that firms are willing to produce more at any particular price level.

Exam tip

Monetary policy is not intended to influence the supply side of the economy, but this is an impact the MPC must take into account when making its interest rate decisions.

Now test yourself

TESTED

5 Why do firms borrow money?

Answer on p. 219

Conflict 3: supply-side policy and fiscal policy

Changes in most supply-side policies will have a direct impact on government spending, i.e. fiscal policy. For example:

- Improving education and health services to encourage people to be more productive requires high levels of government spending.
- Increasing the length of education also means that governments will not receive money via taxes from income those students might have earned had they been at work.

In most cases:

- Supply-side policies tend to *increase* the budget deficit in the short term.
- Supply-side policies can *decrease* the budget deficit in the long term, as improved human capital means higher incomes that can be taxed by the government.

However, some supply-side policies, such as reducing bureaucracy, are unlikely to make a significant impact upon government spending and taxation (G and T).

Some supply-side policies, such as privatisation and cutting benefits, will tend to *reduce* the budget deficit. Privatisation is a one-off fiscal improvement, and cutting benefits could increase long-term costs to the government because of the social problems involved.

Now test yourself

TESTED

6 Why does a cut in bureaucracy improve the supply-side with no impact on the fiscal position?
7 Why do supply-side policies tend to improve human capital?

Answers on p. 219

Typical mistake

Never assume that all supply-side policies work. Many policies take years to achieve, and some might not achieve success at all. The current changes in the education system might be seen as attempt to improve the supply-side of the economy, but if, for example, some young people become alienated by the new exam system then you could argue that the supply-side policy shifts the aggregate supply curve to the left.

Typical mistake

Try to avoid being 'one-sided', for example when assessing supply-side policies such as cutting benefits. Remember that there are two sides to every issue and, if you want to earn evaluation marks, you must weigh up both sides of the argument. Evaluation is worth up to 25% of the marks.

Exam practice

1 Explain the likely impact of a rise in the base rate of interest on the distribution of income. [2]
2 Explain the term indirect tax. Give an example in your answer. [2]
3 Which of the following is correct? If everything else is unchanged, a rise in indirect tax is most likely to cause:
   A aggregate demand to shift to the left and aggregate supply left/decrease
   B aggregate demand to shift to the right and aggregate supply left/decrease
   C aggregate demand to shift to the left and aggregate supply right/increase
   D aggregate demand to shift to the right and aggregate supply right/increase [1]
4 Using an appropriate diagram, explain what is meant by the term 'supply-side policies'. [6]
5 Discuss the use of supply-side policies as a means of addressing a problem of rising youth unemployment. [15]
6 Evaluate whether demand-side policies will be successful in reducing unemployment. [20]
7 Evaluate the likely impact of a rise in the base rate of interest on at least **two** government objectives. [20]

Answers and quick quiz 10 online

ONLINE

Summary

- No objective can be achieved by governments without some form of impact on other objectives. There are seven major economic objectives of governments involving control of:
  1 growth
  2 employment
  3 inflation
  4 balance of payments
  5 fiscal balance
  6 environmental sustainability
  7 distribution of income
- Some of these objectives are possible to achieve together, but for some there is a trade-off, i.e. more of one means less of another. You will need to be able to reason through the relationship between at least two of these seven objectives.
- When a macroeconomic policy is applied, there will be direct effects, which may or may not be seen as a successful outcome, and indirect effects, which may or may not be beneficial.
- The government has to prioritise the objectives that it believes are the most important at any one time, and the economist will try to predict how effective these priorities will be and what the effects of implementation will be on a wide range of variables. No economic policy comes without costs; in addition to knowing what the main macroeconomic policies are (monetary and fiscal) you also need to know the possible side effects.

11 Business growth

A **firm** is a production unit. Its function is to transform factors of production such as raw materials and workers into goods and services.

A **firm** is a production unit.

Size and types of firms

Why do some firms remain small?

REVISED

- **Niche market**. Some firms operate in very small separated areas or sections of a market because the demand for the product is specialised and limited.
- **Lack of economies of scale, or to avoid diseconomies of scale.** We sometimes say that the firm has a small **minimum efficient scale**. This is the smallest output at which a firm can operate having exploited internal economies of scale. Doctors and dentists usually operate in a small firm owned by 'partners', that is the practitioners themselves, who can only operate a certain caseload based on the hours of the working week.
- **Need for a dynamic, responsive, service-led firm.** Firms involved in design are often small and quick to respond to the needs of larger firms which buy in their services.

A **niche market** is a specialised part of the market suited to a business owner's interests or skills, such as a Smart car repair firm with just one make of car, and which is very good at the high-tech skills needed.

Why do some firms want to grow?

REVISED

The reasons why a firm grows will primarily depend on its objectives. If a firm wants to *profit maximise* it may need to grow larger in order to make all the profit that is available. If a firm is *sales* or *revenue maximising* it will want to grow, subject to certain constraints as discussed on page 113.

- **Economies of scale.** Larger firms often have lower costs per unit of output in the long run. These are discussed in more detail on page 123.
- **Increased market share.** A larger firm has more market power, and can control prices and retain consumer loyalty. A larger market share also means that the threat of competitors is reduced.
- **Economies of scope.** Larger firms are less exposed to the risk that firms might have if they are narrowly focused. Especially in times of recession, the dangers of being too uniquely focused can cause uncertainty for a firm's future.
- **Psychological factors.** Managers may gain more job satisfaction from working for a well-known brand and having responsibility for large numbers of people. The larger the firm, the bigger its profile tends to be. Firms may wish to grow because the status of a manager will improve or because workers' motivation is driven by performance-related pay.

Economies of scale occur when an increase in the scale of production results in a fall in long-run average costs.

The divorce between ownership and control: the principal–agent problem

REVISED

Shareholders *own* most large businesses ('principal'), and they appoint directors and managers to *control* business on their behalf ('agent'). Shareholders want to maximise profits (to maximise their dividend), whereas managers might have different motives, such as wanting to increase sales and revenue at the expense of profits. The **principal–agent problem** is when aims diverge and the policies that they choose conflict with the other's aims.

The **principal–agent problem** is when the aims of a firm's owners and controllers diverge and their policies conflict.

Public and private sector organisations

REVISED

The main objective of the firm will depend on whether it is in the **private** or **public sector**.

- **Private sector** firms have to make a profit to survive, so to some extent making a profit has to be a primary objective. Whether private sector firms aim to *maximise* profit is discussed below.
- **Public sector** firms, by contrast, can survive without making a profit because the government can make up any shortfall in revenues. Some public sector firms do aim to make a profit, but tend to have other more important aims such as quality of service. An example is the BBC, which is publicly owned and its primary aim is to entertain and educate. If public sector firms do not make a profit, they may have to compromise on other objectives. For instance, the BBC has had to cut back the range of programming to reduce costs. If public sector firms do not have any ambition to make profit, they may become inefficient and loss-making, which itself compromises the firm's main objectives.

The **private sector** involves assets owned by individuals or groups, not the government. An example is a Bupa hospital. It is funded by private payments from individuals or companies.

The **public sector** involves assets owned by society as a whole, provided through the government. An example is an NHS hospital. It is funded mainly through taxation.

Profit and not-for-profit organisations

REVISED

- We shall look at private sector firms for the majority of this Theme, returning to public sector enterprises in the final section (pages 201–204).
- **Non-profit organisations** or voluntary sector firms are those for which the primary motive is not profit, although they do usually have to cover their costs. They might want to promote education (many private schools, for example), music festivals or the visual arts. The firms are part of the private sector.

Non-profit organisations are private firms for which the primary motive is not profit, although they do usually have to cover their costs.

Business growth

Organic growth

REVISED

Firms can grow from within, by buying new capital, taking on more workers, or increasing the amount of hours people work. This is called organic or internal growth. The main advantages are that this is low risk and often the easiest form of growth to manage. The disadvantages are that the firm might not take on new ideas or people, and might get too specialised in areas becoming out of date. Examples of organic growth can be seen in Lego and John Lewis companies.

External growth

REVISED

Firms can also grow by buying out other firms, either by agreement (mergers) or taking them over (acquisitions), often called M&A. In all of these there are dangers of getting too large and hard to control (diseconomies of scale), and there are financial risks. There is also the risk of investigation by the Competition and Markets Authority, the powerful government organisation that exists to promote competition and consumer interests. Other advantages and disadvantages are listed below.

There are three main ways a firm can grow externally:

Horizontal integration

This is when firms merge at the same stage of the same production process. The firms may not make exactly the same product, and are likely to want to increase the range of products they produce, or are keen to get into new markets around the world.

For example, when Kraft bought Cadbury in 2010 for £11.9 billion, Kraft already made some chocolate products (Terry's chocolate, Oreo chocolate biscuits and Milka chocolate), so they acquired new brands such as Cadbury's Crème Egg but more importantly they gained access to large parts of the European chocolate market.

Advantages:

- economies of scale
- increased market share
- elimination of threatening competition
- remove risk of being bought out

Disadvantages:

- Focus of risk on a narrow range of goods or services.
- Diseconomies of scale.
- The share price of the firm being bought might rise, meaning the buyout is very expensive.
- Some workers might lose their jobs if the roles in the new bigger firm are duplicated, e.g. head of human resources.
- Some workers might have to move or travel further.
- Some assets might be sold off (e.g. duplicated capital equipment) which might be wasteful.

Vertical integration

This is when firms merge at different stages of the production process. This can be broken down into two further types.

Backward vertical integration

This means that one firm buys another firm that is closer to the raw material stage of production. A steel maker buying a coal-producing firm is backward vertical integration because iron/steel production uses coal.

Advantages:

- Control over raw materials means supply is guaranteed.
- Other firms might be prevented from getting the supplies.
- The supplier's mark-up can become profit for the buying firm.

Disadvantages:

- The firm might not need to buy all the supplies.
- The firm might not have specialist knowledge of production.
- The firm might find it hard to adapt to changes in consumer demand, e.g. buying a sugar factory when demand is shifting to artificial sweeteners.

Forward vertical integration

This means buying another firm in the same production process but closer to the customer, for example, a brewery buying a chain of pubs.

Advantages:

- Buying a retail outlet might guarantee that consumers see a firm's products at their best.

- The consumer may not be distracted by competition from other products.
- Market research is more effective and the firm can adapt in response to consumer preferences.

Disadvantages:

- The firm on its own might not offer enough range or choice for consumers.
- The firm might not have marketing and sales expertise.

Conglomerate integration or 'diversification'

This is sometimes also called lateral integration. It occurs when a firm buys another firm in a completely unrelated business. A commonly used example is Virgin, a company owned by Richard Branson, which buys anything from trains and aeroplanes to cable internet providers.

Advantages:

- It spreads the risk — profitable areas can cross-subsidise loss-making areas.
- Different products do well at different parts of the business cycle.
- Brands can become better recognised.

Disadvantages:

- Lack of expertise in new areas.
- Brands might become diluted.

Now test yourself

TESTED

1 In 2013 Penguin Books was bought by the German owners of another large publishing company, Random House. What might be the advantages of this merger?

Answers on p. 219

Constraints on business growth

REVISED

Despite the potential benefits of growth for some firms, there may be powerful constraints preventing a firm from growing:

- **Size of the market.** Some firms could increase output but would have to drop price considerably, or even not find a market at all. For example, there is a limit to the market for A-level textbooks.
- **Access to finance.** Since the credit crisis of 2008 it has become very hard for small and medium-sized firms to borrow, and other forms of finance are limited.
- **Owner objectives** such as control. Some firms like to 'keep it in the family' by employing family members and avoiding taking on people from outside. This may make the firm easier to manage and workers might have greater incentive or loyalty.
- **Heavy government regulation.** Some firms are kept small because the government wants to prevent monopolies developing. This is especially true of commercial banks in the USA, see data on page 138.

Demergers

Demergers occur when firms sell off parts of the firm as a 'going concern', or a viable business in itself. The demerger often means selling off parts that were once owned separately in the past — that is, they had been merged. An example was Pearson, the owners of Edexcel, selling off *The Financial Times* and its controlling stake in *The Economist* in 2015.

Reasons for demergers:

- To focus on core business, and perhaps develop that part to gain benefits of specialisation. For example, Pearson in 2015 wanted to focus on examining activities.
- To raise finance (by selling the shares in the new company).
- To avoid diseconomies of scale. Merged firms can be difficult to manage if they involve different core activities.

Impact of demergers:

- **On businesses.** Mergers and demergers go in cycles, sometimes alongside the business cycle, and are often a matter of business 'fashion' — so they may not be a sign of weakness. Demergers allow focus on the core business, raising funds from selling part(s) of the business, and removing loss-making parts of the business.
- **On workers.** Increased job security if loss-making parts of the business are demerged, reduced conflict between cultures, increased focus on the business to enable it to be more profitable — but some may lose jobs.
- **On consumers.** Greater competition leads to lower prices; more focused businesses are able to better meet consumer needs — but some parts of the service might be limited. For example, when LloydsTSB split into two firms, some found they no longer had a local bank branch near their home.

Revision activity

Draw a sketch of a firm that makes something that interests you. Then show all the ways it can integrate, drawing an upwards arrow for backwards vertical, a downwards arrow for forward vertical etc. This writer usually starts with a brewery!

Now test yourself

TESTED

2 Morgan Motor Company in Malvern produces fewer than 700 cars a year and has a long waiting list. List the factors that might explain why the successful company remains small.

Answers on p. 219

Exam practice

1 Coca-Cola is a firm which manufactures and sells soft drinks, many of which are sold in glass bottles. In 2015 the company announced plans to sell nine production facilities to three of its largest independent bottlers. Explain **one** reason why a vertically integrated firm may decide to sell off assets such as bottling plants. [3]

2 'It is rational for firms to grow as large as possible, in order to exploit economies of scale to the full.' To what extent do you agree with this statement? [25]

Answers and quick quiz 11 online

ONLINE

Summary

- Some firms remain small for sound economic reasons, and others wish to grow, with benefits to many stakeholders.
- A firm's motivation for growth depends on its type, its market and the context.
- Ways in which firms grow may be internal (organic) or by joining with other firms (external).
- When firms grow beyond a certain point, costs start to rise (diseconomies of scale, for example) and this is the main reason for splitting up (demergers).

12 Business objectives

Profit maximisation

Profit maximisation can be looked at in two ways:

- the point where the total revenue and total cost are at their greatest difference apart; or price minus cost per unit, multiplied by quantity, is greatest

or

- the point where the revenue gained from selling one more unit (**marginal revenue**, MR) is exactly equal to the cost of producing one more unit (**marginal cost**, MC). In short, this is written as MR = MC.

It means that the firm is making most money relative to the costs. Often, this means that the firm is not making the most amount of *revenue* possible. This is in fact a different objective called revenue maximisation (see below).

We say that profit maximisation is rational or properly reasoned: if there is an opportunity for a firm to make a profit we assume this is better for the firm than to make less profit. Profit is the reward for risk taking, so it is rational that the risk taker will want to get the greatest reward possible.

While all firms in the private sector have to make a profit in order to survive, not all firms profit maximise.

Exam tip

Profit maximisation is assumed for private sector firms and you should assume this is the aim of a firm unless you are told otherwise.

Marginal revenue (MR) is the change in revenue from selling one more unit of output. If price is constant then price = marginal revenue. But if price has to be lowered to sell more, then marginal revenue falls (it has twice the gradient of the demand curve). Marginal revenue can be positive or negative. When marginal revenue is positive the demand curve is relatively price elastic. When marginal revenue is negative the demand curve is relatively price inelastic. Marginal revenue is the gradient of the total revenue curve.

Marginal cost (MC) is the extra cost of making one more unit of output. Marginal cost is always positive. The marginal cost curve always rises in the short run, as soon as the law of diminishing returns (see page 122) sets in. MC is the gradient of the total cost curve.

Marginal profit is the extra profit gained from selling one more unit. When marginal profit is zero, the firm is maximising profit. Marginal profit = MR – MC.

Now test yourself

TESTED ☐

1 Is profit maximisation an equilibrium point? Is it correct to assume all firms are profit maximisers?

Answer on p. 219

Revenue maximisation

If you ignored all the costs of a firm, or if there were no variable costs, then an alternative to profit maximisation might be that the firm aims to maximise its revenue. This means the firm cuts its price down to the point where the extra revenue received from selling another unit is balanced by the reduced price on every item it is already selling. We say marginal revenue is zero, or MR = 0.

Firms are making as much money as they can but ignoring the fact that, on some units, costs are greater than the revenue they are receiving, so it would be better to cut down on production. It appears to be irrational (see Theme 1).

There are some circumstances, however, that would make revenue maximisation a reasonable choice:

- If a firm is going to have to dispose of all its stock, then effectively the costs are not relevant. For example, for a flower seller who has bought the stock in the morning, and cannot sell it the next day because the flowers will have wilted, maximising revenue is logical.

- If a business is owned and managed by different people, there might be different objectives. The owners might be the shareholders who will want maximum profit, but the managers — that is, the people making the decisions about how much to produce — might be paid according to how much is made or sold, for example through performance-related pay or bonuses based on turnover (revenue). In this case, it would be logical for the managers of the firm to maximise revenue.
- If a firm is about to be taken over by another firm it may be valued on the basis of its revenue. So firms might try to maximise their revenue to ensure that the sale price is as high as possible.

Now test yourself TESTED

2 At the end of a day's trading, a flower seller cuts the prices of all the stock that will not last until the following day. What pricing strategy is this?

Answer on p. 219

Sales maximisation

This occurs when a firm *sells as much as possible* subject to the constraint that it *at least makes normal profit* (see page 120). The firm might increase market share and get rid of competitors by cutting its price. This might be a short-run policy and in the long run the firm might want to return to profit maximisation. This can be shown on a diagram (see Figure 12.1):

- One reason for sales maximisation is to avoid the attention of the competition authorities. The government is often involved as a watchdog for private firms and if firms are seen to be making a large amount of profit they may be subject to investigation.
- Another reason for sales maximisation is that a high level of profitability might attract other firms into the market, so by cutting prices and selling more, new entry is prevented.

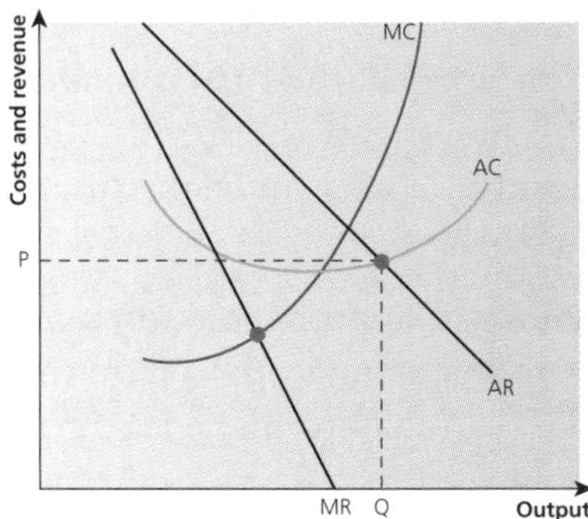

Figure 12.1 Sales maximisation occurs at Q where AC = AR

Typical mistake

Confusing sales maximisation with sales revenue maximisation. The latter is just another name for revenue maximisation (MR = 0) and ignores costs.

Now test yourself TESTED

3 Do sales-maximising firms have lower or higher prices than profit-maximising firms?

Answer on p. 219

Exam tip

Sales maximisation is also sometimes called output maximisation. It means making as much output as possible subject to the condition of making normal.

Satisficing

While it is nice to draw a neat picture using the assumption that firms behave in a rational way, firms' objectives do not always seem to be rational. The human intentions and the interaction of the people who run the firms can have a significant impact on output and pricing decisions.

- The characteristics of the owner or manager will be reflected in the objectives of the firm. For example, if a person wants to run a business with low risk, the business might be kept small, producing just enough to make a certain amount of profit that will pay the costs.

- Firms may wish to keep profits down to avoid being taken over by other firms, and the managers might get some satisfaction from being in control of their own business which is worth more than money.
- Some firms will aim to make just enough profit to keep the shareholders happy and then pursue other objectives. For example, a manager may choose to go and play golf rather than sell a few more items because he knows he has reached his sales targets and making any more money will not be as much fun.

This policy of *satisfying* the shareholders with *sufficient* profit is described by an economics term you need to know: **satisficing**.

As with the objectives above, apart from profit maximisation, we assume there is a divorce or disconnect between the owners and the managers of a firm.

Satisficing is making enough profit to keep shareholders happy, after which managers can aim for other objectives.

Now test yourself

TESTED

4 Why do some firms engage in satisficing?

Answer on p. 219

Revision activity

Draw a short-run diagram for a firm facing a downward-sloping demand curve. Mark on it all the points which represent the main objectives of the firm, to include profit maximising, sales maximising, revenue maximising, productive and allocative efficiency. Go back through this book to check the points are right.

Exam practice

1 Assess reasons why a firm may change its objective from profit maximising to sales maximising. [10]

Answers and quick quiz 12 online

ONLINE

Summary

- We assume that firms in most market structures aim for profit maximisation, a point called MC = MR.
- However, there are reasons why a firm may choose to revenue maximise (MR = 0), sales maximise (AR = AC) or just try to keep stakeholders happy and then aim for another objective (satisficing).

13 Revenues, costs and profits

Revenue

Total revenue and marginal revenue

REVISED

Revenue is the amount of money a firm receives. If everybody pays the same price, the formula is: price multiplied by quantity, P × Q. For example, if I sell 200 doughnuts for 50p each, my total revenue is £100. When we plot the total revenue curve we must consider whether the firm is a **price taker** or a **price maker**.

If the firm is a **price taker**, it is operating in a very competitive market, and it has to offer its product at the same price as everyone else. If it charges a higher price it will not be able to sell anything.

If the firm cuts its price below the market price, it has no advantages because a price taker can sell everything it has at the going rate. A typical example is a fishing boat captain who brings his catch into port in the mornings. The price he gets for his fish will depend entirely on the **demand** and supply for that type of fish at that particular port and that time, and the fisherman has to accept the price offered. When we draw total revenue for a price taker we will draw a straight line going through the origin. (At the end of this chapter you will see two tables of all the definitions, formulae and diagrams you will need.)

However, for most firms, the demand curve is downward sloping.

When we draw total revenue for a price-making firm, the curve is a **parabola** shape. What this means is that as the price falls the revenue will rise, but it rises more slowly each time that price is cut, up to the point of **maximum revenue**. Eventually it reaches the point where revenue will not increase any more. We say the marginal revenue is zero, that is, MR = 0. Marginal revenue is the increase in revenue when one more unit is sold.

You will realise that **marginal revenue** is less than average revenue — or the price that people are prepared to pay — because when price is cut the firm loses money on all the items it is already selling. Where MR = 0, the amount the firm gets from selling one more item is exactly equal to the amount lost by cutting the price on all the items already being sold. So, for example, I am a price-making firm on a beach selling ice creams and I have set the price at £2 per ice cream. I find I cannot sell very many — say 20. My total revenue is £40. I cut the price to £1 to increase my sales and I sell an extra 20 ice creams. My marginal revenue is £20 from selling 20 extra ice creams, but I lose £20 on the ice creams I could have sold at £2 each. My total revenue is still £40; my marginal revenue is zero. The only difference is that I have to sell more ice creams, which in fact will cost me more, so I am actually making less profit.

For a price-taking firm, once the total revenue (TR) has reached a maximum, you will then find that TR starts to fall as you cut the prices. It would be stupid for any firm to operate where TR is falling. It means that by selling another item, the gain is actually negative. We call this **inelastic demand**. When you cut the price, you make less money.

A **price maker** is a firm that has to cut its price in order to sell more.

A **price taker** has to offer its product at the same price as everyone else.

Typical mistake

Thinking that 'charging the same price as everyone else for every product' (price taker) sounds odd in the context of 'perfect competition' is a typical misunderstanding. It does seem as if some other force is dictating prices! However, what is determining prices is the market as a whole, and the individual as a firm has to do as the market dictates or it will make a loss. In practice, most firms have some monopoly power over their local market. Monopoly power means that the firm has control over supply and to some extent it can set prices and is therefore a price maker.

Demand is also known as average revenue (AR).

A **parabola** shape is like a 'U', in this case an upside-down 'U'.

Revenue maximisation is where the firm makes as much money as it can.

The **marginal revenue** is zero.

Price elasticity of demand (PED) and its relationship to revenue

REVISED

PED was studied in Theme 1, and the formula is:

$$\frac{\text{\% change in quantity demanded}}{\text{\% change in price}}$$

The result is called a co-efficient, meaning that it is a number that goes with other numbers and does not have any units of its own. It has a range between zero (perfectly inelastic), to minus infinity (perfectly elastic). The mid-point on a straight-line demand curve is unitary elasticity (minus one) and it is here that marginal revenue is zero (MR = 0). From this we can draw the TR, AR and MR and the key observation is that when the MR is positive PED is elastic, and when MR is negative PED is inelastic (see Figure 13.1).

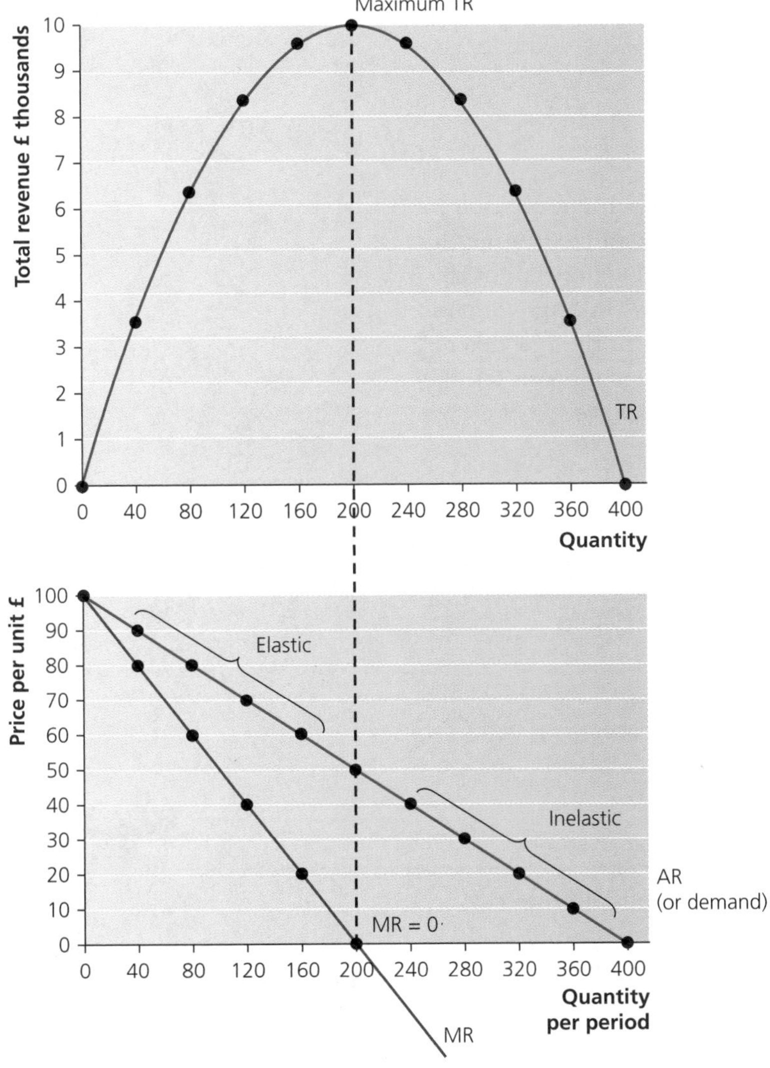

Figure 13.1 A graphical representation of the relationship between TR, AR and MR

Average revenue

REVISED

Average revenue is the price the firm receives per unit sold. An average revenue curve is the same as the demand curve, or price. Just as with total revenue, you can have a price taker and a price maker:

- For average revenue, a price taker has a horizontal demand curve which is perfectly elastic.
- A price maker has a downward-sloping demand curve and we draw marginal revenue on the same graph with a gradient twice as steep. As with total revenue, marginal revenue is the amount received for selling one more unit; it is less than average revenue because cutting prices means losing money on items already sold.

Now test yourself

TESTED

1 If demand for a product you sell is price inelastic, what should you do?

Answer on p. 219

Costs in the short run

Costs are the payments that firms must make in recompense for use of the factors of production. Rent must be paid for the use of land, wages for the use of labour, and an amount we call interest must be allowed for the use of capital goods. Included in costs is a reward for risk taking, which is known as **normal profit**, and this represents the amount the risk taker must receive to keep resources in their current use. Normal profit will be considered as a cost and it is built into the average cost curve.

Costs can be looked at from the point of view of total costs, or the cost per unit, which is also known as average cost.

Now test yourself

TESTED

2 How much profit is normal profit?
3 How do you put normal profit on a diagram?

Answers on p. 219–20

Total costs

REVISED

Total costs are all the costs that the firm faces, and can be split into two components: **total fixed costs** which do not change with output, and **total variable costs** which increase as more is produced. An example of a fixed cost is rent paid for a building. An example of a variable cost is raw materials, such as cocoa beans used to make chocolate. (For the diagram and formulae of these and all the cost curves, see Table 13.2 at the end of this chapter.) The gradient of the total cost curve is the marginal cost.

Typical mistake

Confusing total and average costs. Remember that total costs will never fall and, unless they are fixed costs, they will always be rising (fixed costs stay constant as more is produced).

Exam tip

The gradient of the cost curve shows the increase in the cost of producing one more unit. Because the cost curve is always rising (or zero), marginal cost is always positive (or zero), so you will never see marginal cost as a negative number.

Average costs

REVISED

Average cost (AC) is total cost divided by the amount produced, or quantity (Q). These are also called average total costs (ATC) but many people prefer just to write AC. The cost per unit falls as more is produced because the fixed cost is spread out over more units of output. For example, if you are making chocolate bars, the more you produce the more the cost of the factory is spread out over the number of units produced.

Average fixed cost

Average fixed cost is the cost of overheads such as rent. These are spread out as more is produced. Because fixed costs do not change with output, then by definition fixed cost per unit must always fall.

Exam tip

It is useful to remember the initials of the average fixed cost (AFC) by noting that the words can be replaced with 'always falling curve' — initials AFC.

Now test yourself

TESTED

4 Are wages fixed costs or variable costs?

Answer on p. 220

Average variable cost

Average variable costs are the costs per unit of the factors that change as more is produced. The shape of the average variable cost curve can be explained using the marginal cost curve, which goes through the very lowest point of the average variable cost curve. When marginal cost is below average variable costs, it means the cost of producing the next unit is less than the average cost of producing a unit. So this extra unit produced will bring down the average cost, although the average cost will not fall as much as the marginal cost. When marginal cost is above AVC, AVC always rises.

Marginal cost

REVISED

The marginal cost is the cost to the firm of making one more unit of output.

Here is an example to explain the relationship between the average and the marginal.

Imagine you are playing a game of cricket and the average batsman's score is 23. You go out to bat and you are having a bad day, caught for a golden duck and you are out. Your score is nil. It is also the marginal score and your score will pull down the average for your team. You will not pull everyone down to your score, but you will shave a bit from the average of the team as a whole. Suppose you score 23. Your marginal score is the same as the average, so the average will remain the same. But if you have a fantastic innings, and you make 72, then your marginal score will pull up the batting average. It is exactly the same relationship with marginal cost and average variable cost. If the cost of producing one more is less than the average, then the average cost will fall. If the marginal is the same as the average, then the average remains the same, and if the marginal is greater than the average then the average will rise.

Figure 13.2 illustrates this. Notice that when marginal cost is below average cost the marginal cost could be falling or rising, but average cost will still fall.

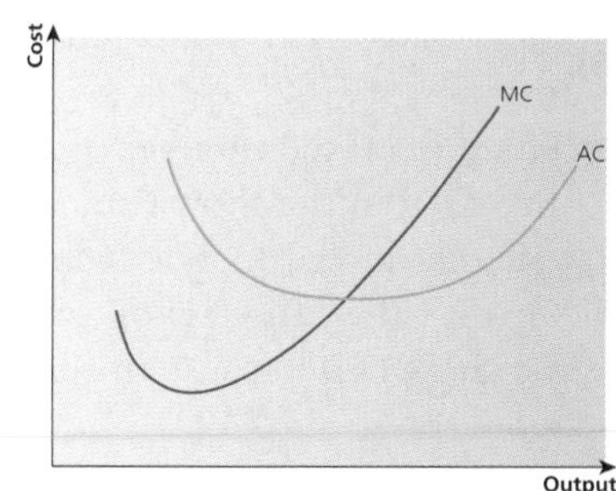

Figure 13.2 The relationship between MC and AC

What explains the shape of the marginal cost curve? The marginal cost curve looks a bit like a tick, or a Nike swoosh. While it might fall a little at the beginning, at some point it starts to rise, and from then it never stops rising. The increasing marginal cost is explained by the law of diminishing marginal returns.

Revision activity

Sketch some U-shaped average cost (AC) curves across a page. Then add marginal costs (MC). Check the MC looks like a Nike tick and goes through the lowest point on each AC.

Derivation of the short-run cost curves from the assumption of diminishing marginal productivity

REVISED

The law of diminishing returns

This concept is a 'law' because logically it is true. It is only applicable in the **short run** when at least one factor of production is fixed. The law states that as more variable factors are added to the fixed factor, the increase in output will eventually fall.

To be able to picture the **law of diminishing returns** in your mind, imagine a farmer with an orchard of 200 apple trees. Working alone, picking apples is a very time-consuming business. If you have someone with you, you can pass down the baskets of apples and someone can move the ladder for you. Some of the apples are hard to pick but some can be gathered easily without climbing the trees.

- The farmer measures her **marginal product** in terms of baskets of apples; these increase as she hires more labourers to pick the apples.
- The **fixed factor** is the orchard; the variable factor is the workers. As more workers are taken on there might initially be a real benefit in having just a few pickers. Two workers might well produce more than double the quantity because of the teamwork and cooperation involved.
- As output begins, the marginal cost curve might even fall, that is the marginal product or the extra output increases when another worker is taken on.
- However, this scenario will reach a point where extra workers cannot increase the output as much as workers employed earlier in the stage of production. This is because the apples will be harder to pick because they are higher up the tree — all the easily picked apples have been collected — and remaining apples cost more time to pick.
- There is a fixed number of apples in the orchard which cannot be increased in the short run, so there must come a point at which it becomes increasingly expensive to get the last apples.
- This is called the law of diminishing returns. It only operates in the short run because in the long run the farmer can plant more apple trees.

The **short run** is the period of time in which at least one factor is fixed.

The **law of diminishing marginal returns** — as more of a variable factor is added to a fixed factor, the increase in output (or marginal product) eventually falls.

Marginal product is the extra output when one more factor of output is added.

A **fixed factor** is the factor of production, such as the size of your apple orchard, which cannot be changed in the short run.

Now test yourself

TESTED

5 Why do marginal cost curves eventually rise?
6 Can the marginal product ever fall?

Answer on p. 220

The relationship between the marginal cost curve and the average cost curve is explained in exactly the same way as the relationship between marginal cost and average variable cost. This is because the only difference between average variable cost and average cost is the average fixed cost, which has absolutely no relationship with marginal cost.

Costs in the long run

Economies of scale

REVISED

In the long run there are no fixed costs, that is, all costs are variable. Because there are no fixed costs, there cannot be the law of diminishing returns, which describes the relationship between inputs and outputs when factors are applied to a *fixed* cost. There are no laws to describe the pattern of costs in the long run, but there are some principles that are often observable — we call these the benefits of large-scale production **economies of scale**, where long-run average costs fall:

- **Managerial economies.** Both large and small firms have just one person at the top. While the manager of a bigger firm might earn more, there are bound to be some duplicated costs when two smaller firms combine to become a bigger one. Larger firms can afford better managers, ones with a good track record, and better management usually means higher profits or long-term sustainability.
- **Financial economies.** Larger firms have access to a wider range of credit than small firms and usually at a lower price. Large firms can issue shares on the stock market and can do deals with lenders to borrow at cheaper rates. Because they have more collateral, large firms are often seen as a safer bet for loans, in other words if their payments dry up there are more assets that can be sold in the firm to pay off the debt.
- **Commercial economies.** Large firms can bulk-buy from their suppliers. Because they buy a large amount at a steady rate they are likely to get better deals. For example, Wal-Mart in the USA cuts a very cheap price from all its suppliers and that is how it keeps prices low.
- **Technical economies.** Doubling the dimensions of any object increases the volume by eight times. So a larger warehouse, or a larger shop or lorry, can carry much more per square metre. You only need to look at the number of pantechnicons on the motorway to see the advantages of large-scale production.
- **Marketing economies.** As a firm grows bigger, the cost of advertising is spread out over a larger number of potential customers. For example, a national advert would not be suitable for a small or regionally based firm.

Economies of scale occur when the average costs per unit of output decrease with the increase in the scale of the output being produced by a firm in the long run.

Diseconomies of scale occur when the average unit costs of production increase beyond a certain level of output.

Minimum efficient scale

REVISED

The **minimum efficient scale** is a concept which applies to firms with very high fixed costs, which find that costs fall very rapidly as output begins, as the costs are being spread out (see Figure 13.3).

At the point where the average costs are at a minimum, the **minimum efficient scale (MES)** of output of a firm or plant is reached.

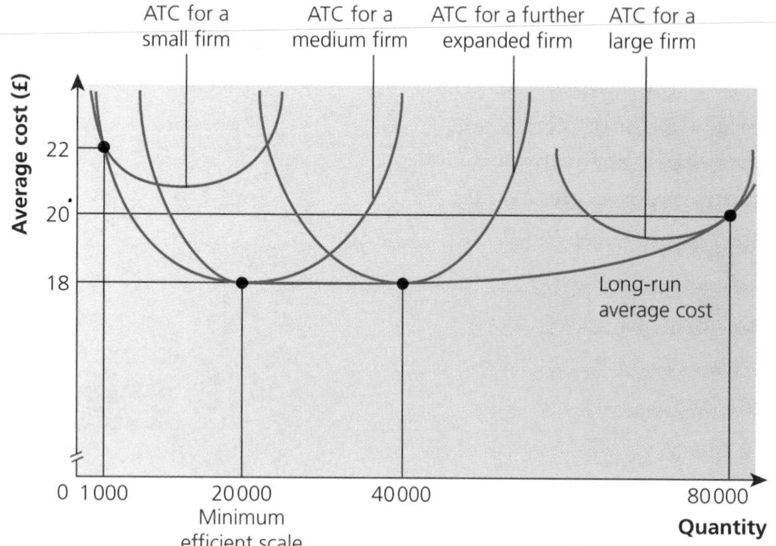

Figure 13.3 Diagram showing minimum efficient scale

Between the range of the minimum and the point just before diseconomies set in, there may also exist constant returns to scale where the average unit costs of production remain unchanged as output increases 20 000 to 40 000. The minimum efficient scale is the point where long-run unit costs of production stop falling, at 20 000 in Figure 13.3. This is the optimum size if it correlates with the total demand or market size. The minimum efficient scale has an important bearing on the number and size distribution of firms in an industry and on concentration.

Now test yourself

TESTED

7 Get a pile of stock cubes or sugar lumps from the kitchen. Imagine these represent storage space in a warehouse. Take one and measure the volume, e.g. 1 cm³. Now double the height, width and breadth of the warehouse. How many cubes do you use?

Answer on p. 220

Diseconomies of scale

REVISED

When firms become big they may face rising long-run average costs.

- **Unwieldiness.** Large firms can become difficult to manage, especially if they are operating in different countries with different cultures, time zones, languages and hours of working. When a firm is difficult to manage, we say it is unwieldy; decisions may take longer to implement and the person making the decision may not have knowledge of the outcome. Unions can become more powerful in a large organisation because they have greater ability to influence working patterns. It is very difficult to manage a large firm where some tasks become redundant, as people can be very keen to hold on to what they do.

- **Slowness.** It takes a large firm a long time to respond in many cases.
- **X-inefficiency** (see page 132). Lack of competition for a large firm may mean that costs are allowed to rise.
- **Communication.** One caricature of large firms involves lots of e-mails flying around and meetings-about-meetings. Workers may experience delays waiting for others to complete their tasks.
- **Lack of engagement.** In a large organisation the management may become very distant from the worker. Workers may then become less loyal to management and the purposes of the firm. This may mean they take more days off sick, or spend working time inefficiently, with no concern for how this directly impacts on the firm's profit.

Now test yourself TESTED

8 If diseconomies of scale have set in, what should the firm do?

Answer on p. 220

External economies of scale

REVISED

Sometimes an industry as a whole grows, with the effect that individual firms can benefit from this growth. Firms based in the Tech City in East London are benefiting from super-fast broadband, new transport links and excellent publicity from the government, which make it cheaper and more effective for any tech firm that is based there. In this situation, the long-run average cost curve of the firm moves downwards without any action by the firm itself as the industry grows. Note, however, that as the industry grows, external diseconomies of scale may set in. For example, firms involved in direct marketing now find themselves in a market so flooded with players that it is very difficult for any one firm to be noticed. As the industry gets bigger, so any one firm will face higher per unit costs.

Now test yourself TESTED

9 What is the difference between internal and external economies of scale?

Answer on p. 220

Profit

What is meant by profit?

REVISED

Profit is the reward for risk taking. It is the difference between revenue and costs.

Profit maximisation

REVISED

Profit maximisation occurs where the firm cannot increase its profits, whether by increasing or decreasing price or output. It is best explained using marginal analysis. For this, you must first understand the key terms marginal cost, marginal revenue and **marginal profit**. (See the definitions given in the key terms box on page 115) and here.

Marginal profit is the extra profit gained when one more unit is produced.

The profit maximisation point is MR = MC. You can rearrange this formula to MR − MC = 0 (see the definition of marginal profit in the key term box). You may also observe that MR = MC when the gradient of the total cost curve and the total revenue curves are the same. Because these are concave to each other this must also be the point at which they are furthest apart vertically. This can be explained using Figure 13.4.

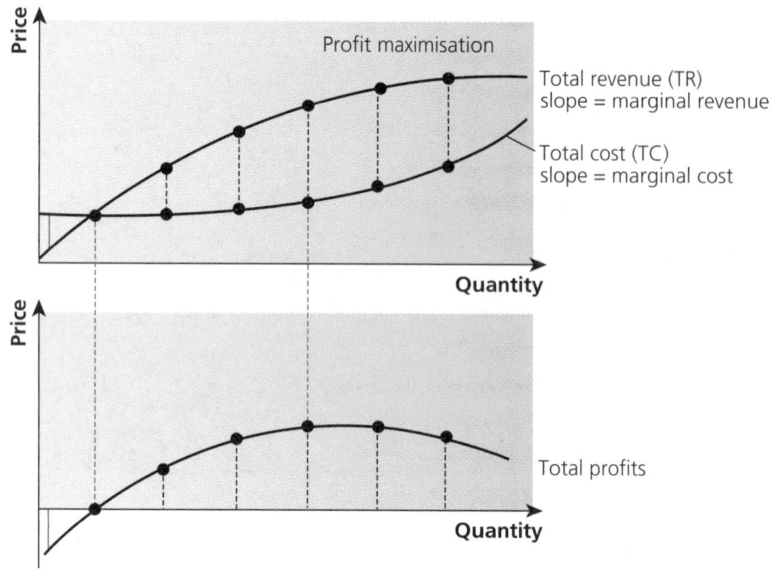

Figure 13.4 The greatest vertical distance apart for TR and TC is where profit maximisation occurs. Notice the gradients of TR and TC are the same, that is, MR = MC

Profit maximisation occurs where the cost of making one more unit is exactly equal to the revenue gained from selling that unit.

Consider the situation if a firm produced at a different output than MC = MR:

- At a lower output, marginal revenue is greater than the cost of producing that unit. There is more profit to be made. That is, the marginal profit is greater than zero. A rational firm would not stop producing when MR > MC because there is more profit (marginal profit) just waiting to be made.
- Likewise consider the situation if a firm is producing at an output higher than MR = MC. The cost of making another unit is more than the revenue received from selling it. The marginal profit is negative. The firm should cut back production — it is giving away its profits if MC > MR.

It follows that a logical decision for the firm would be to operate at MR = MC, and the reasoning in this paragraph is called marginal analysis.

Exam tip

Use marginal analysis in your exam. Examiners like it — it is an efficient way of showing that you understand and you are not just reciting a textbook.

Normal profit, supernormal profit and losses

REVISED

- **Normal profit.** This is the minimum necessary to keep the risk-taking resources in their current use. It is built into the cost curve, and represents the cost of use of the entrepreneurship factor of production. Normal profit occurs when AC = AR or TC = TR. It does not act as a signal for other firms to enter the market, nor does it cause firms to want to leave the market. The size of normal profit varies according to the level of risk involved, and the other investment opportunities available at the time. If you are running your own business 'upcycling' furniture then you probably do not need much profit to keep you in work — just enough to prevent you having to find a job working for someone else. But if you are running an oil exploration firm with a 20-year investment cycle then your normal profits will need to be much higher for you to keep your money in the business. In the first example, normal profit might be £8 000 a year and in the second £8 000 million.

- **Supernormal profit.** This is profit above the minimum required to stay in business. It is the difference between TR and TC.
- A **loss** occurs when a firm's total costs exceed revenues, TC > TR, or the average cost of production is greater than the price per unit. Break-even occurs when TC = TR, and or AC = AR, and the firm will stay in business here because it is earning normal profit (normal profit by definition means there is enough reward to the entrepreneur for the firm to stay in business). However, a firm does not automatically shut down when making a loss.

If a firm is covering its average variable costs it will stay in business. So the point where P = AVC, and any price below that, is the point at which it will shut down. This point is often shown in the same diagram as the break-even point.

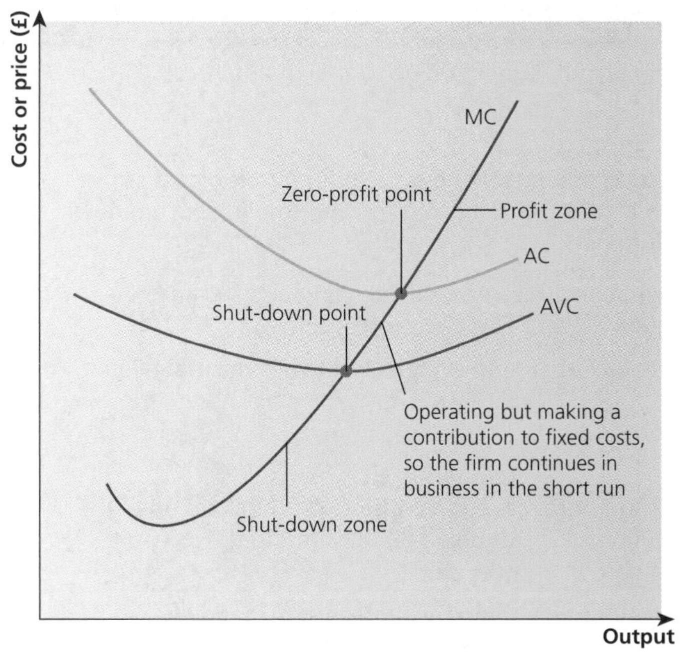

Figure 13.5 Break-even and shut-down points on the average cost diagram

Now test yourself

TESTED

10 What happens when marginal profit is zero?

Answer on p. 220

Exam practice

1 A firm changes its output level from revenue maximisation to sales maximisation. To its surprise it finds that it experiences an increase in its profits in the short run.
Which **one** reason best explains the reason for the increase in profits?
- A Losses were made at MR = 0 and the firm now makes normal profits.
- B Supernormal profits are made where AR = AC.
- C Supernormal profits are made where TR = TC.
- D Demand is relatively inelastic when the firm cuts its price. [1]

2 A firm changes its output level from profit maximisation to sales maximisation.
Which **one** of the following best explains why a rational firm would take this action?
- A The firm wants to increase its price.
- B Supernormal profits are made where AR = AC.
- C Supernormal profits are made where TR = TC.
- D The firm wants to increase market share. [1]

Answers and quick quiz 13 online

ONLINE

Summary

Table 13.1 summarises the definitions, formulae and explanations that you need to know for the theory of individual firms. Revenues and costs are covered in Table 13.2.

Table 13.1 Theory of individual firms

Term	Formula	Explanation
Total profit	TR – TC or (AR – AC) × Q	Supernormal, abnormal or subnormal (a loss)
Normal profit	TR = TC or AR = AC	Return to the entrepreneur is built into the cost curve, which is just enough profit to keep the entrepreneur in this function
Profit maximisation	MR = MC	Marginal profit is zero; or the vertical difference between TR and TC is at a maximum
Sales maximisation	AC = AR or TR = TC, when costs cross revenue from below	Highest level of output consistent with normal profit
Revenue maximisation	MR = 0	Maximum total revenue. Selling another unit adds the same to total revenue as the amount lost from units being sold at a lower price
Price taker/ perfectly elastic demand	AR = MR	TR straight line going through zero, AR and MR horizontal. Price elasticity of demand is infinite
Price maker / monopoly	AR > MR or ΔMR = 2ΔAR	AR downward sloping, MR twice gradient. The firm has some degree of price-setting power
Break-even	AR = AC or TR = TC	Firm covers costs, and makes only normal profit
Shut down	AR = AVC	Firm covers AVC only, makes a loss. If price is above this but below AC there is a loss but the firm *contributes* to AFC so carries on in the short run

Term	Formula	Explanation
Productive efficiency	MC = AC	Minimum point on AC, lowest cost per unit
Allocative efficiency	P = MC or AR = MC	Price charged maximises social welfare, taking into account consumer and producer surplus

Table 13.2 Revenues and costs

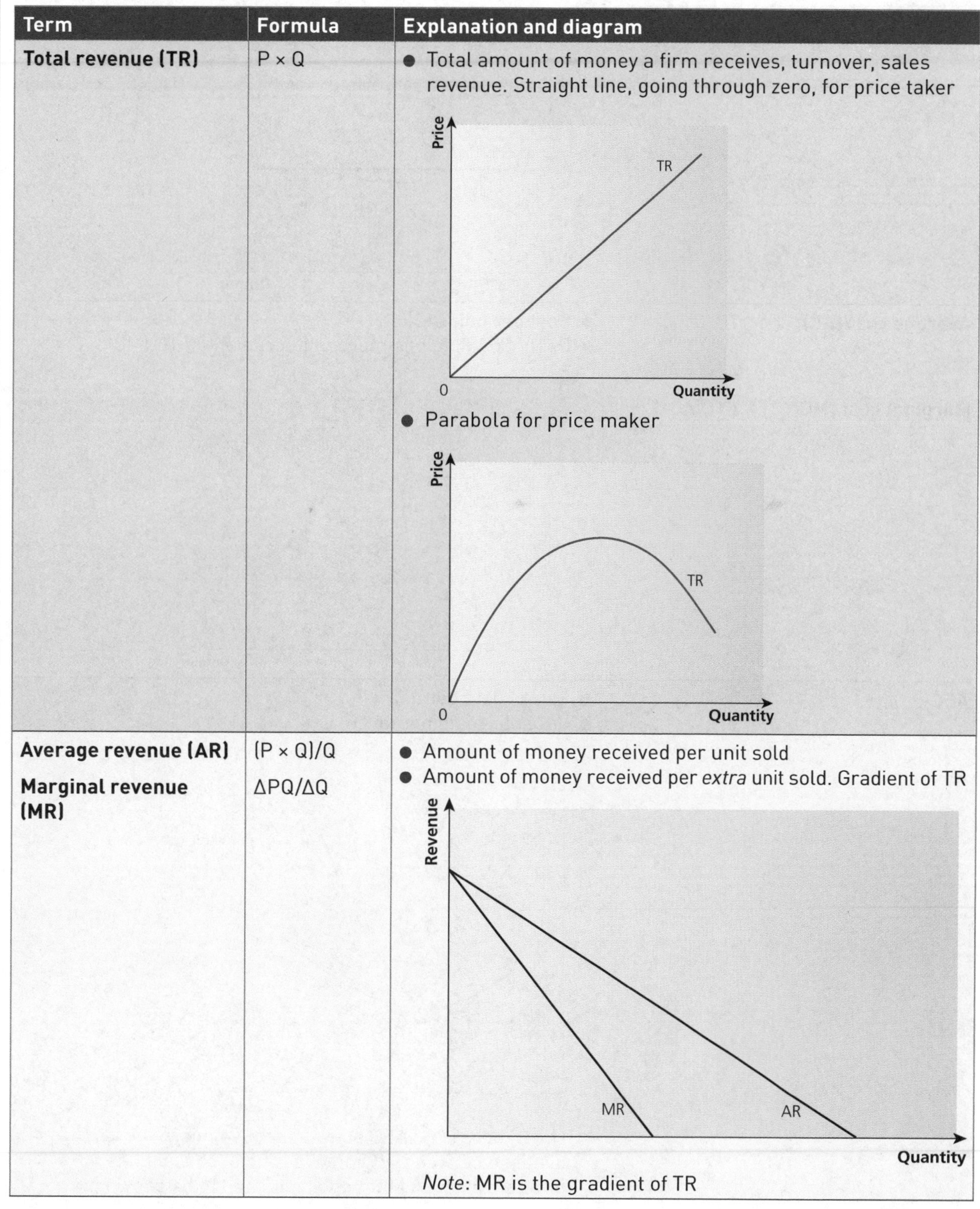

Term	Formula	Explanation and diagram
Total revenue (TR)	P × Q	● Total amount of money a firm receives, turnover, sales revenue. Straight line, going through zero, for price taker ● Parabola for price maker
Average revenue (AR) **Marginal revenue (MR)**	(P × Q)/Q ΔPQ/ΔQ	● Amount of money received per unit sold ● Amount of money received per *extra* unit sold. Gradient of TR *Note*: MR is the gradient of TR

(*Continued*)

(*Continued*)

Term	Formula	Explanation and diagram
Total cost (TC) **Total fixed cost (TFC)** **Total variable cost (TVC)**	TFC + TVC TC – TVC TC – TFC	● Total costs a firm must pay ● Costs incurred when output is zero. They do not change with output ● Costs are zero when output is zero. They *do* change with output 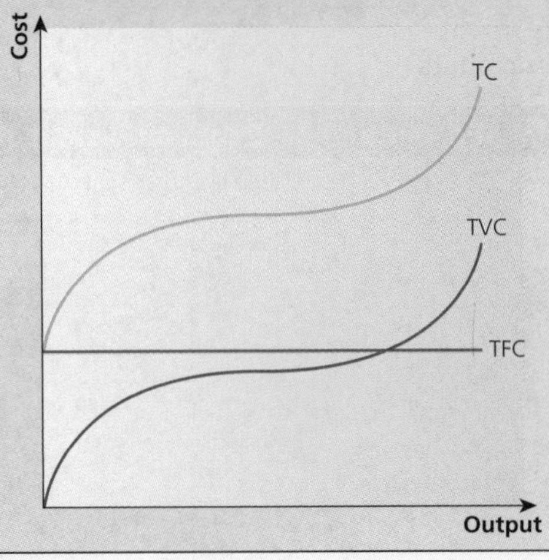
Average cost (AC) **Marginal cost (MC)**	TC/Q or AFC + AVC ΔTC/ΔQ	● Cost per unit (AC) ● Cost of making one more unit, gradient of TC (MC) 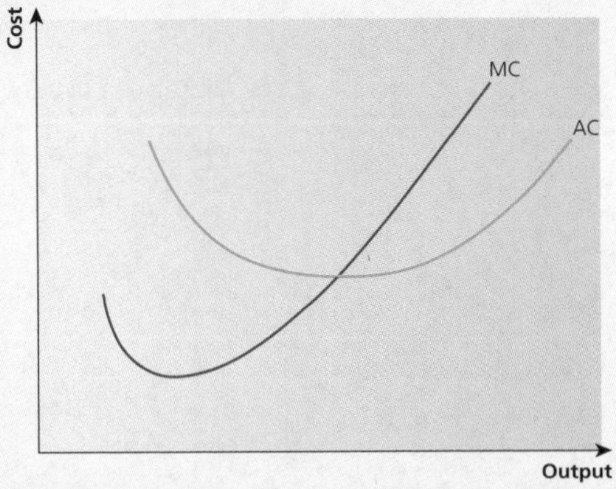
AFC **AVC**	TFC/Q or AC – AVC TVC/Q or AC – AFC	● Fixed costs per unit ● Variable costs per unit 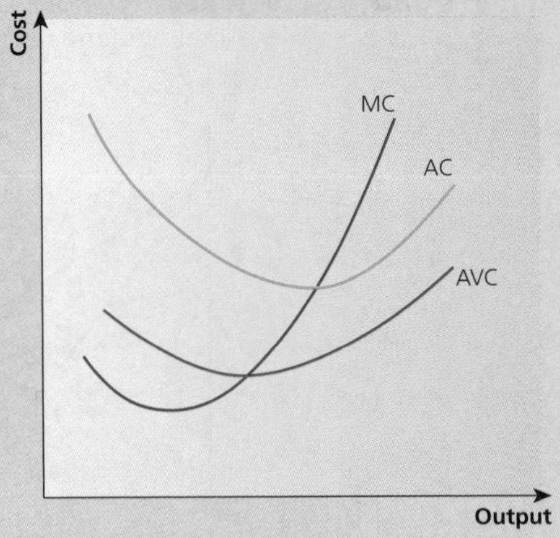 ● Note: there is no AFC shown because this is the vertical distance between AC and AVC, and because it has no relationship with MC it does not need to be shown in diagrams finding equilibrium points with MC

14 Market structures

Efficiency

Efficiency measures how well resources are used, that is, the output relative to some other factor, such as the cost of resources used.

Allocative efficiency

REVISED

Allocative efficiency occurs where the price equals the marginal cost of production, that is P = MC. It means that people are paying the exact amount it costs to produce the last unit. The best way to consider this is the situation where it is *not* true: if people are prepared to pay more than it costs to produce the last unit then it would be better in terms of consumer satisfaction to produce more units — because consumers are prepared to pay more than the cost to society. By contrast, if the consumer satisfaction from the last unit is less than the cost of making the unit then production should be cut back, as consumers do not appreciate the costs involved.

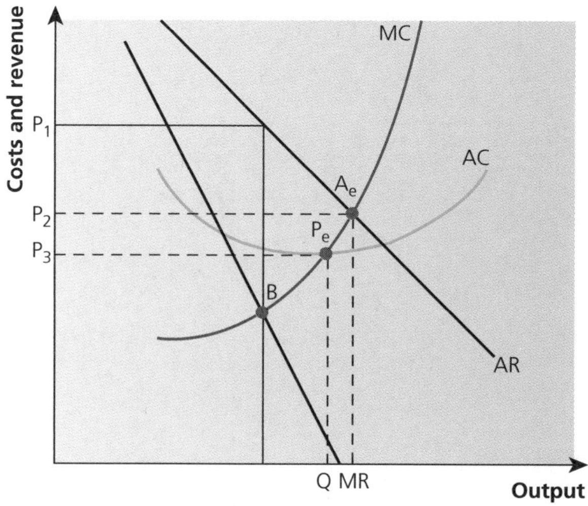

Figure 14.1 The relative prices and outputs of productive efficiency P_e and allocative efficiency A_e

Productive efficiency

REVISED

Productive efficiency occurs where a firm operates on the lowest average cost, that is, the lowest point on the average cost curve. If the price is equal to average cost, then this is the lowest price that the customer can enjoy. So in terms of **consumer surplus** (that is, welfare to the consumer) and effective use of factors of production, this is the optimum output. However, there is very little incentive for a firm to operate at productive efficiency and certainly no incentive to lower the price this far. It occurs where price is equal to marginal cost and equal to average cost. The reason MC = AC is because MC always crosses AC at its lowest point. See the marginal analysis section on page 13.

Dynamic efficiency

REVISED

Some firms do not appear to behave efficiently in the short run because they are aiming to lower long-run costs. A way to measure this is using **dynamic efficiency**, which takes a view over time, and measures a firm's ability to improve productivity over time, for example by innovating, investing in human capital or taking risks.

X-inefficiency

REVISED

This is when costs rise because there is no competition. If you are taking a course at school for which there is no exam you tend to try less hard and never do any homework. This is because there is no competition and no reward for competing well. When you compete with other students in an exam, you work harder. So it is with firms — especially those subsidised or owned by the public sector; when costs start rising there is little incentive to cut back. If wages and employment are not dependent on revenues the workers might not work as hard to raise the volume of sales. See the final section of Theme 3 on ways in which the government might try to reduce x-inefficiency.

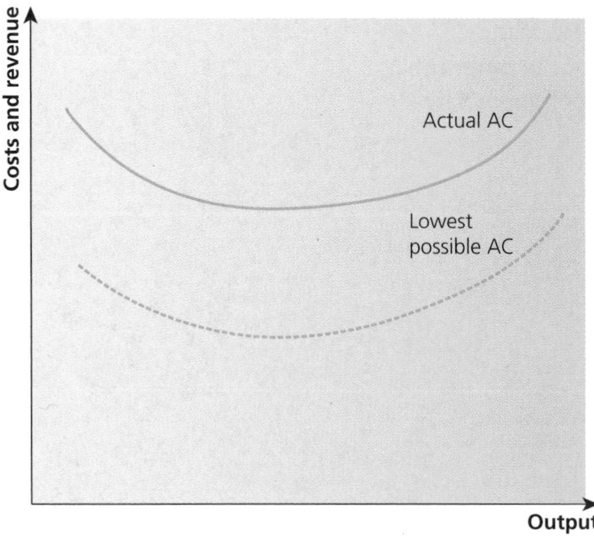

Figure 14.2 X-inefficiency

Now test yourself

TESTED

1 Could productive and allocative efficiency ever occur at the same point?

Answer on p. 220

Here is an example. You are making chocolates to sell in a market. Productive efficiency occurs when you get the costs down to a minimum — you spread out the fixed costs and the rising labour costs do not yet outweigh the falling overheads. Allocative efficiency occurs if you stop making the product when the cost of making the last one is equal to the amount people will pay for the last chocolate on your stall at the end of the day. If it is a perfectly competitive market, these two points will be exactly the same in the long run. But usually productive efficiency kicks in at a lower output than allocative efficiency, as demand curves are downward sloping. Compare points for productive efficiency P_e and allocative efficiency A_e on Figure 14.1 above.

Typical mistake

Many students find it hard to point out productive efficiency on a graph because they do not draw the MC curve going through the lowest point of the AC curve. If you have drawn it correctly, MC = AC at productive efficiency, the lowest point on the AC curve.

Efficiency in different market structures

REVISED

Market structures are the ways in which firms are competing, and they range from monopoly (no competition) to perfect competition. These are discussed in full below, but Table 14.1 is a handy way to apply the efficiency concepts to the market structures you will study:

Table 14.1

Market structure	Productively efficient in the short run?	Productively efficient in the long run?	Allocatively efficient in the short run?	Allocatively efficient in the long run?
Perfect competition	No	Yes	Yes	Yes
Monopolistic competition	No	No	No	No
Oligopoly	No	No	No	No
Monopoly	No	No	No	No

Exam practice 1

Extract: Starbucks

Starbucks, the Seattle-based group, with a market capitalization of $40 billion, is the second-largest restaurant or cafe chain globally after McDonald's. Accounts filed by its UK subsidiary show that since it opened in the UK in 1998 the company has racked up over £3 billion ($4.8 billion) in coffee sales, and opened 735 outlets, but paid only £8.6 million in income taxes, largely because the taxman disallowed some deductions.

Over the past three years, Starbucks has reported no profit, and paid no income tax, on sales of £1.2 billion in the UK. McDonald's, by comparison, had a tax bill of over £80 million on £3.6 billion of UK sales. Kentucky Fried Chicken, part of Yum Brands Inc., the no. 3 global restaurant or cafe chain by market capitalization, incurred taxes of £36 million on £1.1 billion in UK sales, according to the accounts of their UK units.

Analysts, looking at 12 years of stockmarket evidence, reported Starbucks UK as "profitable" and even cited it as an example to follow for operations back home in the United States.

Source: extract (adapted) from *Special Report: How Starbucks avoids UK taxes* by Tom Bergin, 15 October 2012, Reuters

1 Using an appropriate cost and revenue diagram, examine one reason why a firm such as Starbucks can be shown to have a profit and a loss at the same time. [8]

2 Using examples from the passage, discuss the functions of profit in terms of business efficiency. [12]

Answers and quick quiz 14 online

ONLINE

In the following sections we look at the market structure that firms operate in. These structures range from very competitive markets (perfect competition) to monopoly (single seller) or monopsony (single buyer). If a firm sells products very similar to those of other firms, it operates in a relatively competitive market. But if it has a unique product or has strong barriers to entry, it operates with some market power, also known as monopoly power.

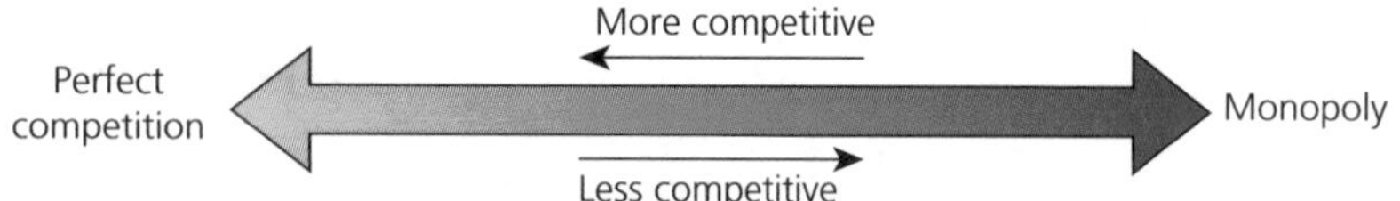

Figure 14.3 Spectrum of competition

Perfect competition

The characteristics of perfect competition

REVISED

The model of perfect competition is a model of an extreme form of competition. In this model, certain assumptions hold:

- There are many buyers and sellers. Neither buyers nor sellers can influence the price. We say they are price takers, and firms face a horizontal demand curve AR = MR.
- There are no barriers to entry or exit (see page 145).
- There is perfect knowledge or information, e.g. about production techniques and sources of cheap raw materials.
- All firms aim to maximise profits, MR = MC.

To draw a diagram for perfect competition, we draw the individual firm facing a horizontal demand curve AR = MR. This means it has no market power, no influence over price. It is also very helpful to add a diagram showing the whole market, that is, the industry demand and supply. Here price is determined, and the demand as a whole is determined, by consumer preferences, showing that as price falls, people demand more.

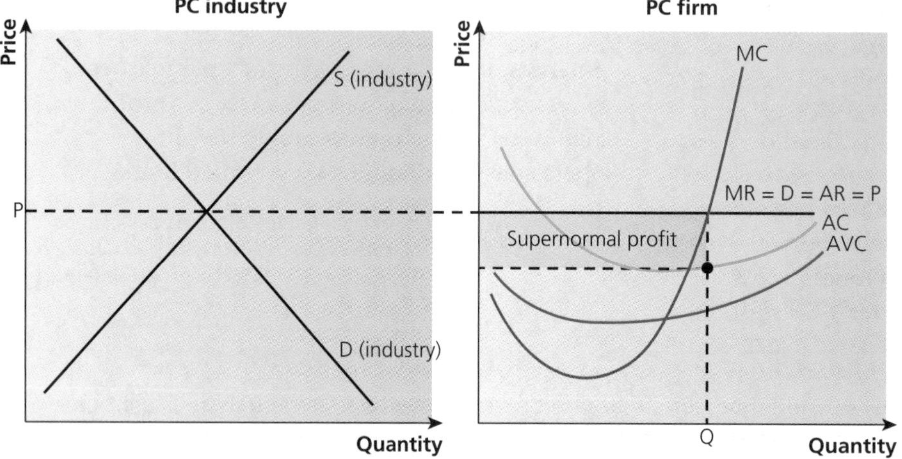

Figure 14.4 Perfectly competitive industry and firm, with short-run supernormal profits being made. Other firms will enter the industry

In Figure 14.4 the firm is enjoying a price which is above the average costs of production. The firm is making supernormal profit. This is shown by the area shaded in yellow. However, the profit acts as a signal to other firms to enter the industry. There are no barriers to entry, so nothing will stop other firms entering. So this excessive profit will soon disappear and we will end up in long-run equilibrium, see Figure 14.5.

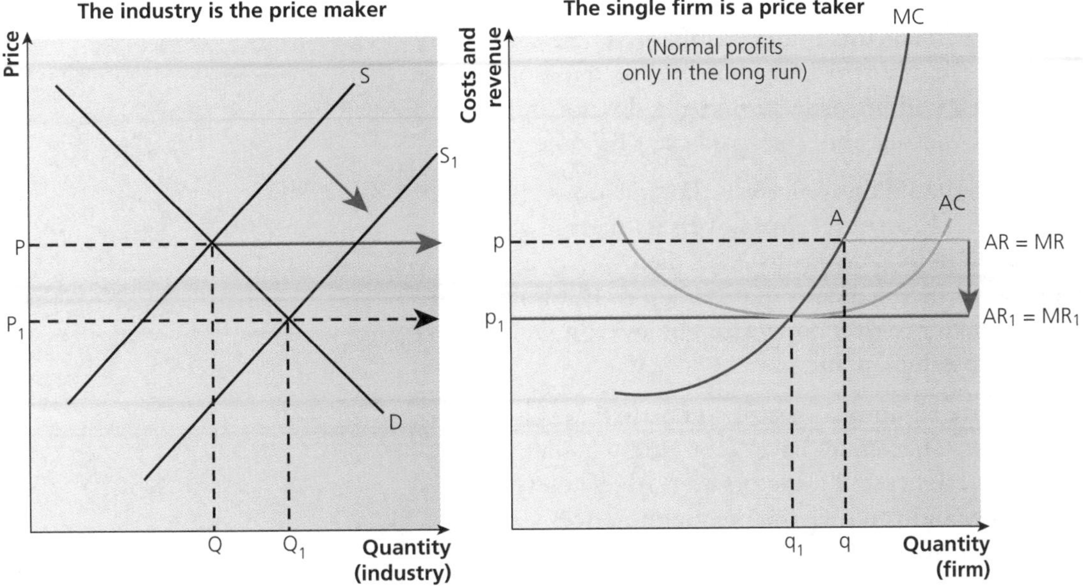

Figure 14.5 Long-run equilibrium

Note that for the individual firm, prices fall, and also that output falls from Q to Q_1 (see Figure 14.5). This is because at lower prices the firm will want to operate at a slightly slower output (MC is lower because MR is lower) but overall the industry supply has increased from Q to Q_1 because there are more firms in the industry.

Firms making a loss

REVISED

Now look at the situation where the perfectly competitive firm is making a loss. Here firms will start leaving the industry, prices will rise, but for the individual firm the output will also rise. This is because there are fewer firms in the market and each one makes just a little more, allowing MC to rise as MR rises. Remember that MC always equals MR.

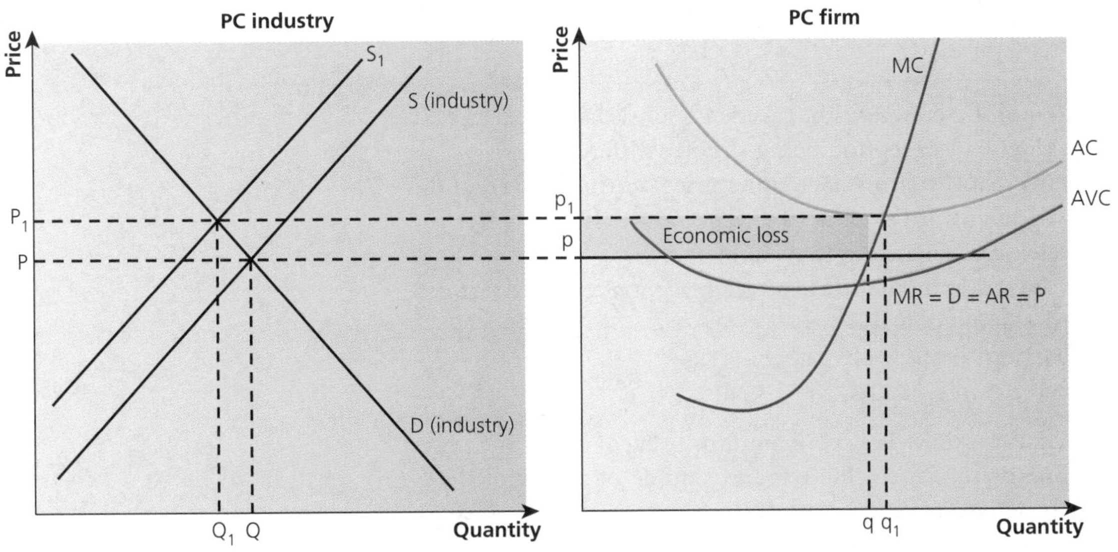

Figure 14.6 Perfectly competitive industry and firm, with short-run losses being made. Firms will leave the industry until the losses disappear

Does the firm in perfect competition automatically shut down when it makes a loss? We know there are no barriers to exit so it seems sensible for the firm to leave the industry straight away. However, before this long-run scenario plays out, there is the short run to consider. A perfectly competitive firm will have fixed costs in the short run. These will have to be paid even if the firm shuts down immediately. The question for the firm is whether a larger loss will be made by shutting down completely (paying the fixed costs) or waiting until the fixed costs become variable.

To discover what the firm should do we look at the shut-down point. This occurs when the price the firm receives covers its average variable costs (AVC). If the firm more than covers its AVC then we say it is making a **contribution** to the fixed costs of production. But if it cannot even cover its AVC, it is better to shut down straight away; it would make less of a loss if it does not produce at all.

Here is an example. You are running a theatre company that is looking for venues to run the show. The venues have to be paid whether the show runs or not and is a fixed cost. The actors are variable costs — if you don't put on the show (and you give them enough notice) you will not have to pay for them. You try selling tickets and realise you are not going to make a profit. Should the show go on? If you have sold enough tickets to pay for the actors then you should run the show, as you will pay a contribution towards the fixed cost of hiring the venue. But if you have not even sold enough tickets to pay for the players, it is better for you if they stay at home.

Now test yourself TESTED

2 Why do firms carry on producing even if they are making a loss?

Answer on p. 220

Monopolistic competition

The characteristics of monopolistically competitive markets

REVISED

The model of monopolistic competition is very close to that of perfect competition, with the main exception being slightly differentiated products. This means that the firms have some price-setting power, and the demand curve is downward sloping (the firms have a little market power). In this model, certain assumptions hold:

- There are many buyers and sellers. Firms are price makers, and firms face a downward-sloping demand curve.
- There are low barriers to entry or exit.
- All firms aim to maximise profits, MR = MC.

In these market structures there is a small amount of local brand loyalty, but no strong brand names. Here is an example of monopolistic competition. A firm offers peanuts on a stall in a busy city centre. No one really remembers the name of the stall but it tends to attract return customers. If the business is profitable, another stall will be set up — and if the firm stops making a profit then the stall will close down.

To draw a diagram for monopolistic competition, we draw the individual firm facing a downward-sloping demand curve AR twice as steep as the MR (see Figure 14.7). This means the firm has some market power, some influence over price. You can add in the profit in the normal way, or a loss if you draw AR below AC, and the diagram works just the same as the monopoly diagram.

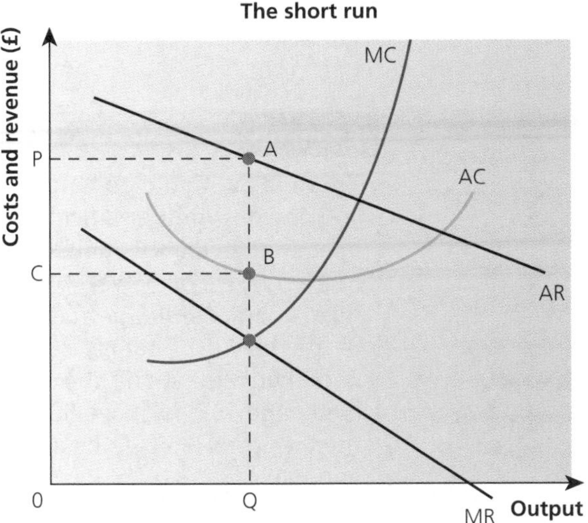

Figure 14.7 **Perfectly competitive industry and firm, with short-run supernormal profits being made. Other firms will enter the industry**

In Figure 14.7 the firm is enjoying a price which is above the average costs of production. The firm is making supernormal profit. This is shown by the area ABCP. However, the profit acts as a signal to other firms to enter the industry. There are no barriers to entry, so nothing will stop other firms entering. So this excessive profit will soon disappear and we will end up in long-run equilibrium (Figure 14.8).

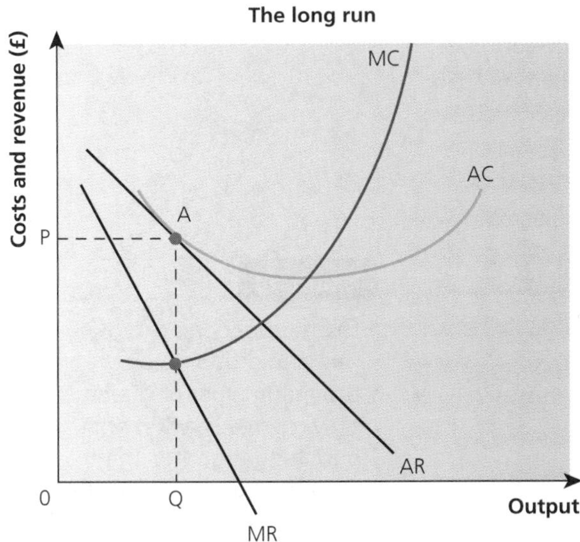

Figure 14.8 **Long-run equilibrium**

Note in Figure 14.8 that the AC and the AR curves are tangential. This is because it is only where AC and AR meet that normal profit exists, so AR will keep shifting until the curves touch just this once (and don't cross).

Now test yourself

TESTED

3 Do firms operating under the conditions of monopolistic competition make profit in the long run?

Answer on p. 220

Oligopoly

Oligopoly is a word of Greek origin: *oligo* means 'a few' and *poly* means 'sellers', so it means a few firms are dominating the market.

Assumptions

The assumptions of oligopoly are similar to monopoly (see page 141):

- A few firms dominate the market (the concentration ratios are *high*).
- There are high barriers to entry and exit.
- Firms aim for profit maximisation — MR = MC.
- The firm faces a downward-sloping demand curve.

But with one key difference.

- *The firms are interdependent.* This means that the actions of one firm are dependent on the actions of another. A firm's decisions on price, output and other competitive activities, such as the level of advertising, can have an immediate effect on other competitors.

Exam tip

There is an 'f-rule' to help you decide whether a firm is operating in an oligopolistic market: 'Five or Fewer Firms control Fifty per cent of the market'. That is, if the concentration ratio (see page 138) is above 50% then there is likely to be an oligopoly.

Measuring market concentration

REVISED

Concentration ratios

Market power is most effectively measured using a concentration ratio. The **n-firm concentration ratio** measures the proportion of the market dominated by the *largest n firms*. For example, the US retail banking market is highly fragmented and has a very low concentration ratio. This is illustrated by the fact that the top ten US banks hold only about 35% of the market share based on total US deposits. This means the ten-firm concentration ratio is 35%, very unlike the UK market where five firms have control of around 70% of the retail banking sector.

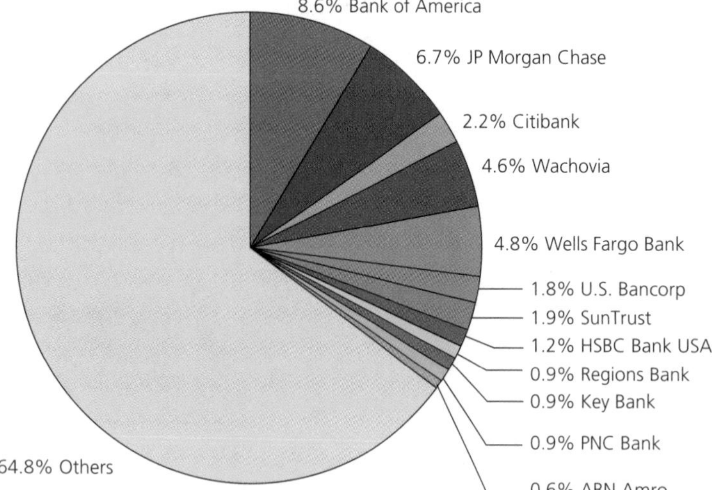

Figure 14.9 The market share of retail banks in the US (2009)

Exam tip

Exam questions often mislead students by providing a list of major players in a market and bunching together the smallest, less significant firms under the tile 'other'. Many students count 'other' in their calculation, as the total of 'other' might well occupy a bigger section than some of the biggest firms. Be careful *not* to include 'other'.

Game theory

REVISED

We can use **game theory** to analyse and evaluate the actions of firms in oligopoly. Game theory is a set of ideas which looks at strategies firms use to make decisions, for example on prices or levels of advertising.

Game theory is the study of strategies used to make decisions.

Simple pay-off matrix

Two petrol stations, R and Q, are situated on the high street leading out of town. The price one charges is highly **dependent** upon the price charged by the other, and vice versa, as shown in the **pay-off matrix** in Figure 14.10.

Interdependence means that the actions of one agent depend on the actions of another.

A **pay-off matrix** is a simple two-firm, two-outcome model.

R \ Q	High price	Low price
High price	R: £100, Q: £100	R: 0, Q: £160
Low price	R: £160, Q: 0	R: £80, Q: £80

Figure 14.10 Simple pay-off matrix

If R and Q agree to charge a high price, they can make supernormal profits per hour of £100. R sees more money can be made and decides to undercut Q. R then gets £160 and Q gets nothing. Q is very unhappy so Q cuts prices too. Both firms find they get only £80 each. Not a very satistfactory conclusion! Perhaps they should both collude again and get £100 each.

As you can see there is a dilemma here. It seems to be worth **colluding**, and also worth breaking the collusion. Once the collusion is broken, it is worth colluding again. This is the **prisoner's dilemma** in action, and explains why **cartels** might form and why they might also be broken.

Non-collusive behaviour occurs when firms act in a way that does not involve collaboration with other players in the market. The kinked demand curve theory explained below provides an example.

A **prisoner's dilemma** is a model used in game theory to question whether firms might not collude, even if it appears that it is in their best interests to do so, or vice versa.

Cartels involve firms acting as one through an agreement.

Pricing strategies used in oligopoly

REVISED

- **Price wars.** These occur when price cutting leads to retaliation and other firms cut prices, meaning the original firms again want to cut prices to increase their sales.
- **Predatory pricing.** This involves cutting prices below the average cost of production (this can also mean prices are below average variable costs). It is a short-term measure only, and once other firms have been forced out of the market the firm raises prices back up again. This is almost always illegal.
- **Limit pricing.** This involves cutting the price to the point where new possible entrants or newly entered higher-cost firms cannot compete. The incumbent firm (the one already in business and engaging in limit pricing) can sustain this position in the long term because it has lower costs. This may or may not be illegal, depending on the specific cases looked at by the competition authorities.
- **Price leadership.** In some markets the dominant firm acts to change prices and others will follow. This is because if other firms try to make changes, this could set off a price war or other sorts of retaliation. The large firm becomes the established leader. Barclays bank has often been regarded as a price leader when it comes to setting inter-bank borrowing rates.

- **Non-price competition.** This is when firms take action to compete without changing the price of their products. This might be through advertising, loyalty cards, free gifts or similar strategies.

Collusion

This occurs when firms operate together, or collaborate. There are two types you need to know about for your exam:

- **Overt collusion.** Overt means 'open'; collusion means 'operating together'. Overt collusion occurs if a firm sends messages to another firm about its prices or other decisions. It is illegal, and easier to detect than tacit collusion.
- **Tacit collusion.** Tacit means 'quiet', or 'unspoken'; collusion means 'operating together'. An implicit understanding might operate between firms. For example, when bidding at an auction there might be a gentleman's agreement — you won't bid as you won the last item, so allowing someone else to get a slightly lower price. This is also illegal, but very hard for the competition authorities to control.

Exam tip

When students talk about non-collusive behaviour they tend to avoid using important economic theory such as brand loyalty reducing price elasticity of demand. The more economic theory you use in your answer, the more marks you can earn.

Now test yourself TESTED

4 A finance director in a firm e-mails her counterpart in a competing firm and asks her what price rises are being planned for the Christmas period. What sort of collusion is this?

Answer on p. 220

Kinked demand theory

REVISED

This is a neat model which can also be used to explain the behaviour of oligopolistic firms.

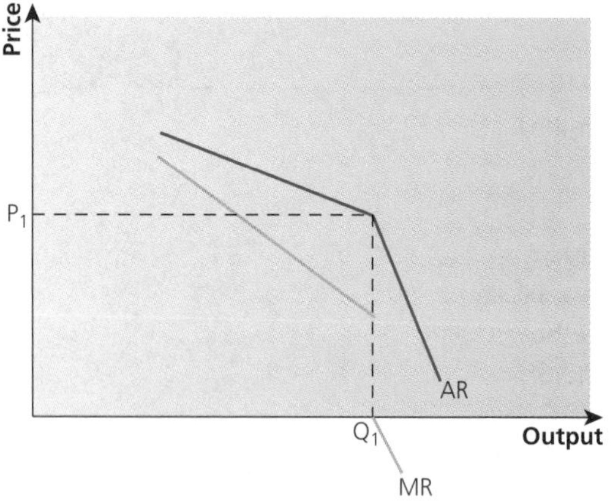

Figure 14.11 Kinked demand theory

The kinked demand curve explains why some prices are 'sticky' — that is, several firms might be charging the same price, and even if costs change the prices do not tend to change. Assume we start at point P_1 and Q_1 in Figure 14.11. Will firms increase revenue by either raising or lowering prices? According to kinked demand theory, no. Raising prices would not be copied by other firms and demand is relatively elastic. Cutting prices would be copied. An example is the price of bread and

Exam tip

A note about the drawing of MR in Figure 14.11. If MR is drawn fully below zero it means that the price elasticity of demand is less than 1, that is, the firm makes less revenue by cutting its price. This means it is definitely not worth the firm cutting prices. However, you can also draw MR above zero. While the price elasticity of demand is not technically inelastic, it is still not worth the firm cutting price because MC will be far below MR. So either way of drawing MR is acceptable, above or below zero, as long as you are careful in the way you describe what happens to total revenue.

milk in supermarkets, which is often the same in Tesco, Sainsbury's and Morrisons, for example. If the supermarkets raised the prices of these essential items, word would get around that these are the supermarkets that charge more, and demand would drop significantly (high level of price elasticity of demand) if prices were raised. However, if prices were cut in one supermarket, the other firms are likely to follow suit immediately. That is, there is a different action or response when prices are raised or if they are cut, and neither action increases total revenue for the firm. The model explains why firms might look as if there is collusion but in fact nothing illegal is happening.

Evaluation of the model

The model does not explain why the prices are what they are in the first place. It only explains some degree of stability and some markets are far more complex. A pay-off matrix gives a much wider range of possibilities and explains cartels and collusion. But the kinked demand curve can provide some simple game theory analysis or evaluation when required.

Exam tip

The kinked demand theory is not required for your exam, but many students find it a logical and easily evaluated concept which can be used to pick up marks in a question on oligopoly.

Now test yourself

TESTED

5 A firm is operating on the kink on a kinked demand curve. What can the firm do to price to raise its revenue? What would you advise this firm to do to increase its profits?

Answer on p. 220

Monopoly

A **pure monopoly** exists where there is only one firm supplying a good or service. It is often more practical to use the **legal** definition of monopoly, that is, that a firm supplies at least 25% of the market.

A **pure monopoly** involves one firm alone dominating the market.

In a **legal monopoly**, one firm dominates 25% or more of the market.

Assumptions of pure monopoly:

- one firm in the market
- high barriers to entry and exit
- firms aim for profit maximisation MR = MC
- firms face a downward-sloping demand curve

Benefits and costs of monopoly

REVISED

There may be advantages to many **stakeholders** when a monopoly exists.

A **stakeholder** is any person or group that has a vested interest in a firm. It includes consumers, suppliers, owners (e.g. shareholders), the government (receivers of corporation tax) and other firms already supplying in the market.

Benefits of monopolies

For consumers:

- Innovation — a monopoly may bring in new ideas and processes, and be able to take the risks of new ideas not working.
- Research and development — large firms are more able to plough back enormous sums into this high-risk enterprise; research more often than not leads to failure.
- Investment — large-scale firms can and will afford to invest, often because they have confidence that they will still be in existence to reap the rewards.

For governments:

- Large firms pay higher rates of **corporation tax**. The more profit the monopoly makes the more the firm will pay in tax.
- Monopolies might have many competitors outside the country. Monopoly power helps to keep jobs within the country and may improve the balance of payments.

Corporation tax is tax on profits.

For workers:

- Monopolies might offer better job security.
- Higher profits for the firm might mean higher bonuses or perks for the workers.

For other firms such as suppliers:

- A monopoly can offer a secure outlet for suppliers. If your company makes car tyres then a monopoly car producer could keep the orders rolling in.
- Firms which buy from monopolies might be more likely to have consistent quality. It is not worth a monopoly taking any risks with the quality of a well-known brand, as there is too much to lose.

Costs of monopolies

For consumers:

- Less choice — large firms keep to the brands that make the most profit.
- Higher prices — monopolists can increase price to maximise their profits.
- Lower quality — firms with no competition might not have the incentive to produce better goods or services, and the after-care service might be very limited. The good thing about competition in banking, for instance, is that if you do not get the service you need you can change bank.

For governments:

- Monopolies can find it easy to avoid paying tax, and employ expensive tax consultants to help them do so.
- Inequality tends to increase, as the rich get richer.

For workers:

- In a monopoly the worker does not have strong bargaining power. If a worker is not happy, it might not be easy to transfer to a similar company, as there is just one employer in that industry. Wages might also be kept down for this reason.
- Monopoly workers do not necessarily have any more job security than in more competitive industries. Monopoly profits can be used to invest in new machinery which can replace workers.

For other firms:

- Firms which buy from monopolies can be exploited. Small computer outlets, for instance, have no choice over range and price when dealing with Apple products.
- Other firms can be deliberately forced out of the market (by limit pricing or predatory pricing) because they have not yet had the chance to establish themselves.

Now test yourself

TESTED

6 Two firms each have 26% of a market. Is this monopoly, oligopoly, or something else?
7 Why do governments want to limit the power of monopolies?

Answer on p. 220

Price discrimination by a monopoly firm

REVISED

Price discrimination occurs when a firm with some degree of market power charges more than one price for the same good or service.

In the model for price discrimination there are three conditions:

- There are different submarkets with different price elasticities of demand.
- Consumers cannot move between the submarkets — we say there is no 'arbitrage'.
- The cost of keeping the markets separate is less than the increased profits gained from so doing.

In the diagram we draw two separate submarkets, one with relatively inelastic demand and one with price elastic demand. We can plot the demand marginal revenue in the firm as a whole by combining the demand and marginal revenues from the two submarkets. The equilibrium for the two submarkets can be found from the whole market where MC equals MR in the third diagram (see Figure 14.12). This is the marginal cost the firm will operate at, but not the marginal revenue. For this we need to draw out the marginal revenue, that is, pull a line out to the left from the diagram on the right.

Exam tip

Do not confuse price discrimination with the more common product discrimination, where different prices are charged for slightly different products. For example, meals for children are half price at Ikea — but the meals are much smaller than the adult meals.

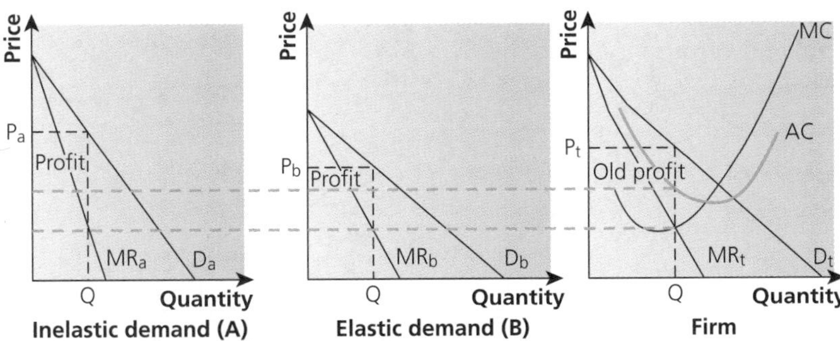

Figure 14.12 Price discrimination in two separate submarkets, A and B, with the firm as a whole shown in the third set of axes

When the marginal cost hits the marginal revenue in each of the other two markets (MR_a and MR_b), we draw a vertical line to show the quantity (Q) in each of the submarkets. The vertical line is extended upwards and meets the demand in each of the two markets, and we find the price in each market, P_a and P_b. The price is higher in the relatively inelastic demand market.

Exam tip

Always make sure the price is higher in the relatively price inelastic market, and lower in the more elastic market.

Now test yourself

TESTED

8 Why is price discrimination focused on markets with monopoly power?

Answer on p. 220

Monopsony

A **pure monopsony** is a firm which is the sole buyer of resources or supplies. Many firms have *some* degree of monopsony power, which means firms have *some control* over their suppliers.

Exam tip

You do not need to be able to draw or interpret a monopsony diagram in your exam, although you might find one more efficient than just using words. Any valid economics you use can earn credit, even if it is not required in your course.

Benefits of monopsony

REVISED

The benefits of monopsony to firms and consumers include:

- Power in buying means the firm can make more profits as suppliers cannot overcharge.
- Lower buying costs might be passed on to the consumer in retail prices.
- Higher profits of monopsony can be used to invest and innovate.
- Monopsony power can give power to buyers in the face of monopoly supply of resources. For example, cosmetic producers such as L'Oréal can charge very high prices for their products but supermarkets can force their suppliers to cut their costs.

Costs of monopsony

REVISED

The costs of monopsony to firms and consumers include:

- Suppliers can be squeezed out of business.
- Choice for consumers could be limited, as monopsony acts as a barrier to entry for new firms.
- Higher profits of monopsony can mean inequality.
- Firms might be investigated by the competition authorities.

Exam tip

You need to know the possible benefits and costs of monopsony power, in the context of data provided.

Now test yourself

TESTED

9 What is the difference between monopoly power and monopsony power?

Answer on p. 220

Contestability

The threat of competition

REVISED

Contestability is a measure of the ease with which firms can enter or exit an industry.

- High barriers to entry and exit make a market less contestable.
- **Sunk costs** are the key reason for low contestability. Any costs which cannot be recouped such as goodwill (see page 145) reduce contestability.
- A high level of competitiveness may be a sign that barriers to entry are low, but this is not the same concept. Even a monopoly can be perfectly contestable, if it is the only firm in an industry that no other firm wishes to enter because profits are low.
- A high level of concentration is a sign that contestability is low.

Sunk costs are unrecoverable costs, costs which cannot be recouped if the firm closes down.

Typical mistake

Confusing competitiveness and contestability, or concentration and contestability.

Signs of a high level of contestability include:

- low levels of supernormal profits
- low barriers to entry or exit
- low concentration ratios
- low sunk costs
- low levels of collusion or other signs of oligopoly
- new firms entering or leaving the market

Exam tip

Make sure you can evaluate whether a market is contestable or not. If you are provided with some data you will be able to give evidence on both sides of the argument.

Barriers to entry and exit

REVISED

- **Barriers to entry** are any obstacles that prevent a firm from setting up or extending its reach into new markets.
- **Barriers to exit** are any factors which prevent a firm from leaving a market, or which make it more unprofitable for a firm to leave than to stay in business, even if it is operating at a loss. Examples include sunk costs, which are irretrievable costs such as advertising or the value of the goodwill in a business.

Types of barriers to entry and exit

There are three main types:

1. Some are deliberately imposed and can be seen by the regulators as illegal anti-competitive measures:
   - predatory pricing
   - limit pricing
2. Many barriers to entry exist simply due to the nature of the business or the market, for example:
   - economies of scale
   - minimum efficient scale
3. Some barriers to entry are imposed by the authorities, in cases where too much competition might be seen as working against the interest of the consumer:
   - legal barriers, such as patents
   - state-owned franchises, such as the rail network
   - legislation to allow firms to operate, such as 4G licences

Let's take an example of a butcher who is making a loss. He can sell the shop, but this might be difficult in a recession as people might not be able to find the credit, or they may be unwilling to take the risk. He can sell his specialised equipment, but the second-hand market is also unreliable in a recession for reaching the values that might normally be expected. But probably worst of all, the reputation that the butcher has built up over the years, the loyalty of his customers, his good service records and word-of-mouth recommendations are all goodwill elements that cannot be sold on with the firm.

- If barriers to entry and exit are high, the firms are likely to be operating with strong market power.
- If the barriers to entry are extremely high, the market is likely to be a monopoly (for example, Apple computers face no direct competition and have some product lines which are strongly dominating the market).
- If the barriers to entry are high but not impossible to overcome, then the firms are likely to be operating in an oligopoly (see page 138).
- If barriers to entry are low, then the firm is operating in a fairly contestable market, and might be in monopolistic competition or, in the case of no barriers to entry and exit, the market is called perfect competition.

Revision activity

Contestability is a common area for questions with a high mark base, and it is easy to get a low score by writing about competition instead of contestability. One of the most effective ways to revise is to look at an answer that has scored full marks on a high-mark question. You can find a good example of such a type by reading the Results Plus document on Paper 6EC03 of the old specification for Edexcel Economics. Try June 2014 as a good place to start, on the Pearson Qualifications website.

Now test yourself

TESTED

10 Are barriers to entry the only factor determining market power?
11 What are the benefits of high levels of contestability?

Answer on p. 220

Exam practice 2

Entry costs to London Dungeons, 2012

ONLINE SAVER TICKET	DOOR PRICE (not including priority entrance)	WEB PRICE (including priority entrance)	WEB SAVING
Adult (16+)	£24.00	£16.00	£8.00
15 and under	£18.60	£10.00	£8.60

3 Using examples from the data provided, explain what is meant by price discrimination. [5]
4 Examine the benefits of price discrimination to firms such as the London Dungeons. [8]

Answers and quick quiz 14 online

ONLINE

Summary

- There are four main types of efficiency to consider at A-level:
  - allocative efficiency where the price is equal to marginal cost
  - productive efficiency at the lowest point of the average cost curve
  - dynamic efficiency, where costs are optimised in the long run
  - falling x-inefficiency, where firms see costs fall as the threat of competition drives them down

Different market structures exhibit these efficiencies to different degrees. In general, the more the competition and contestability, the more efficient the market — although there are many important exceptions to this.

- There are four main market structures for firms selling their output that you need to know, and they range from many sellers to just one seller. These structures are: perfect competition, oligopoly, monopoly and monopolistic competition.
- There is also a market structure showing the market conditions where there is one powerful buyer, monopsony.
- For each of these market conditions, you must be able to show price and output equilibrium points, and be able to show what happens when there are supernormal profits or losses being made.
- You must be able to show what happens when there is an increase or decrease in demand (shift AR and MR) and what happens where there is a change in costs (shift AC and MC if there is a change in variable costs, and shift just AC if there is a change in fixed costs).
- Remember that game theory can be used for your analysis of oligopoly because the firms in this market structure are interdependent.
- Contestability is a measure of the ease with which firms can enter or exit a market. It is concerned with barriers to entry and exit and sunk costs.

15 Labour market

The demand for labour

The demand for labour is the amount that firms are willing to pay for a certain amount of workers. The price of workers is the wage, and the demand varies inversely with wage.

The demand for labour is influenced by:

- worker productivity — when workers become more productive. For example, new methods in farming mean that output is more efficient so firms may be prepared to pay workers more
- the cost of capital (a substitute for labour) — firms can choose to use capital if it is cheaper, more efficient or more reliable
- the level of consumer demand for the product being made — the extra output made by any one worker multiplied by the amount that output can be sold for is called the **marginal revenue product** and is a key determinant of wages in competitive markets
- labour costs as a percentage of total costs — the demand for labour is less elastic when labour costs overall are small, so workers in a nuclear reactor, for example, can earn more than workers on a clothes production line

Labour is a **derived demand**, based on what the output they produce can earn for the firm, and the market is often called a factor market, because it is the price of resources used to make other goods and services.

Derived demand means that the demand for labour is dependent on demand for the final goods and services that the workers produce.

The supply of labour

The **supply of labour** varies in direct relationship with the wage. More people are willing to work, and for longer hours, when wages rise.

The **supply of labour** is the number of workers willing and able to work at any given wage.

The supply of labour is influenced by:

- the quality of education and training
- migration
- income tax and out-of-work benefits
- the strength of trade unions
- the opportunity cost of leisure (the next best alternative for the workers)

Market failure is common in the supply of labour because it is often difficult for workers to move easily between jobs compared to the other factors of production. Reasons include:

- **Geographical immobility.** Some workers find it hard to move to different places to seek and find work. This may be due to family ties, the cost of travel or the cost of accommodation.
- **Occupational immobility.** Some workers find it hard to move between jobs as they lack the appropriate skills or training. As an economy shifts from having a manufacturing base to a service sector base, many manufacturing workers find it difficult to transfer to jobs in the service sector as they lack the required skills.

Exam tip

One of the most common errors is to confuse demand and supply factors. This is because, with labour, demand is firms and supply is workers. It might be helpful to see the market for labour as 'the other way around' from other markets.

Wage determination

Wage determination in competitive markets

REVISED

The wage rate is the *price* of labour, that is, where the demand and supply of labour meet, in competitive markets. If wages are too high, labour supply will be high but labour demand will be low — there is excess supply leading to unemployment. To clear the market, workers will have to accept lower wages or go without a job, meaning the wage rate will tend to fall to the market clearing wage rate.

If wages are lower than the equilibrium, labour demand will be high but supply will be low — there is excess demand and therefore there will be a labour shortage. The deficit will not disappear until wages rise, and firms will have to pay workers more (demand contracts) to convince people to work (supply expands).

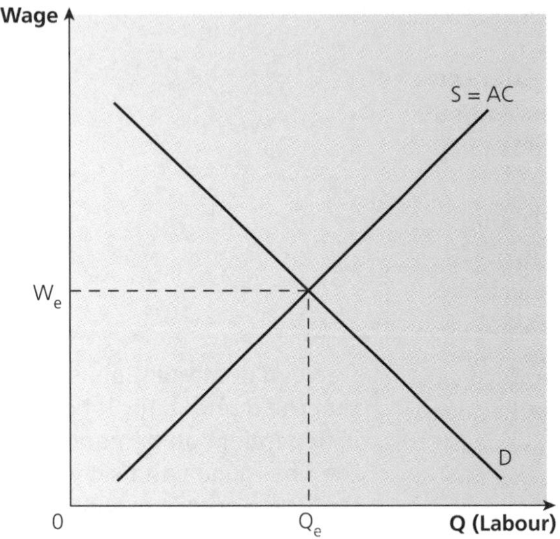

Figure 15.1 The determination of wages in competitive markets

- The **labour force participation rate** is calculated as the labour force divided by the total working-age population.
- **Unemployment** measures the number of people who are willing and able to work but not currently employed.
- **Underemployment** occurs when there are workers who are highly skilled but are working in low-skill jobs, and when there are part-time workers who would prefer to be full-time or work more hours.

The **labour force** is the sum of people employed and unemployed.

Now test yourself

TESTED

1 Is it true that measures to increase the size of the labour force include 'cutting JSA'?

Answers on p. 220

Wage determination in non-competitive markets

REVISED

In a non-competitive market there is market power — either buyers have monopsony power (the employers, for example the NHS, can force prices or wages down) or suppliers have monopoly power (trade unions, for example, force up wages). Here we cannot assume that an employer pays the employee the value the worker adds to the firm — essentially the firm 'exploits' the workers, or takes advantage of their weak market power, and forces wages down. Conversely, some employers have weak power and the employees have huge power. Think about the cost involved in employing a lawyer, for example. You are an individual, and the profession will have high fees for the smallest service, because the lawyer knows you are in a weak bargaining position.

Current labour market issues

REVISED

These include:

- skills shortages in certain areas, such as maths teachers in inner cities
- unemployment, e.g. problems accessing the labour market and youth unemployment. This may become less of a problem with the introduction of the National Living Wage (see below) of £9 an hour by 2020, but this only applies to those over 25
- increasing retirement ages, to cope with the problems in funding pensions because we live so much longer
- underemployment — many people are working in jobs which do not require the skills they have gained, e.g. graduates in non-graduate jobs, and many people do not have enough hours
- temporary, flexible and zero-hour contracts — these make it hard for people to make investments, and there are problems with delays in benefits for people moving in and out of work
- tax credits — are these an incentive to rejoin the labour market, or a disincentive to work full time? The current policy is to try to reduce these but it is not universally agreed

The **National Minimum Wage (NMW)** is the minimum firms are allowed to pay their workers, by law. A recent development in the UK is the National Living Wage, a premium paid to over 25-year-olds, from 2016. This is significantly higher than the previous trend of minimum wages, and was introduced by the chancellor of the exchequer in the Budget as a way to 'make work pay'.

In perfectly competitive markets, a minimum wage, set at W_1, will result in a wage above the market equilibrium wage, W_e (Figure 15.2). The higher wage will result in an extension of the supply of labour to Q_1 but firms

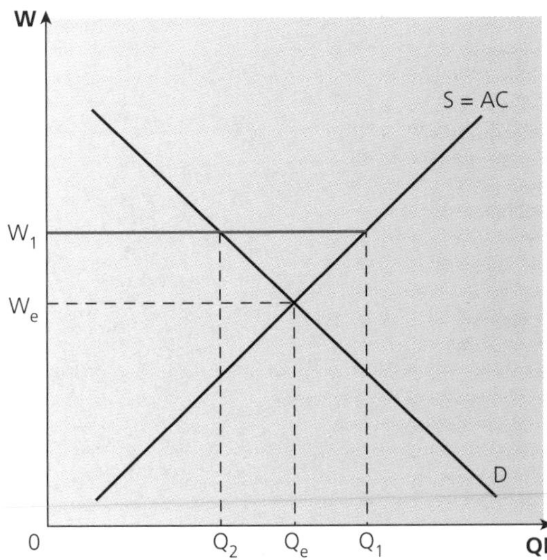

Figure 15.2 Real wage unemployment

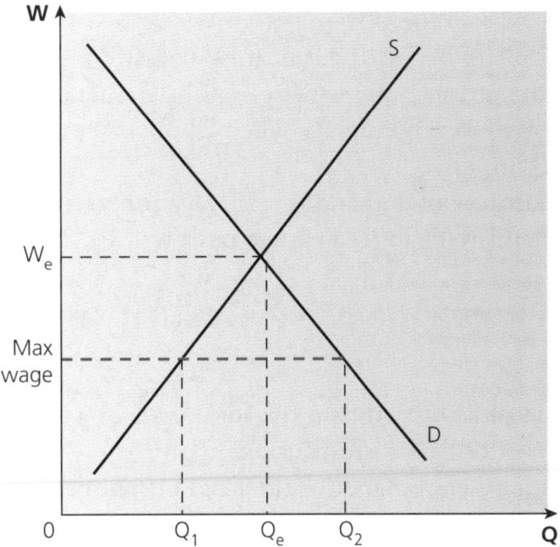

Figure 15.3 Effects of imposition of a maximum wage

will contract demand to Q_2. This leads to excess supply and Q_1–Q_2 will be unemployed, called 'real wage' or classical unemployment. Up to 2015 there was no evidence that the NMW caused this type of unemployment.

A **maximum wage** has been suggested to reduce the rate at which the top earnings are racing away from median earnings. The targeted groups are bankers and footballers. See Figure 15.3.

Benefits and costs of minimum and maximum wage

The aim of minimum and maximum wages is to reduce income inequality.

- Minimum wages can prevent very low wages, which can mean poverty, people struggling to stay in work, and an unemployment trap, where it is financially better not to go to work and to rely on benefits.
- Maximum wages are seen as a way to prevent the top 1% of earners 'creaming off' the profits in the business, and would allow higher wages to be earned by a wider group of the workers.

However:

- Minimum wages can lead to a surplus of workers, in competitive markets.
- Minimum wages need to reflect the cost of living. In an expensive city such as Edinburgh you would want a higher minimum wage (if there is going to be any impact on poverty) than in a city such as Dundee (if you want it to prevent unemployment). But a 'regional minimum wage' would be hard to enforce.
- Maximum wages can lead to a shortage of certain types of worker. If top footballers have their wages capped in the UK, they might choose to go and play abroad.
- Maximum wages can destroy incentives. If a bank needs to be transformed, it needs to attract the top businesspeople in the field, and capping wages means they will not be attracted to the job.

The government is a major employer, and through its own **public sector wage setting**, it can directly impact the labour market, rather than doing so indirectly through minimum and maximum wages. It can also set policies to tackle labour market immobility, such as training programmes and relocation subsidies.

The wage or price **elasticity of demand for labour** refers to how responsive the demand for labour will be to changes in wages. It is estimated to be −0.4 in the UK.

- If the price elasticity of demand is relatively **elastic** (−1 to minus infinity), businesses will cut back aggressively on employment if wage rates increase, and will expand rapidly when labour becomes cheaper relative to other factor inputs.
- If the price elasticity of demand is relatively **inelastic** (0 to −1), the response by firms to changes to wage rates will be smaller.

What determines the price elasticity of demand for labour?

- the proportion of labour costs in the total costs of a business
- the ease and cost of factor substitution
- the price elasticity of demand for the final output produced by a business
- the time period under consideration

The wage or price **elasticity of labour supply** to an occupation measures the responsiveness of labour supply to a change in the wage rate.

- If the price elasticity of supply is relatively **elastic** (1 to infinity), workers respond quickly if wage rates increase and supply will expand rapidly when wages rise.
- If the price elasticity of supply is relatively **inelastic** (0 to 1), the response by workers to changes to wage rates will be smaller.

What determines the price elasticity of supply of labour?

- In low-skilled occupations, labour supply is elastic because a pool of labour is available to take the job.
- Where jobs require specific skills, training or qualifications, the labour supply will be more inelastic because it is hard to expand the workforce in a short period of time when the wage for workers has increased.

The significance of these elasticities is that we can use them to explain wage differentials and changes in wage rates. The higher the elasticities, the lower the wages will tend to be.

Now test yourself

TESTED

2 The demand for labour is often seen as a product of the marginal physical product of a worker (what is actually made) and the price that the product is sold for. What happens to the demand for labour if the price of the product rises?

3 What is the main difference between a competitive and a non-competitive labour market?

Answers on p. 220

Exam tip

Use a selection of demand and supply of labour diagrams to explain wage differentials. Remember to use the slope of the demand and supply curves to illustrate elasticities.

Revision activity

Make a list of reasons why London Tube train drivers earn so much more than nurses. Make sure that you look at demand as well as supply factors.

Exam practice

1 Evaluate the possible microeconomic and macroeconomic effects on the UK economy of increased immigration. [25]

2 Evaluate the possible microeconomic and macroeconomic effects on the UK economy of a decision by the government to raise the national minimum wage. [25]

Answers and quick quiz 15 online

ONLINE

Summary

- In competitive labour markets, wages are determined by the demand and supply of labour.
- Market failure means that governments often want to intervene to influence some wages and labour immobility.

16 Government intervention

Competition policy refers to the set of rules and powers that are used to increase competition within markets. Competition authorities, the government's means of intervening in markets, take increasingly strong action to control mergers and monopolies, promote competition, and protect suppliers and employees. Examples of competition authorities are:

- the Competition and Markets Authority (CMA) in the UK
- the Antitrust Commission in the USA
- the European Competition Commission

These organisations aim to promote the interests of the consumer: prices, profit, efficiency, quality and choice.

Types of government intervention

Prevention of mergers

REVISED

The competition authorities can prevent mergers from happening, or intervene to ensure mergers only occur with certain restrictions in place. The CMA can also force firms to demerge, for example LloydsTSB was forced to split into separate firms in 2013.

Action to prevent abuse of monopoly power

REVISED

The regulator looks at aspects of monopoly behaviour and has various means of addressing problems it uncovers.

Monitoring of prices and price capping

- Price changes can be hidden from customers because price charts or tariffs are often overcomplicated or not clearly presented to consumers. In response, for example, a decision by the gas and electricity regulator, Ofgem, meant that tariffs had to be simplified and customers would have to be told the best deal they could get.
- The regulator can impose a limit on price increases by firms. This is usually done in line with the retail price index (RPI) measure of inflation. Prices are allowed to rise by RPI − X where X is a measure of the amount of efficiency savings the regulator believes the firm can make. Sometimes a value is added to this to allow for investment in the industry, given the letter K. For example, water companies currently have an RPI − X + K formula where K allows a price rise to take account of the required increase in investment.

Exam tip

In past papers you will see references to the Office of Fair Trading (OFT) and the European Competition Commission. You do not need to know their detailed individual powers or history, but you should understand the functions of competition authorities as a whole. You should be able to refer to at least one case where the CMA has had a significant impact on firms.

Profit regulation

The government can set a maximum percentage profit relative to a firm's assets. The problem here is often that the firm has no incentive to be efficient in its capital spending.

Quality standards

The government can control the forms of competition and therefore choice for customers by offering a limited quantity of licences or permission to operate in some markets, depending on quality being of a certain high standard. This is made more effective by giving a limited franchise period, which will not be renewed if quality is unacceptable.

Performance targets

These can be set for service quality. For example, the Office of Rail Regulation, the regulator of the railways in the UK, measures train punctuality and ensures passengers can get refunds for late arrivals of trains.

Private sector involvement in public organisations

The government pays the costs but market forces are involved in producing goods or services. There are many forms in which this operates. Two important forms for your exam are:

- **Private finance initiative (PFI).** This is a form of financing major public projects such as motorway construction or the building of schools and hospitals. The private sector funds the building and maintains the service, and rents or leases the service to the government over a guaranteed period, usually 25–30 years. It was introduced in 1992 in the UK, and has had a significant impact on the government's finances because it can achieve projects today without having to raise the funds in the current period.
- **Contracting out.** Many governments use the private sector to provide some services, for example office cleaning, grounds maintenance, leisure services and the management of sports centres, public libraries and arts centres. Since 1988 local councils have been required to test their existing arrangements against the best the private sector could offer. Many councils found that they could make substantial savings by contracting out to commercial firms. This is thought to reduce waste and inefficiency in the public sector and to increase the level of competition in the private sector, which leads to lower prices and more choice for consumers.

Exam tip

The regulatory period is important. Regulation is imposed on firms for a period of time, and consideration of the length of any control is useful for evaluation. The longer the regulatory period, the longer the firm can adapt to the controls and make profits within the parameters set. However, if the period is too long, the firm might not be forced to make more efficiency savings or may be prevented from making profits which would enable it to adapt and grow.

Promoting competition and contestability

- **Deregulation.** Removing direct controls on firms can allow more competition in markets. The post services in the UK have been subject to large-scale deregulation, which you will notice on your mail as you now see very few letters carrying Royal Mail postage payments. By allowing firms to compete for postal services — meaning the postal worker brings your letters from a large number of suppliers — you have more choice, and hopefully better service and lower prices.
- **Privatisation.** This is the selling of public sector assets to the private sector. The action can force the firm to increase its profitability because it can no longer rely on government subsidy. The competition from other firms might also increase competition, removing x-inefficiency, that is the organisational slack and unwieldiness that comes when there is no competition.
- **Competitive tendering** is when government acquires goods or services by extending to suppliers an invitation to bid or 'tender' a proposal. In general, the bid with the lowest price wins the order, although factors related to quality, shipping, timeliness and efficiency will be considered. The process forces suppliers to compete and consequently (so the theory goes), the purchaser and taxpayer will gain better 'value for money'.

Protecting suppliers and employees

Suppliers to large powerful firms (monopsonies) may be protected by government intervention. For example, from 2015 a Groceries Code Adjudicator independently ensures that large supermarkets treat their direct suppliers lawfully and fairly, investigates complaints and arbitrates in disputes, such as when supermarkets change orders at the last minute when the crops have been harvested.

Nationalisation

Government can take firms back into the public sector to protect workers and other firms which rely on the failing firm. In the 2008 financial crisis the government nationalised or part-nationalised Lloyds, RBS and other major banks.

Nationalisation is when private firms are taken back into public or state ownership. The government may purchase all the privately-held shares.

The impact of government intervention

The aim of government intervention is to:

- promote competition between firms, meaning that prices are lower and choice for consumers is wider
- ensure profitability is not at the expense of abusing market power
- make markets work efficiently. Competing firms tend to be careful to keep costs low and find ways to reduce wasteful procedures
- contribute towards improved efficiency in individual markets and enhanced competitiveness of UK businesses more significantly now we have voted to exit the European Union (EU) single market
- ensuring minimum standards of quality and preventing action such as mergers which might reduce consumer choice

However, government intervention may fail to bring about the socially optimal position; for example, through **regulatory capture**. This means that the regulators are 'taken in' by the firm, for example when a firm persuades the regulators that it is a good firm. It is also important to consider how **asymmetric information** could make it difficult for the authorities to investigate and discover anti-competitive practices, because the people operating the businesses are likely to know much more about the market than the regulators.

Exam tip

If exemplar papers are a guide, in Paper 3 there will be two essay questions (from a choice of 2 + 2), which will require you to look at **microeconomic and macroeconomic effects**. In all aspects of the course, make sure you think about the micro impact, e.g. effects on firms, workers or consumers, even during macro topics such as competitiveness or changes in exchange rates.

Now test yourself

TESTED

1. Why do governments want to increase competition in markets?
2. What is the difference between symmetric information and asymmetric information?
3. Does the relatively low number of CMA cases recommending action for firms mean that the CMA is ineffective?

Answers on p. 220

Revision activity

Make a list of three **merger** cases that the CMA has investigated in recent years. One should be where the merger was allowed, one with some recommendations, and one where it was prohibited. Can you see how this might be useful in writing an evaluation of the role of the CMA in the current context?

Exam practice

A competitive market for the supply of healthcare services is being introduced in the UK. This began with the development of the internal market in the 1990s and the plan includes the introduction of patient choice, foundation trusts, payment by results (the system used to pay hospitals for the episodes of care they provide to patients) and independent sector treatment centres.

1 Which reason best explains why the public sector is introducing competition in the NHS?
   A The government has no experience of building or running hospitals.
   B The government has a budget surplus.
   C It is cheaper for the private sector to borrow than for the public sector.
   D The government believes that competition provides efficiency incentive. [1]

Extract: New watchdog to monitor competition law

There is a new watchdog regulating UK firms. Legal experts are divided over whether it will live up to the government's billing of a nimble hunter of price-fixers and monopolistic mergers, or whether it will be a bloated, toothless political lapdog.

In the biggest shake-up of British competition law in decades, the creation of the new Competition and Markets Authority has taken on the anti-monopoly powers of the Office of Fair Trading and the entire Competition Commission. Everything from cartel enforcement to merger analysis is now done under one roof, as well as new responsibilities, such as undertaking wide-ranging studies of markets if politicians judge it to be in the public interest.

The redesign of the regulatory architecture has been a long time coming since the OFT was formed in 1973. The government said it would make it easier for prosecutors to bring criminal cartel cases because they would no longer have to prove defendants acted dishonestly, but just show they had not been open in their dealings. 'The OFT has suffered from a lack of experience, poor judgment exacerbated by a lack of robust checks and balances, and a failure to attract enough high quality competition lawyers,' said Robert Vidal, head of competition at Taylor Wessing.

Source: adapted from 'New watchdog to monitor competition law', Caroline Binham, FT.com, 15 March 2012

2 Using examples from the passage, explain the ways in which governments aim to maintain competition between firms in the UK. [5]

3 Using examples from your own knowledge, discuss the effectiveness of competition policy in the UK. [15]

Answers and quick quiz 16 online

ONLINE

Summary

- Governments intervene in markets either to increase competition or to prevent action which would reduce the level of competition.
- Where increased competition will not improve the welfare of consumers, the government may use regulation, using direct controls to ensure that firms behave in the interests of consumers and other stakeholders.

17 International economics

Globalisation

From a purely economic perspective, **globalisation** refers to the increased economic integration between countries. Globalisation is not a new phenomenon but the pace of globalisation has increased significantly in the last 50 years with the exception of the period following the financial crisis of 2008.

Globalisation refers to the increased integration between countries economically, socially and culturally.

The key characteristics of globalisation include:

- **Increased trade as a proportion of GDP.** It can be seen from Figure 17.1 that world trade has been increasing at a faster rate than world GDP.

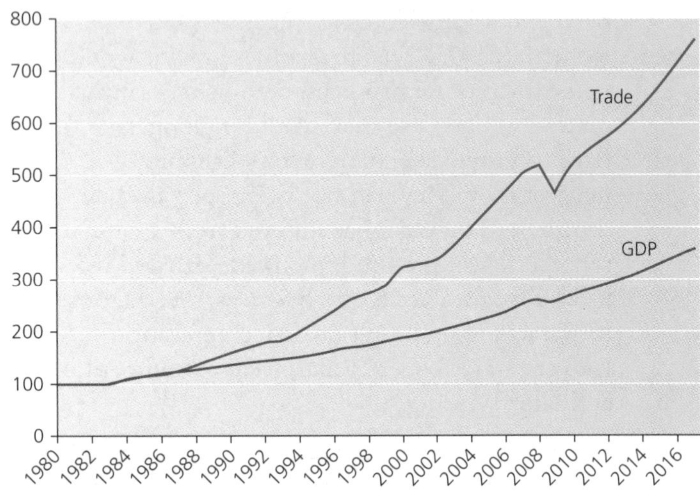

Figure 17.1 World GDP and global trade as a percentage of GDP, 1980 = 100
Source: IMF WEO

- Increased **foreign direct investment (FDI)**. The trend in FDI inflows is illustrated in Figure 17.2.

Foreign direct investment occurs when a company in one country establishes operations, e.g. a factory, in another country or when it acquires physical assets or a stake in an overseas company.

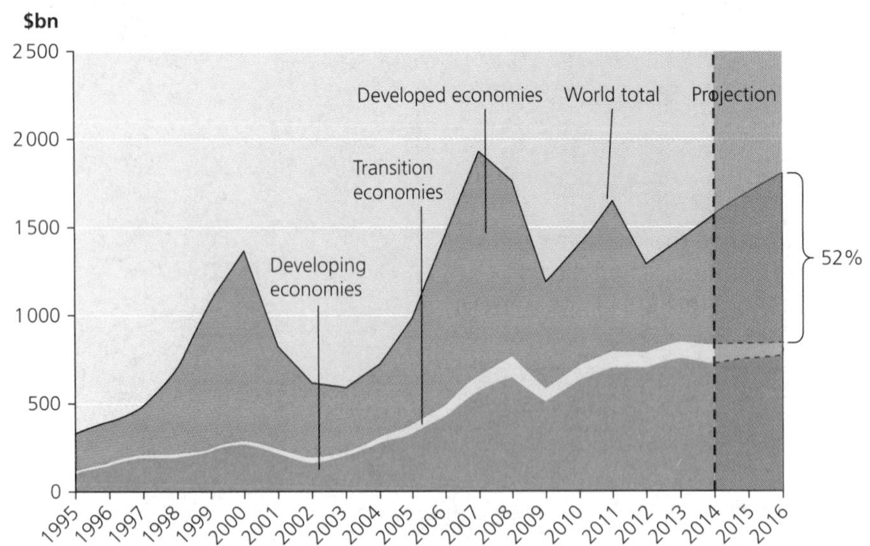

Figure 17.2 FDI inflows, global and by group of economies, 1995–2013 and projections, 2014–16 (billions of US dollars)

- Increased **capital flows** between countries. These have increased as cross-border acquisitions and mergers of companies have grown in different countries.
- Increased movement of people between countries.

Capital flows refer to all the money moving between countries as a consequence of investment flows into and out of countries around the world.

Exam tip

Although globalisation may be interpreted very broadly, you should focus on its economic aspects when answering questions in economics exams.

Now test yourself

TESTED

1 Identify two factors which could limit globalisation.
2 Suggest three reasons why trade between countries is likely to increase in the next 20 years.

Answers on p. 221

Causes of globalisation

REVISED

These include:

- a **decrease in transport costs** — for example, containerisation resulted in **economies of scale** and falling long-run average costs
- a **decrease in the cost of communications** especially as a result of the internet
- a **reduction in world trade barriers** engineered by The General Agreement on Tariffs and Trade (GATT) and its successor, the World Trade Organization (WTO)
- the **opening up of China** and the **collapse of communism in Eastern Europe**
- the **growth of trading blocs** (see page 163)
- the **increased importance of global companies or transnational companies (TNCs)** — TNCs have undertaken much FDI, which frequently involves moving manufacturing to a country where production costs are lower — a practice known as **offshoring**.

Economies of scale refers to falling in long-run average costs when output increases.

Offshoring refers to companies transferring manufacturing to a different country.

Now test yourself

TESTED

3 Why is the internet a significant cause of globalisation?

Answers on p. 221

Impacts of globalisation

REVISED

- **On individual countries.** With lower trade barriers and increased trade, countries can specialise in producing goods in which they have a **comparative** advantage (see page 159). This results in higher world output and, therefore, to an **increase in living standards**. However, a country which does not have a competitive advantage may come to rely increasingly on imports, which would cause a **deterioration in its current account of the balance of payments**. Further, it is argued that globalisation has resulted in **increased inequality** within countries. One reason for this is that the demand for unskilled labour has decreased in developed countries, so increasing the earnings gap between the highest-paid and lowest-paid workers. An additional issue is that the **risk of contagion is increased**.

- **On governments. Tax revenues** will increase, which may be used on public services such as health and education or for infrastructure. However, some TNCs engage in a form of tax avoidance referred to as **transfer pricing**.
- **On producers.** Firms will be producing on a larger scale and so will benefit from **economies of scale** and higher profits. Further, **technology transfer** is likely to occur — that is when TNCs invest in other countries they are likely to bring modern technology with them. Similarly, TNCs are likely to introduce **modern managerial techniques** designed to increase productivity. In turn, both these may be adopted by local producers, resulting in increased productivity. However, local producers who are uncompetitive may be forced out of business.
- **On consumers.** Consumers can expect lower prices (**increased consumer surplus**) and greater choice.
- **On workers.** Workers can expect **increased employment opportunities**. However, TNCs might exploit workers in developing countries by paying low wages for long working hours.
- **On the environment.** There will be **increased external costs**. Increased trade will increase road and air transport and associated noise and air pollution. Further, FDI by countries in search of raw materials may result in exploitation and depletion of resources.

Transfer pricing refers to the price that has been charged by one part of a company for products and services it provides to another part of the same company. This system enables TNCs to declare profits in the country in which corporation tax is lowest.

Consumer surplus refers to the difference between consumers' willingness to pay for a product and the market price.

External costs refer to costs to third parties who are not party to the transaction. They are not reflected in the price mechanism.

Now test yourself TESTED

4 Identify two benefits of globalisation to firms.

Answers on p. 221

Exam tip

Notice that some of the benefits of globalisation are similar to those for free trade.

Specialisation and trade

Absolute advantage

REVISED

Absolute advantage implies that a country can produce more of one product than another country can with the same amount of resources. Figure 17.3 illustrates a situation in which country A has an absolute advantage in the production of maize and country B has an absolute advantage in the production of smartphones.

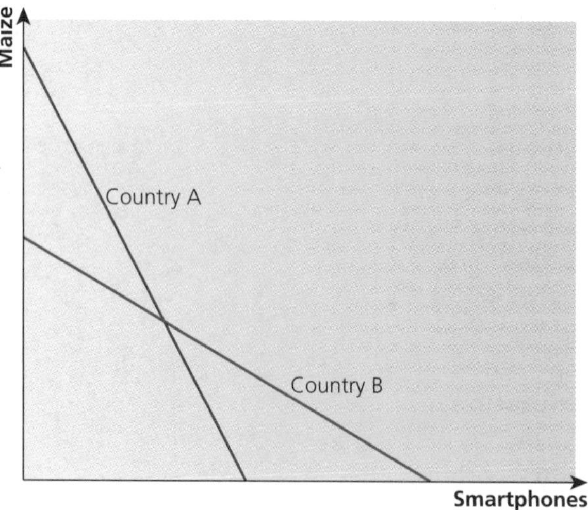

Figure 17.3 Country A has an absolute advantage in maize and country B has an absolute advantage in smartphones

In this case, it is clear that each country could benefit by specialising in the product in which it has an absolute advantage.

Comparative advantage

REVISED

If a country has a **comparative advantage** it can produce a good with a lower opportunity cost than that of another country.

One country has **comparative advantage** over another in the production of a good if it can produce it at a lower opportunity cost.

David Ricardo demonstrated that trade between the two nations can be beneficial to both if each specialises in the production of a good in which it has a comparative advantage (even if one has an absolute advantage in both products). The crucial requirement is that there must be *a difference in the opportunity cost* of producing the products.

The law of comparative advantage

Assumptions:

- Constant returns to scale. This would imply that the production possibility frontiers are drawn as straight lines.
- No transport costs.
- No trade barriers.
- Perfect mobility of factors of production between different uses.
- Externalities are ignored.

Exam tip

The law of comparative advantage is not only fundamental to an explanation of international trade, but it also applies to specialisation and the division of labour.

Exam tip

Some of the assumptions underlying the law of comparative advantage are unrealistic and so could be used in evaluating the law.

Typical mistake

Confusion between absolute with comparative advantage.

Comparative advantage illustrated diagrammatically and numerically

Figure 17.4 illustrates the principle of comparative advantage.

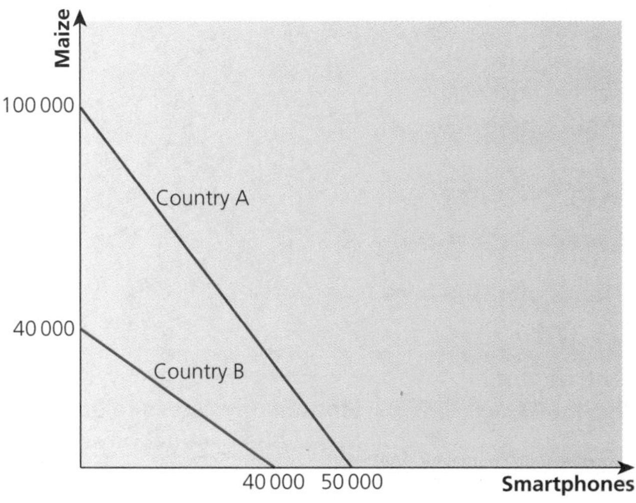

Figure 17.4 Country A has an absolute advantage in both products

In our example, countries A and B both produce two products, maize and smartphones. Suppose they can both produce the following amounts of these products with the same quantity of resources:

Country	Maize		Smartphones
A	100 000	or	50 000
B	40 000	or	40 000

Clearly, country A has an absolute advantage in the production of both maize and smartphones. If each country devotes half its resources to the production of each product then output would be as follows:

Country	Maize	Smartphones
A	50000	25000
B	20000	20000
Total	**70000**	**45000**

To determine whether trade will be worthwhile, the **opportunity costs** must be calculated:

Opportunity cost is the next best alternative which has been foregone when a choice is made.

Country	Opportunity cost of producing 1 kg of maize	Opportunity cost of producing 1 smartphone
A	½	2
B	1	1

From the table it can be seen that country A has a comparative advantage in maize (because the opportunity cost is lower) while country B has a comparative advantage in smartphones.

For trade to be beneficial, the **terms of trade** (see page 162) must lie between the opportunity cost ratios. In this case, the terms of trade must lie between 1 and 2 kg of maize for 1 smartphone.

Terms of trade measure the price of a country's exports relative to the price of its imports.

Now test yourself

TESTED

5 Absolute advantage implies that one country can produce more of a product than another country with the same amount of resources. What is the difference between absolute advantage and comparative advantage?

Answers on p. 221

Limitations of the law of comparative advantage

- Free trade is not necessarily fair trade (i.e. the rich countries might exert their **monopsony power** to force producers in developing countries to accept very low prices).
- The law of comparative advantage is based on unrealistic assumptions such as constant costs of production, zero transport costs and no barriers to trade.
- If the opportunity costs were the same, then there would be no benefit from specialisation and trade.

Monopsony refers to a sole buyer of a product or service (see also pp. 143—44). In this case, **monopsony power** refers to the buying power of rich developed countries.

Advantages and disadvantages of specialisation and trade

REVISED

The advantages of specialisation and trade include:

- higher living standards and increased employment resulting from an increase in world output
- lower prices, increased choice

- transfer of management expertise and technology transfer
- economies of scale
- reduction in power of domestic monopolies

The disadvantages of specialisation and trade include:

- a deficit on the **trade in goods and services balance** if a country's goods and services are uncompetitive
- danger of **dumping** — firms in countries with surpluses of goods might 'dump' them on other countries. This could cause local producers to go bankrupt. In the long run, the country could then become dependent on imports
- increased unemployment in some countries (resulting from the above factors)
- increased risk of contagion and disruption resulting from problems in the global economy
- unbalanced development — international specialisation based on free trade means that only those industries in which the country has a comparative advantage will be developed, while others will remain undeveloped. This could cause **sectoral imbalance**, which could limit economic growth
- TNCs may become global **monopolies**

Developing countries may face problems for a variety of reasons, including:

- infant industries may be unable to compete and go out of business
- monopsony power of firms in developed economies might force producers in developing countries to accept low prices for their products
- declining terms of trade for countries dependent on primary products

Exam tip

In considering the advantages of international trade, it is important to refer to theory, e.g. the law of comparative advantage.

Trade balance (trade in goods and services balance) refers to the value of exports minus the value of imports.

Dumping occurs when a product is sold in a foreign country for less than the cost of making the product. Under the rules of the WTO, this practice is illegal.

Sectoral imbalance refers to an imbalance in the three main sectors of the economy — primary, secondary and tertiary sectors.

Monopolies are sole suppliers of a product.

Now test yourself

TESTED

6. From the perspective of consumers and workers, identify two advantages and two disadvantages of free trade.
7. From the perspective of a firm, identify two advantages and two disadvantages of free trade.

Answers on p. 221

Patterns of trade

Key factors influencing patterns of trade between countries include:

- comparative advantage (see above)
- the growth in exports of manufactured goods, especially from low wage countries to developed economies
- the growth of global supply chains
- the increased importance of emerging economies as trading partners (see page 181)
- the growth of trading blocs and bilateral trading agreements (see page 163)
- changes in relative exchange rates

Figure 17.5 illustrates the share of selected countries' world trade over a 30-year period, and how this is expected to change.

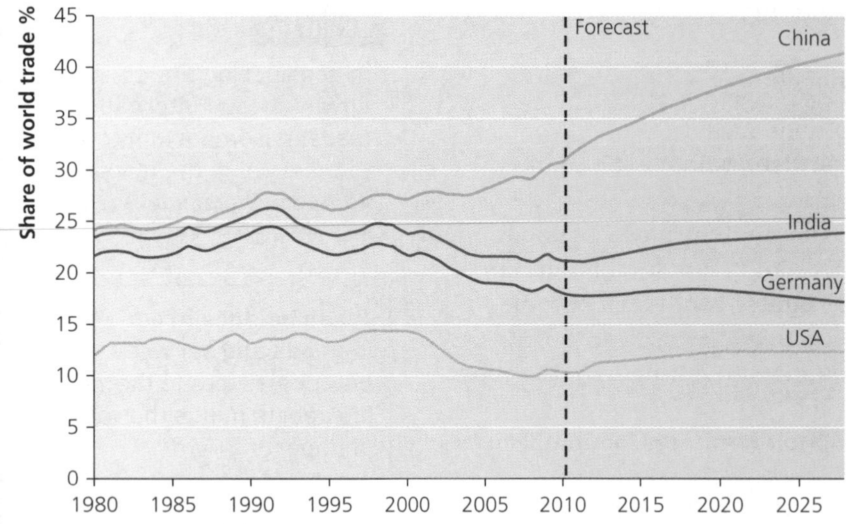

Figure 17.5 Share of world trade for USA, Germany, China and India, 1980–2025

Source: Oxford Economics

Now test yourself

TESTED

8 Suggest three reasons why China's share of world trade has increased.

Answers on p. 221

The **terms of trade** measure the price of a country's exports relative to the price of its imports.

Terms of trade

Calculation

REVISED

$$\frac{\text{index of export prices}}{\text{index of import prices}} \times 100$$

Factors influencing a country's terms of trade

REVISED

- the country's rate of inflation relative to other countries
- the country's productivity relative to that of other countries
- tariffs
- the country's exchange rate

The effect of an increase in a country's terms of trade

REVISED

These include:

- **higher living standards** — the country can import more for a given quantity of exports
- **deterioration in the current account of the balance of payments** — although an increase in the terms of trade is referred to as an 'improvement' because of its implications for living standards, such an increase would cause a decline in the competitiveness of its goods and services

A decrease in a country's terms of trade would have the reverse effects of those described above.

Exam tip

Note that the concept of terms of trade is also relevant when discussing primary product dependency in developing countries.

Now test yourself

TESTED

9 Calculate the terms of trade in year 2 resulting from the following changes, assuming that the base year is year 1:
   (a) a 20% increase in the price of exports combined with a 10% increase in the price of imports
   (b) a 10% fall in the price of imports combined with a 10% increase in the price of exports

10 What is the likely effect of a fall in the UK's terms of trade on its living standards?

Answers on p. 221

Trading blocs and the World Trade Organization (WTO)

What is a trading bloc?

REVISED

A **trading bloc** is a group of countries usually within a geographical region designed to significantly reduce or remove trade barriers between member countries. The world is now increasingly divided into trade blocs, most of which are in specific geographical regions. For example, the East African Community (EAC), the Common Market for Eastern and Southern Africa (COMESA), and the Southern African Development Community (SADC).

Trading blocs are groups of countries that agree to reduce or eliminate trade barriers between themselves.

Typical mistake

Assuming incorrectly that trading blocs mean blocks or restrictions on international trade.

Exam tip

It is useful to know examples of trading blocs so you can include these in your answers.

Types of trading blocs

REVISED

Trading blocs or regional trade agreements take several forms, which include:

- **Free trade areas.** In these trading blocs trade barriers are removed between member countries but each member can impose trade restrictions on non-members.
- **Customs unions.** There is free trade between member countries combined with a common external tariff on goods from countries outside the customs union.
- **Common markets.** These have the same characteristics as customs unions but include the free movement of factors of production (e.g. labour) between member countries.
- **Monetary unions.** These are customs unions which adopt a common currency. The Eurozone is an example of such a monetary union.

Typical mistake

Assuming that all trading blocs have the same characteristics.

Costs and benefits of regional trade agreements/trading blocs

REVISED

Costs of regional trade agreements include:

- **Trade diversion.** In most trading blocs there are tariffs and/or other restrictions on imports from outside the bloc. Consequently, trade may be diverted away from low-cost producers outside the bloc to high-cost producers within the bloc.
- **Distortion of comparative advantage.** Trade barriers against non-members are likely to cause a decrease in specialisation and to a fall in world output.

Trade diversion occurs when trade is diverted from a more efficient exporter towards a less efficient producer.

In addition, there are various costs associated with **monetary unions** such as the Eurozone:

- **Transition costs.** These are one-off costs associated with changing menus, price lists and slot machines when the currency is introduced.
- **Loss of independent monetary policy.** Countries no longer have control of their own interest rates. In the Eurozone's case, the European Central Bank (ECB) controls monetary policy.
- **Loss of exchange rate flexibility.** Individual members of the Eurozone no longer have their own currencies.

Benefits of regional trade agreements include:

- **Trade creation.** The removal of trade barriers between member countries will result in increased trade between them.
- **Increase in Foreign Direct Investment (FDI).** TNCs would have unrestricted access in selling goods to consumers in the bloc.
- **Increase in economic power.** A large trading bloc might be in a better position to negotiate trade agreements with other countries and trading blocs.

Trade creation occurs when trade is created as a result of the formation of a free trade agreement between a group of countries by the establishment of a trading bloc.

In addition, monetary unions may enjoy further benefits including:

- **Elimination of transactions costs.** These are costs involved in changing currencies when goods are imported or exported.
- **Price transparency.** Consumers have the ability to compare prices more easily across national borders.
- **Elimination of currency fluctuations between member countries.** This could encourage increased investment by businesses.

The role of the World Trade Organization in trade liberalisation (WTO)

REVISED

The WTO now has 164 members. The key roles of the WTO are:

- to promote free trade — this is achieved through various rounds of talks
- to settle trade disputes between member countries

Possible conflicts between regional trade agreements and the WTO

REVISED

Regional trade agreements restrict trade with non-member countries, which conflicts with the aims of the WTO. However, both the number and the size of these regional trade agreements have been increasing, so they have played an important role in promoting free trade.

Now test yourself

TESTED

11 What is the theoretical basis for the World Trade Organization?
12 Distinguish between trade creation and trade diversion.

Answers on p. 221

Restrictions on free trade

Reasons for restrictions on free trade

REVISED

- to correct a deficit in the trade in goods and services balance
- to prevent dumping
- to reduce unemployment
- to reduce the risk of disruption resulting from problems in the global economy
- to prevent sectoral imbalance: international specialisation based on free trade means that only those industries in which the country has a comparative advantage will be developed
- to limit the monopoly power of global companies

Developing countries may have particular reasons for restricting trade, including:

- to protect infant industries
- to limit monopsony power of firms in developed economies

Now test yourself

TESTED

13 Why might **protectionism** against dumping be justified?
14 Explain why a developing country might use protectionist policies.

Answers on p. 221

Protectionism means methods of restricting free trade.

Types of restrictions on free trade

REVISED

Examples of trade barriers are shown in Figure 17.6.

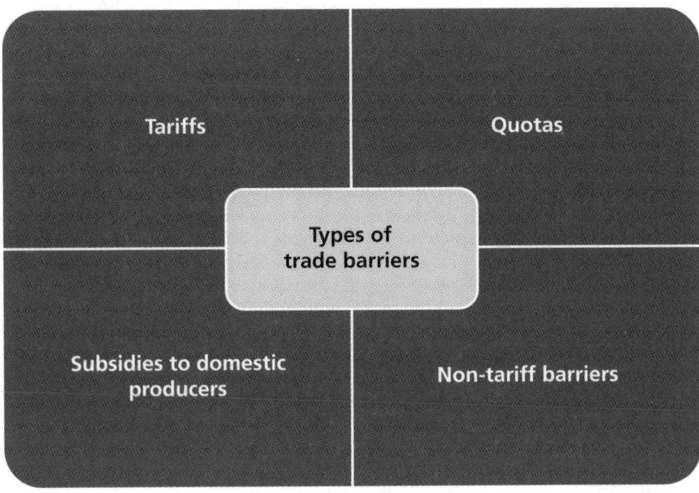

Figure 17.6 Types of trade barrier

Tariffs

Tariffs and customs duties are taxes placed on imports that artificially raise the price of imported goods. Figure 17.7 shows the impact of a tariff on a particular product both on domestic output and on the level of imports.

Tariffs are taxes on imported goods.

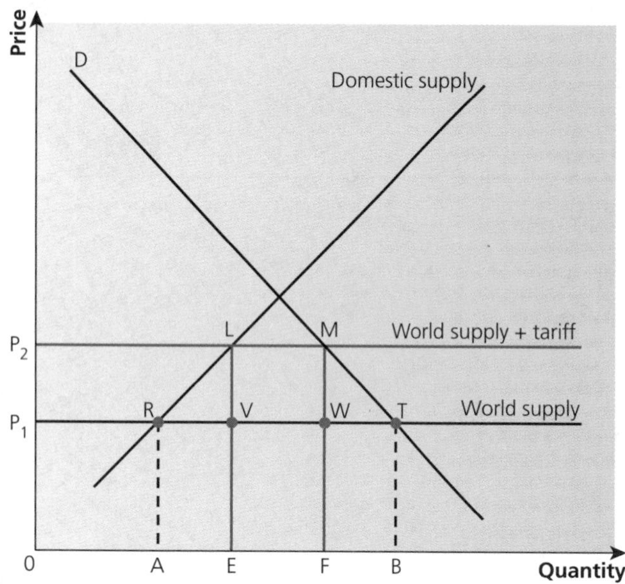

Figure 17.7 The effects of a tariff on cars

The table below summarises the effects of the tariff on cars, with reference to Figure 17.7.

	Before tariff is imposed	After tariff is imposed
Price paid by consumers	P_1	P_2
Domestic output	0A	0E
Imports	AB	EF
Tax revenue	Zero	LMWV
Net welfare loss	Zero	RLV and WMT

Quotas

Quotas are limits on the physical quantity of a product which may be imported. As with tariffs, the price to domestic consumers will increase and domestic output will rise.

Quotas are limits on the quantity of a product imported.

Subsidies to domestic producers

Subsidies are government grants to firms which reduce costs of production, so causing the supply curve of domestic producers to shift to the right. Figure 17.8 illustrates the impact of subsidies.

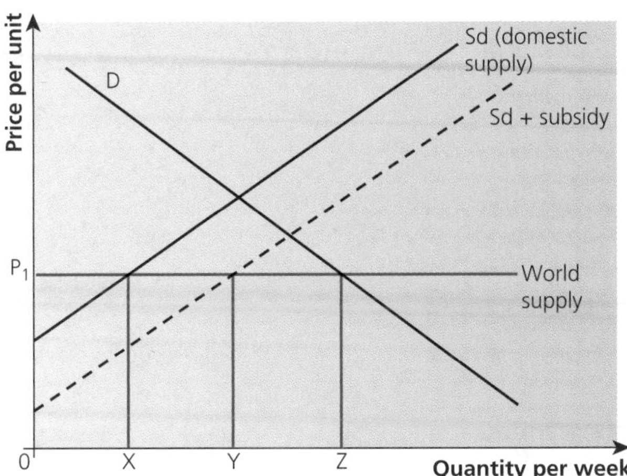

Figure 17.8 The effect of a subsidy

The effects of a subsidy to domestic producers, with reference to Figure 17.8, are summarised in the table below.

	Before subsidy	After subsidy
Price paid by consumers	P_1	P_1
Domestic output	0X	0Y
Imports	XY	YZ

It can be seen that the effect on imports is similar to that of tariffs but in this case the price of imports does not change and the government does not receive any tax revenue. Indeed, this method involves public expenditure to finance the subsidies to domestic producers.

Exam tip

This analysis is essentially the same as that for subsidies covered in Theme 1. However, it is given a global context by including world supply.

Non-tariff barriers

Given that GATT and WTO agreements have reduced tariffs, countries have resorted to a wide range of alternative methods to restrict imports. These include:

- health and safety regulations
- environmental regulations
- labelling of products
- bureaucracy, e.g. requiring importers to complete a vast number of forms

All these may raise the cost of imports and/or deter foreign companies from attempting to export goods to the country imposing the restriction.

The impact of protectionist policies

REVISED

- **On consumers.** Tariffs and quotas result in higher prices and a reduction in both consumer surplus and consumer choice.
- **On producers.** Domestic firms face less competition and have less incentive to produce at lowest average cost. Further, they may cause retaliation by other countries which might impose protectionist measures.
- **On governments.** If tariffs are imposed then a government would receive tax revenue.
- **On living standards.** Protectionism distorts comparative advantage. This means that specialisation is reduced, resulting in lower output.

Exam tip

Understanding the disadvantages of protectionism can help in evaluating the benefits of free trade.

Now test yourself

TESTED

15 Identify two differences in the effects of a tariff and a subsidy to domestic producers.
16 How might quotas affect consumers and producers?

Answers on p. 221

The balance of payments

There are two main components of the **balance of payments** accounts: the **current account** and the **capital and financial account**.

The **balance of payments** is a record of all financial transactions between one country and those in the rest of the world.

The **current account** of the balance of payments shows a country's day-to-day transactions with other countries.

The **capital and financial accounts** of the balance of payments show long-term investments and short-term capital flows.

The current account

REVISED

The current account consists of several elements, the most important of which are:

- the **trade in goods balance** — value of goods exported minus value of goods imported
- the **trade in services balance** — value of services exported minus value of services imported
- **investment income (now called the primary balance)** — income earned from assets owned overseas minus income paid to foreigners for assets owned in the UK
- **current transfers (now called the secondary balance)** — payments received from foreign institutions (e.g. the EU) minus payments paid abroad (e.g. to the EU or food aid to developing countries)

The sum of the above items will give the current account.

If the result is negative, there is said to be a **current account deficit**.

If the result is positive, there is said to be a **current account surplus**.

A **current account deficit** of the balance of payments occurs when more money is flowing out of the country than is flowing in.

A **current account surplus** on the balance of payments occurs when more money is flowing into the country than is flowing out.

Exam tip

Remember that the balance of payments is concerned with external balance (related to trade and financial transactions between countries).

The capital and financial account

REVISED

This part of the accounts is concerned with changes of ownership of the UK's foreign financial assets and liabilities. It comprises several elements, including:

- **foreign direct investment** — investment by foreign companies into the UK minus investment by UK companies abroad

- **portfolio investment in shares and bonds** — purchase of UK shares and bonds by foreigners minus purchase of foreign shares and bonds by UK citizens
- **short-term capital flows**, often referred to as **hot-money flows** — hot-money flows into the UK minus flows out of the UK to other countries
- **changes in foreign currency reserves**

Exam tip

The balance of payments is a set of accounts and so it must balance each year. Therefore, if there is a current account deficit, there must be a corresponding surplus on the capital and financial account.

Causes of deficits on the current account

REVISED

These include:
- relatively low productivity
- the relocation of many manufacturing industries from developed countries to countries where labour costs are significantly lower, such as China
- an increase in the country's exchange rate against that of other countries
- continuous economic growth, resulting in an increase in imports

Causes of surpluses on the current account

REVISED

Current account surpluses could be caused by the opposite of the above points.

Now test yourself

TESTED

17 For each of the following, state whether they would be part of the current account or financial account and whether they would have a positive or negative impact on the UK's balance of payments:
 (a) the UK selling JCBs to Brazil
 (b) a UK citizen taking a holiday in Bali
 (c) investment by Toyota into an extension of its UK car factory
 (d) wine imported into the UK from Chile
 (e) dividends paid to US shareholders of Kraft as a result of profits made by Cadbury, its UK subsidiary

18 Explain how each of the following would affect the UK's trade in goods balance:
 (a) an increase in real incomes of the UK's major trading partners
 (b) an increase in the UK's inflation rate
 (c) a decrease in the UK's productivity rate
 (d) a decrease in the UK's income tax rates

19 Given the following information, calculate the country's current account balance.

Exports of goods	$150 bn
Imports of goods	$165 bn
Export of services	$60 bn
Import of services	$50 bn
Net current transfers	–$25 bn
Net investment income	–$10 bn

Answers on p. 221–2

Measures to reduce a country's imbalance of the current account

REVISED

Measures to reduce a current account *deficit*:

- **Expenditure-reducing policies**. These include deflationary fiscal and monetary policy, which would reduce aggregate demand and, in turn, lead to a reduction in imports.
- **Expenditure-switching policies**. These include tariffs, quotas and export subsidies (see pages 100 and 166).
- **Devaluation/depreciation** of the country's currency (see page 171)
- **Supply-side policies** are often viewed as the most effective way of reducing current account deficits for some countries. These could include:
  - cut in corporation tax
  - improved infrastructure
  - provision of superfast broadband
  - training and education
  - reduction in regulation and red tape
  - reduction in employers' national insurance contributions
  - improved/subsidised childcare provision

A current account *surplus* could be reduced by using the opposite of the above measures.

Expenditure-reducing policies are policies designed to reduce aggregate demand, e.g. deflationary fiscal and monetary policy.

Expenditure-switching policies are policies designed to alter the pattern of a country's expenditure between domestic and imported goods and services.

Exam tip

When considering how a country might reduce its current account deficit, the context is key. For example, countries in the EU cannot unilaterally raise tariffs or give subsidies to firms unless they are acting under an EU agreement.

Now test yourself

TESTED

20 Explain how demand-side policies might be used to reduce a current account deficit.

Answers on p. 222

Significance of global trade imbalances

REVISED

Global trade imbalances arise when some countries run persistent and large current account deficits, such as the USA and the UK, while others run persistent and large current account surpluses, for instance China, Germany and many oil-exporting countries. These differences in current accounts are often associated with differences in savings ratios.

Global trade imbalances occur when some countries have large current account deficits while other countries have large current account surpluses.

Figure 17.9 shows that, since the financial crisis of 2008, global imbalances have decreased.

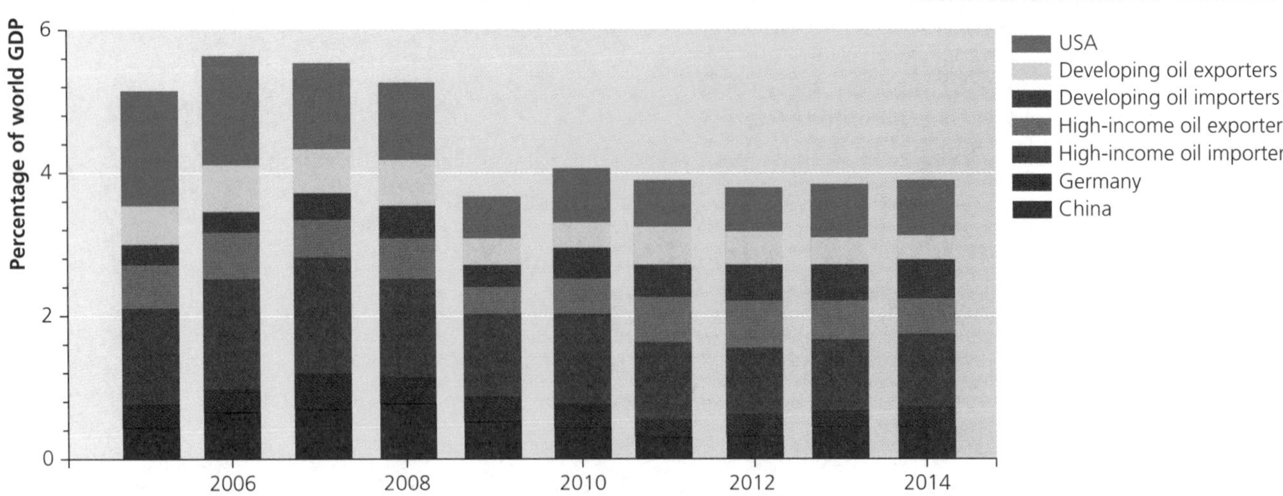

Figure 17.9 Global imbalances as a percentage of global GDP

A **persistent current account deficit** may be undesirable because:

- it could indicate that the county's goods and services are uncompetitive
- in turn, this may result in an increasing rate of unemployment
- ultimately, the country may be forced to borrow foreign currency from other countries or from the International Monetary Fund (IMF), see page 194
- further, under a system of floating exchange rates, it could result in a depreciation of the exchange rate

On the other hand, a current account deficit may not be regarded as a major problem if:

- it is caused by imports of capital goods
- it is only a short-run problem
- it can be financed easily by inflows into the financial account

Similarly, a **persistent current account surplus** may be undesirable as:

- it could result in inflation, since aggregate demand will be increasing
- it may imply that living standards are falling, since there are fewer goods and services available for domestic consumption
- it could cause an appreciation in the value of the country's currency
- it might cause other countries to impose restrictions on imports

Exchange rates

The exchange rate is the rate at which one currency exchanges for another, or the value of one currency in relation to other currencies. One currency may also be valued against a basket of other currencies weighted according to their relative importance in world trade. This is called the **trade-weighted index**.

Exchange rate systems

REVISED

- **Floating.** Under this system the exchange rate is determined by market forces, i.e. by the forces of supply and demand.
- **Fixed.** In this case the country's currency is fixed against those of other currencies.
- **Managed.** This is essentially a floating exchange rate but one which is subject to intervention by the central bank in the foreign exchange market in order to influence the exchange rate of the country's currency.

Revaluation and appreciation; and devaluation and depreciation

REVISED

- A **revaluation** is when a country decides to increase the exchange rate of its currency under a system of **fixed exchange rates**.
- An **appreciation** refers to an increase in the exchange rate of a country's currency under a system of **floating exchange rates**.
- A **devaluation** is when a country decides to decrease in the exchange rate of its currency under a system of **fixed exchange rates**.
- A **depreciation** refers to a decrease in the exchange rate of a country's currency under a system of **floating exchange rates**.

Factors influencing floating exchange rates

REVISED

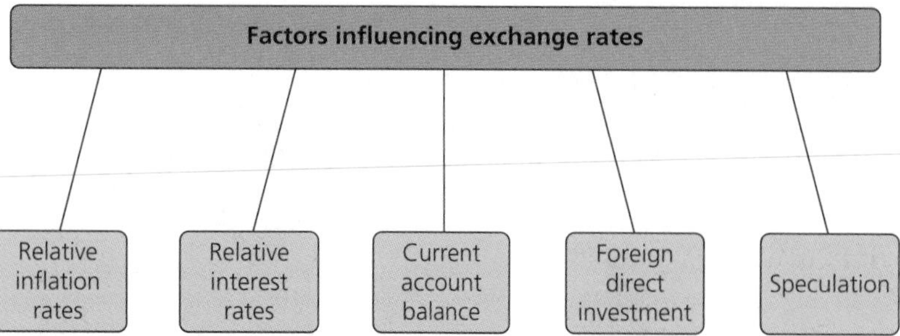

Figure 17.10 Factors influencing exchange rates

- **Relative interest rates.** If a country has much higher interest rates than others, this may attract money into its banks from abroad, causing increased demand for the currency and so causing its value to rise.
- **Relative inflation rates.** If a country has a higher inflation rate than its competitors, then its purchasing power will fall relative to its competitors and, in the long term, it is likely that its value will fall. This may be explained in terms of **purchasing power parity**.
- **Current account balance.** Therefore, the supply of the country's currency is increasing relative to the demand for it, resulting in a depreciation in its currency.
- **Foreign direct investment.** A country which is a net recipient of FDI will experience an increased demand for its currency, so causing its value to appreciate.
- **Speculation.** Speculation arises for a number of reasons, e.g. the expected state of the economy. Greater pessimism about the future state of the economy would cause the country's exchange rate to depreciate.

Government intervention in currency markets

REVISED

- **Foreign currency transactions.** If the aim is to reduce the exchange rate of the country's currency, then the central bank would sell its currency on the foreign exchange market. This increase in supply of the domestic currency would cause a fall in its value.
- **Interest rates.** To reduce the exchange rate of the country's currency, the central bank would reduce the base interest rate. This would make it less attractive for foreigners with cash balances to leave them in that country, so causing an increase in supply of the currency on the foreign exchange market and so causing a reduction in its value.

Competitive devaluation/depreciation

REVISED

To improve rates of economic growth, a country could try to engineer a depreciation in its exchange rate with the aim of improving its net trade balance (exports – imports). If other countries follow suit then a '**currency war**' might break out. Ultimately, currency wars could result in increased protectionism as a means of gaining a competitive advantage.

Currency war refers to a situation where a number of nations seek to deliberately depreciate the value of their domestic currencies in order to stimulate their economies.

Impact of changes in exchange rates

REVISED

The current account of the balance of payments

A devaluation/depreciation would cause:

- a decrease in the foreign currency price of a country's exports
- an increase in the domestic price of its imports

These two factors would cause an increase in the competitiveness of the country's goods and services and to an improvement in its balance of payments on current account.

However, this will only happen if the **Marshall–Lerner condition** holds. This states that the current account of the balance of payments will only improve if the sum of the price elasticities of demand for exports and imports is greater than 1.

Further, there may be different effects in the short run and in the long run, as illustrated by the **J-curve effect** shown in Figure 17.11.

The **Marshall–Lerner condition** states that a depreciation or devaluation of the currency will only lead to an improvement in the trade balance if the sum of the price elasticities of the demand for imports and exports is greater than one.

The **J-curve effect** describes the situation in which a country's trade balance initially worsens following a devaluation or depreciation of its currency and only improves in the long run.

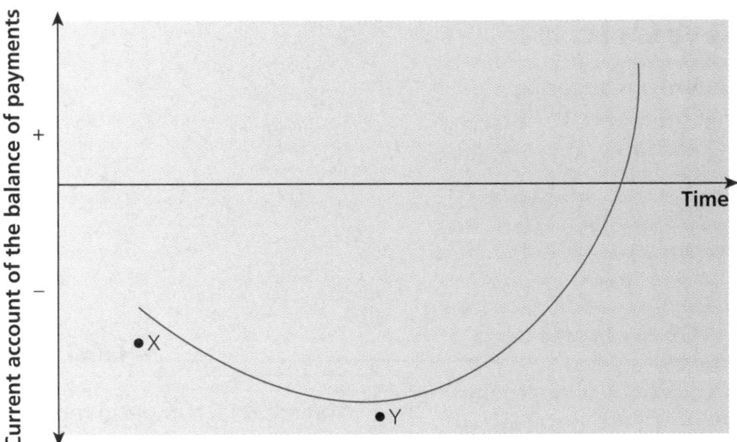

Figure 17.11 The J-curve effect

In the short run, a devaluation/depreciation might cause a deterioration in the current account of the balance of payments because:

- the demand for imports might be price inelastic if firms have stocks or if they are tied into contracts
- the demand for exports might be price inelastic because consumers take time to adjust to the new, lower prices

Consequently, it will only be in the long run, when these factors are no longer relevant, that there would be an improvement in the current account of the balance of payments.

Economic growth and employment/unemployment

In terms of aggregate demand/aggregate supply analysis, a devaluation/depreciation should lead to an increase in aggregate demand because net exports should rise, causing a rise in real output. In turn, this would lead to an increase in employment and a fall in unemployment.

Rate of inflation

The increased price of imported commodities and raw materials would cause an increase in costs of production, so leading to cost-push inflation. Further, the increase in aggregate demand described above could also cause an increase in the rate of inflation.

Foreign direct investment (FDI) flows

A depreciation in the value of the Japanese yen would make it cheaper for, say, an American company to invest in Japan because a dollar would be worth more in yen than before the depreciation.

Now test yourself

TESTED

21 Which of the following is likely to cause an appreciation of the US dollar?
 (a) a rise in inward investment into the USA
 (b) a rise in US inflation above that of its main competitors
 (c) a rise in interest rates in other major economies
 (d) an increase in confidence in the future state of the US economy

22 Outline the likely effects of an appreciation of a currency on the country's economy.

23 Explain how a central bank might be able to bring about a depreciation in the value of its currency.

Answers on p. 222

International competitiveness

International competitiveness is a measure of a country's advantage or disadvantage in selling its products in international markets at a price and quality that is attractive in those markets. Two types of competitiveness may be distinguished:

- price competitiveness
- non-price competitiveness

Measures of international competitiveness

REVISED

International competitiveness is measured in a variety of ways, including:

- **Relative unit labour costs.** According to the OECD, **unit labour costs** (ULC) measure the average cost of labour per unit of output and are calculated as the ratio of total labour costs to real output. A rise in labour costs higher than the rise in labour productivity may result in a fall in the economy's cost competitiveness.
- **Relative export prices.** A country's export prices relative to those of its major competitors are significant for competitiveness.
- **The Global Competitive Index (GCI).** A composite index based on a range of indicators including macroeconomic stability, labour market efficiency, infrastructure, health and primary education.

International competitiveness is a measure of the cost of a country's goods and services exports relative to those of other countries.

Unit labour costs measure the average cost of labour per unit of output and are calculated as the ratio of total labour costs to real output.

Factors influencing international competitiveness

REVISED

Competitiveness may be affected by a variety of factors, including:

- **Unit labour costs.**
- **Productivity.**
- **The real exchange rate.** This is the nominal exchange rate adjusted for changes in price levels between countries. It may be calculated as follows:

$$\text{real exchange rate} = \frac{\text{nominal exchange rate} \times \text{domestic price level}}{\text{foreign price level}}$$

There will be a depreciation in the real exchange rate if the nominal exchange rate falls or if the prices of goods abroad rise relative to prices in this country.

- **Labour taxes or subsidies.** Employers' national insurance contributions are regarded as a tax on jobs and so could reduce the competitiveness of a country's goods and services.
- **Government laws and regulations.** These include environmental and health and safety regulations; employment protection; and a national minimum wage.
- **Research and development (R&D).** This might result in technological advancement and increased productivity.

Revision activity

Make a chart showing the distinction between the following groups of terms.
(a) trade blocs and tariffs
(b) appreciation; revaluation; depreciation; devaluation
(c) fixed, floating and managed exchange rate systems

Now test yourself

TESTED

24 How might each of the following affect the competitiveness of a country's goods and services?
(a) a depreciation in its exchange rate
(b) a reduction in employer national insurance contributions
(c) an increase in the national minimum wage
(d) an increase in expenditure on research into new technology
(e) an improved apprenticeship scheme for school-leavers

Answers on p. 222

The significance of international competitiveness

Benefits of being internationally competitive:
- an improvement in the current account of the balance of payments
- a reduction in unemployment
- an increase in economic growth because an increase in net exports will cause an increase in aggregate demand and have a **multiplier** effect on national income

The **multiplier** describes the process by which a change in an injection (government expenditure, investment or exports) causes a more than proportionate change in national income.

Problems of being internationally uncompetitive:
- an increase in unemployment
- a deficit on the current account of the balance of payments
- a depreciation in the country's exchange rate (under a system of floating exchange rates), leading to an imported inflation

Exam practice

Extract: Trends in world trade

From the end of the Second World War until the end of the twentieth century world trade (a significant aspect of globalisation) expanded significantly. For many decades world trade grew at twice the rate of the global GDP. However, world trade declined significantly during the financial crisis and subsequently grew relatively slowly. In the 1990s, a 1% increase in global income was associated with a 2.2% increase in world imports. But in the 2000s, a 1% increase in world income was associated with only a 1.3% increase in world imports.

More seriously, forecasts for world trade growth in 2015 were reduced considerably, largely as a result of the slowdown in China's economy and very slow growth in the European Union.

Further, there has been a structural shift in the global economy, meaning that growth in world trade is unlikely to increase for some time. For example, the USA has changed from being

(Continued)

(Continued)

a net importer of energy to a net exporter of energy. This change, coupled with a decision by manufacturers to shorten global supply chains and 'reshore' production back into the USA, has also contributed to a reduction in world trade.

During the economic downturn of 2008–09, protectionism has increased in the form of both tariffs and subsidies to domestic producers who have faced difficulties. One reason was that many countries were facing pressure from their electorates because unemployment levels were increasing rapidly. More recently, countries have been responding to slowing economic growth by adding even more protectionist measures. Chinese companies have been the target of the most trade measures by other countries.

A further problem was that some countries, including developing countries, that had developed tourism, faced particular difficulties because the financial crisis resulted in a sharp downturn in tourist numbers, especially from developed countries to exotic destinations such as Barbados, Kenya and the Far East. Further, terrorist attacks in 2015 have had a severe impact on tourism in Tunisia, Egypt and France.

1 (a) Explain the key features of globalisation. [5]
(b) With reference to the information provided and your own knowledge, analyse the causes of the change in income elasticity of demand for world imports. [8]
(c) With reference to the first two paragraphs of the extract, assess the reasons for the slowdown in world trade in 2015. [12]
(d) Evaluate the likely microeconomic and macroeconomic effects of an increase in protectionism on the world economy. [25]
Or
(e) In the light of the information provided, evaluate the microeconomic and macroeconomic effects of a terrorist incident for a country which is heavily dependent on tourism. [25]

Answers and quick quiz 17 online

ONLINE

Summary

You should have an understanding of:

- Globalisation: meaning; causes; costs and impacts.
- Absolute and comparative advantage.
- Advantages and disadvantages of specialisation and trade.
- Factors influencing the patterns of trade.
- The terms of trade.
- Trading blocs: types; costs and benefits.
- The World Trade Organization.
- Types of and reasons for restrictions on free trade.
- The meaning and components of the balance of payments.
- The causes of current account deficits and surpluses.
- The significance of current account imbalances and measures to correct them.
- Fixed, floating and managed exchange rates.
- Devaluation and depreciation; revaluation and appreciation of currencies.
- Factors influencing the exchange rate of a currency and impact of changes.
- Measures of international competitiveness.
- Factors influencing international competitiveness and significance.

18 Poverty and inequality

Poverty

Distinction between absolute poverty and relative poverty

REVISED

- **Absolute poverty** is defined as the minimum amount of resources a person needs to survive, including food, shelter, clothing, access to clean water, sanitation, education and information.
- **Relative poverty** is measured in comparison with other people in a country and will vary between countries. People are considered to be in relative poverty if they are living below a certain income threshold in a particular country.

Measure of absolute poverty

REVISED

In October 2015, the World Bank updated the international poverty line to US$1.90 a day. This new line preserves the real purchasing power of the previous line (of $1.25 a day in 2005 prices) in the world's poorest countries.

Measures of relative poverty

REVISED

A poverty line is set, which is a percentage of average income. Commonly, these poverty lines range from 40–70% of household income. In the EU people falling below 60% of median income are said to be 'at risk of poverty'.

There are some problems with the concept of **relative poverty**, including the following:

- It is highly subjective.
- It changes over time.
- It cannot easily be used to make international comparisons.

Absolute poverty occurs when a person has insufficient resources to meet basic human needs, e.g. food, shelter, clothing.

Relative poverty— people are classified as relatively poor in a country if their incomes are below those of the average income.

Other measures of poverty

REVISED

- **The United Nations Human Poverty Index.** There are two indices, the first of which, HPI-1, is a measure of deprivation in the poorest countries of the world, whereas HPI-2 is more relevant to developed countries. Both of these are composite measures which combine components such as life expectancy, literacy rates, long-term unemployment and relative income.
- **Ratio method.** Poverty is measured by calculating the proportion of income spent on basic necessities such as food or energy.

Typical mistake

Confusion between absolute and relative poverty.

Now test yourself

TESTED

1 If absolute poverty is falling, will relative poverty be falling also?

Answer on p. 222

Causes of changes in absolute poverty and relative poverty

REVISED

Changes in:

- the level of indebtedness
- the level of unemployment
- health or education
- access to public services
- the state of the economy and real incomes
- distribution of income

Now test yourself

TESTED

2 Identify two factors which could cause a reduction in absolute poverty.

Answer on p. 222

Inequality

Distinction between wealth inequality and income inequality

REVISED

- **Income** is a flow concept, e.g. the money earned by a person over a period of time. Therefore, income inequality refers to the unequal distribution of earnings between individuals.
- **Wealth** refers to the stock of assets a person owns. So wealth inequality refers to difference in the value of stocks of assets owned by individuals.

Measurements of income inequality

REVISED

The Lorenz curve

The **Lorenz curve** is a graphical representation of income distribution.

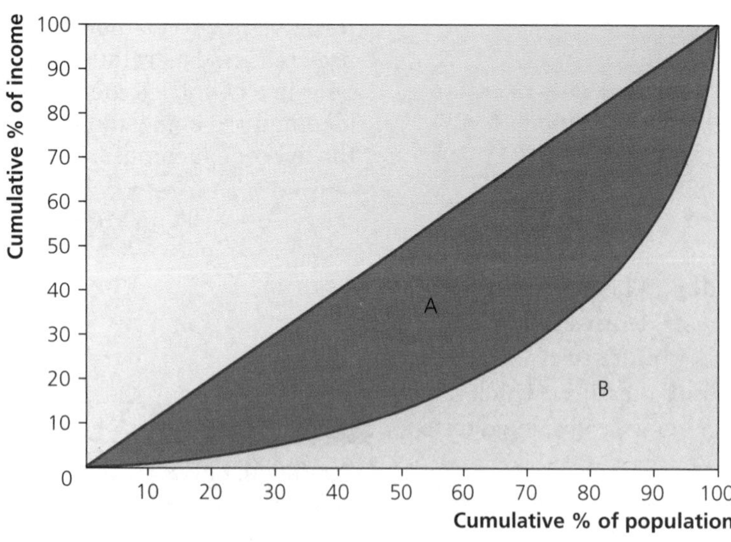

Figure 18.1 The Lorenz curve

It can be seen that the **Lorenz curve** plots the cumulative percentage of the population against the cumulative percentage of total income. The 45° line represents perfect equality. The curved lined represents the income distribution for a particular country.

Typical mistake

Incorrect labelling of the Lorenz curve axes.

Now test yourself

TESTED

3 How would an increase in inequality be illustrated on a Lorenz curve diagram?

Answer on p. 222

The Gini coefficient

To determine the degree of inequality, the **Gini coefficient** may be calculated. The following formula indicates how this may be done:

$$G = \frac{A}{A + B}$$

A represents the area between the diagonal line and the Lorenz curve and B represents the area under the Lorenz curve. The Gini coefficient will have a value between 0 and 1, with 0 representing absolute equality (the 45° line) and 1 representing absolute inequality (i.e. the Lorenz curve would lie along the horizontal and vertical axes).

The Gini coefficient may also be expressed as a percentage:

$$G = \frac{A}{A + B} \times 100$$

The **Gini coefficient** is a numerical calculation of inequality based on the Lorenz curve with a value of zero being perfect equality and a value of 1 representing perfect inequality.

Causes of income inequality and wealth inequality *within* countries

REVISED

A variety of factors may cause inequality within a country, including:

- globalisation (see page 156)
- education, training and skills
- wage rates
- strength of trade unions
- degree of employment protection
- social benefits (see page 54)
- the progressiveness of the tax system (see page 206)

Now test yourself

TESTED

4 Identify two factors which influence wealth inequality.

Answer on p. 222

Causes of income inequality and wealth inequality *between* countries

REVISED

Income and wealth inequality between countries may be caused by differences in:

- natural resources
- geography, e.g. whether a country is land-locked or close to large markets
- history, e.g. the impact of colonialism on a country's economic growth
- degree of political stability
- macroeconomic policies
- amount of foreign direct investment (FDI) attracted by different countries
- degree of trade liberalisation
- degree of technological change

Typical mistake

Confusion between income and wealth.

Impact of economic change and development on inequality

REVISED

This is illustrated by the Kuznets curve, as shown in Figure 18.2.

This shows that when the economy is at an early stage of development and primarily agricultural, there is a relatively low level of income inequality. Industrialisation results in increased inequality but at some point it starts to decrease. However, in the 30 years before the financial crisis there was evidence that inequality in many advanced economies was increasing.

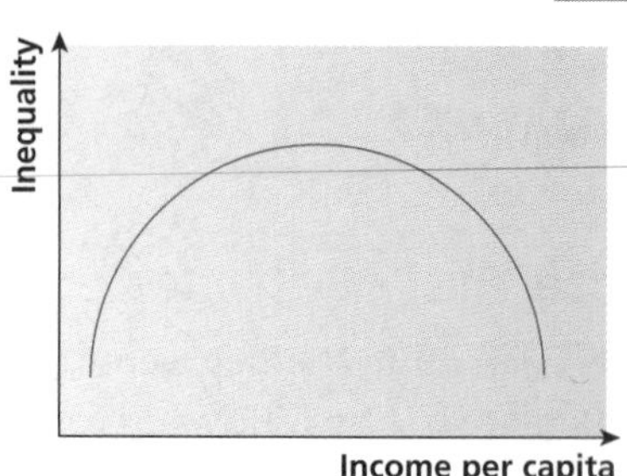

Figure 18.2 The Kuznets curve

Significance of capitalism for inequality

REVISED

A capitalist society is characterised by the split between, on the one hand, the owners of the resources required for producing and distributing goods and, on the other, the working class, who sell their labour to the owners of resources in exchange for wages. Typically, the owners of resources will have more wealth and income than workers, so contributing to inequality.

Now test yourself

TESTED

5 Why is inequality inevitable in a capitalist economy?

Answer on p. 222

Revision activity

Make a list of the causes of inequality.

Exam practice

1 The following table shows the Gini coefficients for four countries:

Country	Gini coefficient
The Netherlands	0.28
France	0.33
Brazil	0.53
Haiti	0.61

(a) Explain how the Gini coefficient is calculated. [5]
(b) Illustrating your answer with a Lorenz curve diagram, analyse differences in inequality for the Netherlands and Haiti. [8]
(c) Assess the possible causes of differences in inequality between the Netherlands and Brazil. [12]
(d) Evaluate measures by which a government could help to reduce inequality in a country. [25]

Answer and quick quiz 18 online

ONLINE

Summary

You should have an understanding of:

- Absolute poverty.
- Relative poverty.
- Measures of absolute and relative poverty.
- Causes of changes in absolute and relative poverty.
- Distinction between wealth and income inequality.
- Measures of inequality: Lorenz curves and Gini coefficients.
- Causes of income and wealth inequality within countries and between countries.
- Measures to reduce inequality.

19 Emerging and developing economies

Measures of development

The Human Development Index (HDI)

REVISED

The HDI is a composite measure which is used in the United Nations Development Report and which consists of three elements:

- GDP per head — measured at purchasing power parity.
- Health — measured in terms of life expectancy at birth.
- Education — measured in terms of mean years of schooling at age 25 and expected years of schooling at age 4.

Exam tip

When discussing economic development, it is useful to know a range of development indicators.

Typical mistake

Inability to distinguish between economic growth and economic development.

Advantages and limitations of using the HDI

REVISED

Advantages of the HDI

- It is a broader measure than GDP per capita.
- According to the United Nations Programme, the three essential contributors to development are for people to *lead a long and healthy life*, *to acquire knowledge*, and *to have access to the resources needed for a decent standard of living.*

Limitations of the HDI

- It is too narrow, as it only comprises three aspects of development.
- It is only concerned with long-term development outcomes.
- It is an average measure and so disguises disparities and inequalities within countries.

Other indicators of development

REVISED

These include:

- the proportion of the population with access to clean water
- the proportion of the male population employed in agriculture
- energy consumption per person
- the proportion of the population with internet access
- mobile phones per thousand of population
- the degree to which people are entitled to civil rights
- the degree of democracy
- the degree of inequality

Now test yourself

TESTED

1 Name the three elements of the HDI.
2 Name two other indicators of economic development.

Answers on p. 222

Factors influencing growth and development

The impact of economic factors in different countries

REVISED

Figure 19.1 summarises a number of factors which affect growth and development.

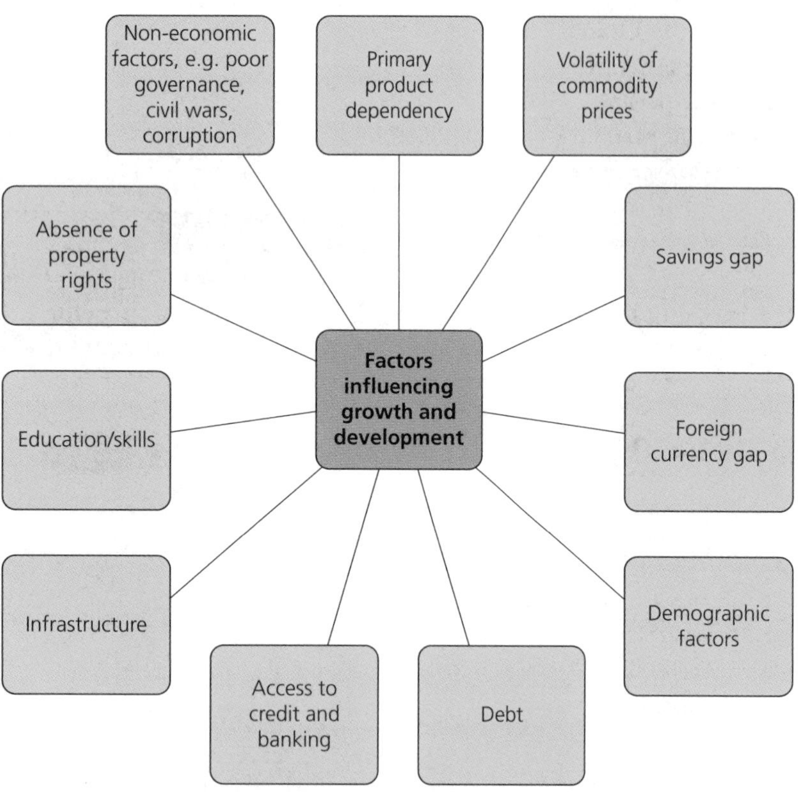

Figure 19.1 Factors influencing growth and development

Primary product dependency and volatility of commodity prices

There are two broad types of primary product:

- **Hard commodities** are usually those that are mined or extracted, e.g. copper.
- **Soft commodities** are usually agricultural goods, e.g. rice.

For countries dependent on primary products, there are various issues:

- **Extreme price fluctuations.** Since both the supply of, and the demand for, primary products tend to be inelastic, any change in the conditions of supply or demand will cause large price fluctuations.
- **Fluctuations in producers' revenues resulting from price fluctuations.** These make it more difficult to plan investment and output.
- **Fluctuations in foreign exchange earnings.** Revenues from exports of primary products will also fluctuate, making it more difficult for the government to plan economic development.
- **Protectionism** by developed countries.
- **Shortages of supplies for domestic consumption.** Cash crops are usually exported, meaning that there is little left for domestic consumption.

Primary product dependency occurs in countries where the value of production of primary products accounts for a large proportion of GDP.

- **Finite supplies of hard commodities.**
- **Appreciation of the currency.** Demand for a particular commodity will cause an increase in demand for the country's currency.
- **Falling terms of trade.** See page 162 and the **Prebisch–Singer hypothesis** below.

The Prebisch–Singer hypothesis

According to this hypothesis:

- The demand for primary products tends to be income inelastic whereas the demand for manufactured goods is income elastic.
- Therefore, as real incomes rise, the demand for manufactured goods will increase at a faster rate than the demand for primary products.
- As a result, the prices of manufactured goods will rise more quickly than the prices of primary products.
- Consequently, the terms of trade of developing countries will fall relative to those of developed countries.

However, some **criticisms** of the Prebisch–Singer hypothesis include:

- The developing country may have a comparative advantage in the primary product.
- The real price of primary products might increase over time with rising world incomes and population.
- FDI has increased significantly in recent years in countries dependent on primary products.

Exam tip

This area of the specification involves many concepts introduced earlier in the course, e.g. elasticity of demand and the balance of payments.

Now test yourself

TESTED

3 (a) Calculate the change in the terms of trade from the following information: import prices rise by 4% while export prices rise by 12%.
(b) Outline two implications of this change in the terms of trade.
4 Explain why primary product prices are likely to fluctuate.

Answers on p. 222–3

Savings gap: the Harrod–Domar model

The Harrod–Domar model illustrates the problem of how countries with a low GDP per head will experience low savings ratios. Low savings mean that it will be difficult to finance investment and, therefore, capital accumulation will be limited. This will translate into low output and low GDP, as illustrated in Figure 19.2.

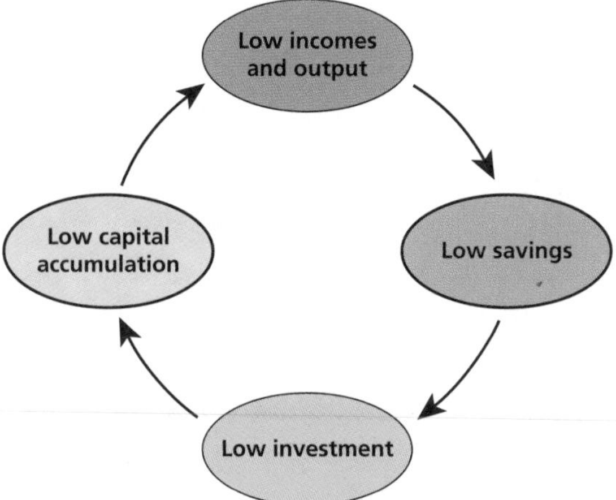

Figure 19.2 The Harrod–Domar model

However, this model may be criticised for the following reasons:

- It focuses on physical capital and ignores the significance of human capital.
- It assumes a constant relationship between capital and output.
- The savings gap may be filled by means other than domestic savings, e.g. from FDI.

Now test yourself

TESTED

5 What is the main cause of the savings gap in developing countries?

Answers on p. 223

Foreign currency gap

Countries may face shortages of foreign currency, which could be caused by:

- dependency on the export of primary products
- dependency on imports of oil and manufactured goods
- interest payments on debt to foreign countries
- **capital flight**, which occurs when individuals and countries decide to transfer cash deposits to foreign banks or to buy shares or assets in foreign countries

Capital flight occurs when assets or money are taken out of a country.

For these reasons, the country may have insufficient foreign currency to purchase imported capital goods which would be needed to increase its productive capacity.

Now test yourself

TESTED

6 How might the foreign exchange gap constrain economic development?

Answers on p. 223

Demographic factors

Thomas Malthus predicted that famine was inevitable because population grows in geometric progression whereas food production grows in an arithmetic progression. In countries where population growth is greater than the growth of GDP, then GDP per head would decline.

Ageing populations result in smaller working populations, who will have to support much larger proportions of elderly people. This will be significant issue for China and other developing countries.

Now test yourself

TESTED

7 Under what circumstances would an increase in economic growth be associated with a fall in GDP per head?

Answers on p. 223

Debt

Causes of debt include:

- dependency on primary products and falling terms of trade
- developing countries borrowing money at times of low interest rates, but struggling to service the debt (i.e. pay interest on it) when interest rates increase
- these countries having to borrow to pay for imports when oil prices increase
- loans taken to finance prestigious investment projects
- depreciation in the value of the currencies of developing countries, which increases the burden of the debt
- loans taken to finance expenditure on military equipment

Now test yourself

TESTED

8 How might debt affect the foreign exchange gap?

Answers on p. 223

Access to credit and banking

This is important both for new entrepreneurs who need to borrow money to finance their start-up expenses and for existing businesses which may need money to finance expansion and for cash-flow reasons.

Infrastructure

A country's infrastructure refers to the physical and organisational structures and facilities which are required for the efficient operation of a society and its enterprises.

If a country's infrastructure (e.g. roads, rail and electricity generation) is poor, it is likely to deter both domestic investment and foreign direct investment.

Education/skills

If the school enrolment ratio is low then the levels of literacy and numeracy are likely to be low. In turn:

- the productivity of the workforce is likely to be low
- this will act as a deterrent to FDI

Absence of property rights

Hernando de Soto has argued that a strong market economy depends critically on property (ownership) rights and the rule of law. For example, if a person owns no assets then it will be very difficult to secure a bank loan because he/she will not have collateral.

Property rights are the the exclusive authority to determine how a resource is used, whether that resource is owned by government, collective bodies, or by individuals. In other words, property rights are ownership rights.

The impact of non-economic factors in different countries

REVISED

Poor governance, political instability and civil wars

If there is weak or inefficient government then it is unlikely that resources will be allocated efficiently. Further, government failure may occur, that is intervention by the government in the economy might result in a net welfare loss.

Civil wars can have a devastating effect on the infrastructure of the country, deter investment and so hinder growth and development.

Corruption

Corruption is undesirable if it causes:

- an inefficient allocation of resources
- an increase in the costs of doing business in the country
- a decrease in foreign direct investment
- capital flight

Strategies influencing growth and development

Figure 19.3 indicates a number of strategies which might be adopted to promote growth and development:

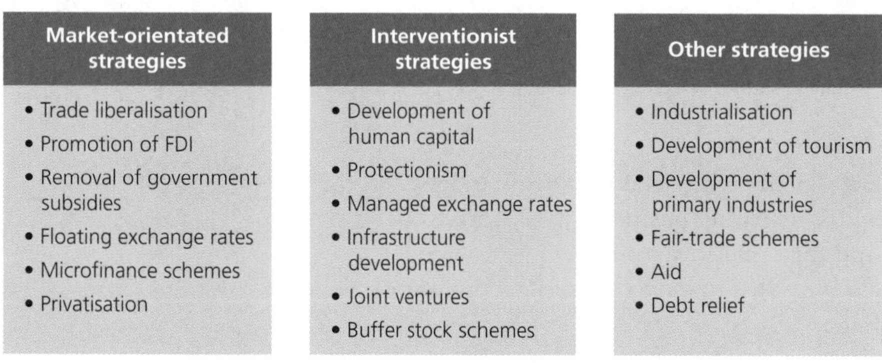

Figure 19.3 Strategies to promote growth and development

Market-orientated strategies

REVISED

Trade liberalisation

This refers to the removal of trade barriers. Consequently, it results in an increase in trade and the associated welfare benefits of, for example, lower prices and increased consumer surplus. This is illustrated in Figure 19.4.

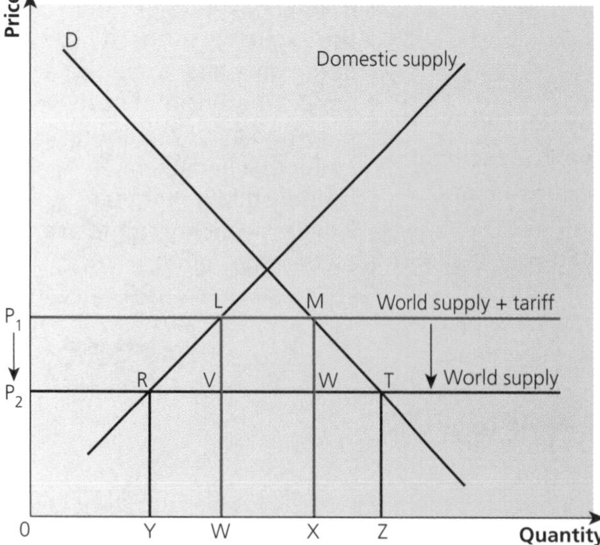

Figure 19.4 The effect of trade liberalisation

At the original price of P_1, domestic supply is 0W and imports are WX. After the tariff has been eliminated, the price falls to P_2, domestic supply falls to 0Y and imports rise to YZ.

In turn, this is likely to encourage FDI.

Now test yourself

TESTED

9 What is meant by trade liberalisation?
10 Give two reasons why trade liberalisation might help to promote development.

Answers on p. 223

Promotion of FDI

FDI may be encouraged by a variety of measures, including:

- trade liberalisation
- deregulation of capital markets
- measures to make it easier and cheaper for global companies to build factories in developing countries
- tax incentives

Removal of government subsidies

Subsidies to domestic producers might result in an inefficient allocation of resources because competition (e.g. from imports) is reduced and so there is less incentive for firms to minimise costs.

Floating exchange rate systems

A system of floating exchange rates might result in a depreciation of the exchange rate, which would make the country's goods and services more internationally competitive.

Microfinance schemes

These schemes are a means of providing extremely poor people with small loans (microcredit) to help them engage in productive activities or to grow their tiny businesses.

The main clients of microfinance are women (97% of clients), the self-employed, small farmers in rural areas and small shopkeepers.

However, microfinance schemes have been criticised because of the high interest rates charged on loans and because they have not been very successful at creating prosperous businesses in the long run.

Now test yourself

TESTED 

11 What constraint on economic development does microfinance help to solve?

Answer on p. 223

Privatisation

Since the profit motive and competition are characteristics of firms operating in the private sector, it is argued that privatised firms will be more efficient than those run by the state.

Interventionist strategies

REVISED

Development of human capital

Human capital refers to the skills, knowledge and talents of the workforce and it includes the idea that there are investments in people, such as education and training, which increase an individual's productivity.

Protectionism

Protectionist policies would include tariffs, quotas and, in particular, subsidies to domestic producers. (See Chapter 17.)

Managed exchange rates

Under a system of managed exchange rates (see page 188), the central bank could engineer a depreciation of the country's currency, so increasing the competitiveness of its goods and services.

Infrastructure development

Investment in infrastructure tends to be very expensive but is vital to a country's economic development and prosperity. Such projects may be funded publicly, privately or through public–private partnerships.

Promoting joint ventures

In a **joint venture**, the foreign investor and a local partner business establish a jointly owned firm to conduct operations in the host country. The advantages of joint ventures include:

- reduction in the costs and risks
- less vulnerability to hostile actions if there is political instability

However, there are several potential problems for the foreign investor:

- possible loss of control of technology and expertise to the local partner
- possibility of the partners having different strategic interests

Joint venture refers to an enterprise undertaken jointly by two or more firms which retain their distinct identities.

Buffer stock schemes

The key features of these schemes include:

- a ceiling price — the maximum price which would be allowed
- a floor price — the minimum price which would be allowed
- a buffer stock, which involves the storage or release of stocks in order to reduce price fluctuations to the agreed limits

A **buffer stock scheme** is a scheme designed to reduce price fluctuations and which involves the buying and selling of stocks to maintain price within agreed limits.

The diagram in Figure 19.5 illustrates the operation of a buffer stock scheme:

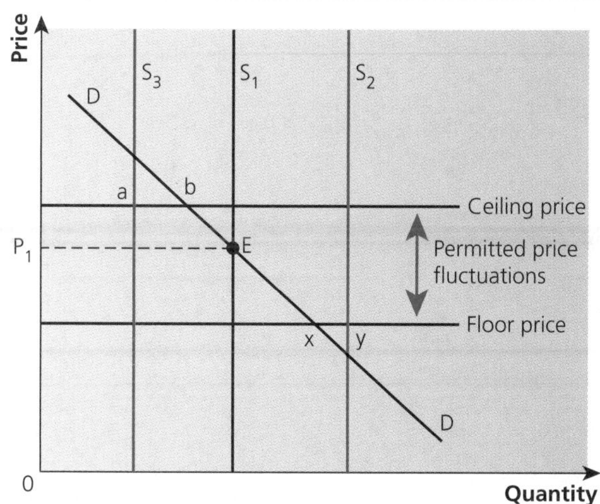

Figure 19.5 Operation of a buffer stock scheme

- In year 1, the equilibrium price is P_1 so no action is required because the price is within the permitted price range.
- Suppose supply is S_2 in year 2, then, to prevent the price from falling below the floor price, xy would be removed from the market and stored in a buffer stock.
- If supply fell to S_3 in year 3, then, to prevent the price rising above the ceiling level, ab would be released from the buffer stock.

Critique of buffer stock schemes

- If the floor price is set too high, then there will be surpluses each year.
- If the ceiling price is set too low, then there may be insufficient stocks available in years of shortage.
- Costs of storage.
- Cheating by one of the members.

Typical mistake

Drawing inaccurate diagrams. This problem can be minimised by using the diagram in Figure 19.5.

Exam tip

The analysis is more straightforward if the supply is assumed to be perfectly inelastic. This is a reasonable assumption because a set amount will be produced each year.

Now test yourself TESTED

12 What is the main purpose of buffer stock schemes?
13 Under what circumstances is a buffer stock scheme most likely to be successful?

Answers on p. 223

Other strategies

REVISED

Industrialisation: the Lewis model

Lewis's structural change (dual sector) model considers many developing countries at an early stage of development to have two sectors:

- a primarily subsistence agricultural economy, characterised by low productivity, with a large proportion of the population living in rural areas
- a small modern industrial sector, characterised by high productivity, monetary exchange and people living in urban areas

Lewis's view is that economic development can only occur if there is industrialisation. This is illustrated in Figure 19.6 (overleaf).

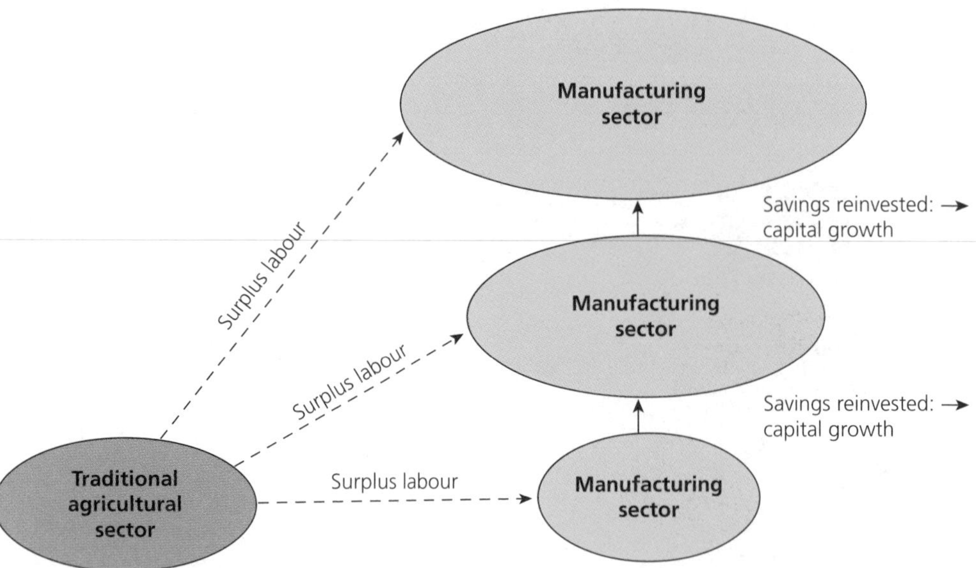

Figure 19.6 The Lewis structural change (dual sector) model

The key features of the Lewis model include:

- The transfer of surplus labour from the low-productivity agricultural sector to a higher-productivity industrial sector.
- The **marginal productivity** of agricultural workers would be zero or close to zero because of the excess supply of workers. This analysis is based on the law of diminishing returns (see page 122).
- Therefore, the opportunity cost of the transfer of workers from the agricultural to the industrial sector would be zero or close to zero.
- Industrialisation requires investment, which will increase productivity and profitability and result in higher wages, so attracting workers from the rural areas.
- Increases in the savings ratio and in profits as a proportion of GDP will lead to more investment, so further increasing economic growth.

Marginal productivity is the change in output resulting from the addition of one more unit of the variable factor.

However, there are various criticisms of the Lewis model, including:

- Profits made by TNCs may be repatriated to the foreign owners.
- The assumption of surplus labour in the agricultural sector and full employment in the industrial sector is contradicted by the evidence, e.g. the favelas in South America.
- Agriculture and primary products have formed the basis of growth and development in some countries.

Now test yourself

TESTED

14 How might industrialisation affect the following?
   (a) the distribution of population between rural and urban areas
   (b) the degree of inequality
   (c) the environment

Answers on p. 223

The development of tourism

The expansion of tourism has strong attractions for a variety of reasons:

- **Source of foreign exchange**.
- **Investment by global (transnational) companies.** Investment in hotels and associated services will have multiplier effects on GDP.

- **Improvement in infrastructure.** Global companies may help to finance new roads and houses as part of agreements to allow them to build hotels.
- **Employment opportunities.**
- **Increased tax revenues**, which may be used to reduce absolute poverty, improve public services and to redistribute incomes.
- **Demand for tourism is income elastic.** When real incomes are rising, demand will increase more than proportionately.
- **Preservation of natural heritage.**

However, there are various **drawbacks** in pursuing tourism as a means of development, including:

- **Adverse effect on the current account of the balance of payments**
  - imported capital goods are required for the building of hotels and equipment
  - imported food and gifts are demanded by tourists
  - profits may be repatriated to foreign shareholders of global companies
- **Fluctuations in demand associated with the trade cycle.**
- **External costs.** Tourists may cause an increase in waste, pollution, destruction of ancient monuments and water shortages for local people.
- **Changes in fashion.** Tourism is subject to changes in tastes, preferences and fashions as well as to climate change.
- **Terrorism.** The tourist industries in countries such as Kenya, Tunisia and Egypt have been adversely affected by terrorist incidents.
- **Employment may be low paid and seasonal.**

Now test yourself TESTED

15 Why might foreign currency earnings from a developing country with a large tourist sector fluctuate?

Answers on p. 223

Development of primary industries

Some countries have achieved rapid rates of growth and development as a result of development in their primary sectors. This approach to economic development may be appropriate if:

- the demand for the primary products being produced is income elastic
- the country has a comparative advantage in the production of primary products
- FDI is attracted by the existence of primary products

Fair-trade schemes

The primary aim of fair-trade schemes is to guarantee that producers receive a fair price for their products.

Advantages of fair-trade schemes

- Producers receive a price higher than the market price for their products.
- Producers can use increased revenues to improve the quality of products.
- Extra money is available to spend on development programmes, e.g. education and health.
- Producers are protected from wildly fluctuating prices, enabling them to plan investment and output.

Criticisms of fair-trade schemes

- The extra money available to spend on development projects may be very small.
- Some poorer or remote farmers are unable to join the scheme, while others will be working for larger producers who are excluded from many fair-trade product lines.
- Distortion of market forces — the artificially high prices encourage existing producers to increase output and new producers to enter the market, so driving down prices for products not in the scheme.
- There is little incentive for producers to improve the quality of their products.
- Certification of Fairtrade is based on normative criteria.
- A significant proportion of the higher price for fair-trade goods goes to the profits of the retailers rather than to the producers.

Now test yourself

TESTED

16 Why might a fair-trade scheme not necessarily benefit banana producers?

Answers on p. 223

Aid

Aid refers to the voluntary transfer of resources from one country to another or to loans given on concessionary terms, i.e. at less than the market rate of interest.

Official development assistance (ODA) relates specifically to aid provided by governments.

The purpose of aid

- to reduce absolute poverty in the long run
- to provide emergency, short-term relief following natural disasters or extreme weather events; or for refugees following a civil war

Types of aid

- **Tied aid.** This is aid with conditions attached. For example, there might be a requirement to buy goods from the donor country or the aid might be given in return for political and economic reforms.
- **Bilateral aid.** This is aid given directly by one country to another.
- **Multilateral aid.** This is aid provided by individual countries but channelled through organisations such as the World Bank to developing countries.

The case for aid

- To reduce absolute poverty and inequality.
- As a means of filling the savings gap and foreign exchange gap (see page 184).
- To provide funds for investment.
- To improve human capital.
- Benefits to developed countries if aid results in increased incomes in developing countries.

The case against aid

- According to dependency theory, aid reinforces the dominance of developed economies over developing economies.
- Danger that a dependency culture will result.
- One aid is going to relatively rich countries such as Turkey and Brazil.
- Corruption.
- Aid may distort market forces.
- Donor countries may exert political influence over recipient countries.
- Interest must be paid on concessional loans, i.e. loans at below the market rate of interest.

Now test yourself TESTED ☐

17 Give two reasons why aid may not stimulate economic development.

Answers on p. 223

Debt relief

Debts are usually owed to all or to some of the following: the IMF; the World Bank; governments and banks in developed countries.

The Heavily Indebted Poor Countries (HIPC) initiative

- Devised by the International Monetary Fund (IMF) and World Bank in 1996 and enhanced in 2005 by the Multilateral Debt Relief Initiative (MDRI).
- Aimed at reducing the external debt of the poorest countries of the world to sustainable levels.
- Helped to achieve the 2015 goal of halving absolute poverty by 2010.
- By 2012, 36 countries had approval for debt-reduction packages under the HIPC initiative.

Arguments for debt cancellation

In addition to the arguments for aid (see 'The case for aid' above), the following may be added:

- Increased business confidence, leading to an increase in investment.
- Environmental gains: conditions might be attached to the cancellation of debts.

Arguments against debt cancellation

In addition to the arguments against aid (see 'The case against aid' above), the following may be added:

- Length of time to agree a debt cancellation programme.
- **Moral hazard problem.**
- Corruption.
- Adverse impact on financial institutions and their shareholders in developed countries.

The **moral hazard problem** occurs when the person/firm/country taking the risk may not be the one who bears the consequences of that risk.

Now test yourself

TESTED

18 What is the difference between aid and foreign direct investment?

Answers on p. 223

Typical mistake

Confusion between aid and foreign direct investment.

International institutions

REVISED

The World Bank (International Bank for Reconstruction and Development)

The original role of the World Bank or IBRD was to provide long-term loans for reconstruction and development to member nations which had suffered in the Second World War.

In the 1970s, its role changed to setting up agricultural reforms in developing countries, giving loans and providing expertise.

The World Bank imposes **Structural Adjustment Programmes (SAPs)**, which set out conditions on which loans are given. The aim is to ensure that debtor countries do not default on the repayment of debts.

SAPs were based on free-market reforms. However, they have been criticised because they did little to help the world's poor; they increased inequality; and they resulted in social and political chaos in many countries.

Following these criticisms, the World Bank now focuses on poverty reduction strategies, with aid being directed towards countries adopting sound macroeconomic policies; healthcare and broadening education; local communities rather than central governments.

The International Monetary Fund (IMF)

The IMF was founded in 1944 with the objective of increasing international liquidity and providing stability in capital markets through a system of convertible currencies pegged to the dollar. It also lends to countries with temporary balance of payments deficits on current account.

Membership and finance

There are now 189 members of the IMF.

When a country joins, it is required to pay a quota which is broadly based on the relative size of the country in the world economy (calculated in terms of its GDP). Up to 25% of this quota or subscription must be paid in the Special Drawing Rights or currencies which are generally acceptable, such as the US dollar, the pound sterling, the yen or the euro.

Impact of the 2008 global financial crisis

Following the financial crisis, the IMF:

- increased lending
- provides forecasts, analysis and advice to individual countries

Non-government organisations (NGOs)

The work of NGOs has brought **community-based development** to the forefront of strategies to promote growth and development (i.e. the focus has moved away from state-managed schemes).

Revision activity

Draw a mind map to show the links between the factors influencing growth and development and concepts in other themes, e.g. primary product dependency and income elasticity of demand.

Exam practice

Extract 1: Sub-Saharan Africa

Growth in sub-Saharan Africa is forecast to slow to 4.2% in 2015, slower than previously expected and lower than the 5% population growth rate of many African countries. This mainly reflects falling oil prices which have considerably reduced growth in commodity-exporting countries such as Angola and Nigeria. Further, there are constraints on growth in South Africa such as energy shortages and weak investor confidence due to the expected tightening of monetary and fiscal policy.

Another negative factor affecting sub-Saharan Africa is the Ebola crisis, while China's slowdown, tightening of monetary policy in the United States, and the fragility of the recovery in Europe, remain as key external risks.

Between 2000 and 2014, sub-Saharan countries increased their trade with emerging economies such as Russia and China: these countries were importing raw materials such as oil, cotton, iron ore and copper from sub-Saharan Africa. However, the problems of this have been illustrated by the slowdown in China. Further, some development economists think that the path to development lies in industrialisation, not greater dependence on primary products.

Extract 2: Mobile phones in sub-Saharan Africa

The mobile phone industry in sub-Saharan Africa contributed more than US$100 billion to the region's economy in 2015, equivalent to 5.7% of the region's GDP. Mobile phone operators directly contributed US$31 billion, representing 1.7% of GDP. This economic contribution is set to increase in future as mobile operators continue to extend connectivity across the region and develop new mobile broadband networks and services.

The mobile phone industry has helped to promote economic growth and employment in sub-Saharan Africa. In 2014, it directly employed approximately 2 million people with the majority working in the distribution and retail sectors and approximately 325,000 employed by mobile operators. A further 2.4 million jobs were indirectly supported as a result of the demand generated by the mobile sector, bringing the total to 4.4 million. It is forecast that the industry will grow to support more than 6 million jobs by 2020. The mobile phone industry also made a contribution to the public finances of the region's governments through general taxation of approximately US$15 billion in 2014.

Mobile operators in the region invested US$9 billion in network infrastructure development in 2014. Mobile technology is also playing a central role in sub-Saharan Africa by addressing a range of socio-economic challenges, particularly digital and financial inclusion, and enabling access to vital services such as education.

1 (a) Explain why, despite positive growth rates, some sub-Saharan African countries faced a fall in average living standards. [5]

(b) With reference to the information provided, analyse problems faced by countries which produce and export oil. [8]

(c) Apart from dependence on oil exports, assess the reasons for the fall in the economic growth rate in countries of sub-Saharan Africa. [12]

(d) Evaluate the significance of mobile phones to the economies of sub-Saharan Africa. [25]

Or

(e) Evaluate measures a sub-Saharan African country might take to improve economic development. [25]

Answers and quick quiz 19 online

ONLINE

Summary

You should have an understanding of:

- Measures of economic development.
- Factors influencing growth and development.
- Strategies influencing growth and development.
- International institutions.

20 The financial sector

Financial markets

A financial market covers any marketplace where buyers and sellers participate in the trade of assets such as equities, bonds, currencies and derivatives. Therefore, the financial sector provides the means of channelling funds to households, firms and governments.

> **Exam tip**
>
> This section relates to other parts of the syllabus including, for example, demand-side policies especially monetary policy instruments and the role of the Bank of England in Theme 2; macroeconomic policies in a global context in Theme 4; market failure and government failure in Theme 1.

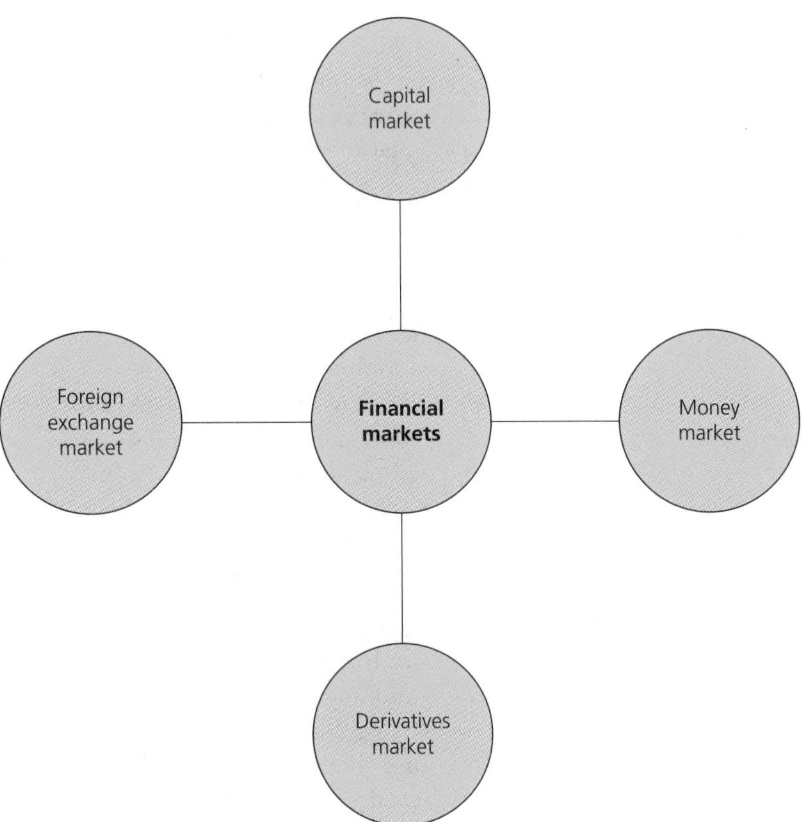

Figure 20.1 Financial markets

Some of the key financial markets include:

- **Capital markets.** These enable individuals and institutions to trade financial securities, so enabling organisations and firms in both the private and public sectors to gain long-term finance. Two examples are stock markets and bond markets.
  - Stock markets allow investors to buy and sell shares in limited companies.
  - Bond markets are markets for loans to companies or governments.
- **Money markets.** These are markets for short-term loans such as treasury bills and certificates of deposit.
- **Derivatives markets.** Derivatives are financial instruments, e.g. futures contracts whose price depends on the value of the underlying asset.
- **The foreign exchange (FOREX) market.** This is the market in which currencies are traded.

Now test yourself

TESTED

1 Give four examples of financial markets.

Answers on p. 223

The role of financial markets

The functions of financial markets include the following:

To facilitate saving

REVISED

Financial institutions enable households and businesses to save money by providing a range of accounts with varying degrees of risk and rates of interest.

To lend to businesses and individuals

REVISED

Financial institutions enable the connection between households and businesses which have savings with those which need to borrow.

To facilitate the exchange of goods and services

REVISED

The financial system handles millions of transactions every day. These allow people to:

- make payments in shops and online
- receive wages, welfare payments from the government and other incomes
- settle debts

To provide forward markets in commodities and contracts

REVISED

Essentially, forward markets set the price of an asset, e.g. a commodity such as wheat, or of a financial instrument, e.g. a foreign currency for future delivery.

Forward contracts may be used for both hedging and speculation. A hedge is an investment to reduce the risk of adverse price movements in an asset.

To provide a market for equities

REVISED

An equities or stock market is one in which stocks and shares are issued and traded. A stock market gives companies access to capital and investors a share of ownership in a company.

Now test yourself

TESTED

2 Which financial market provides a means for:
(a) buying and selling shares
(b) buying and selling currencies?

Answers on p. 223

Market failure in the financial sector

Asymmetric information

REVISED

This is a situation in which one party involved in a financial contract has less information than the other party.

Examples of asymmetric information include:

- The market for health insurance relies heavily on accurate information but those seeking insurance generally have better information about their own health than the health insurance providers.
- In the banking industry, relatively few investors understood the risks associated with derivatives traded prior to the 2008 financial crisis.
- In the stock market, there will be differences in knowledge between buyers and sellers about productivity and profitability of companies.

Moral hazard

REVISED

Before the financial crisis some bankers engaged in trading highly risky securities to enhance their bonuses. In the event, these risky loans resulted in huge losses that were so great that some banks, for example RBS, had to be rescued by the UK government. This could create a further moral hazard (and government failure) because banks might continue to engage in risky behaviour in the knowledge that they would be bailed out by the government if they were in danger of going bankrupt.

Speculation and market bubbles

REVISED

The period between 2000 and 2007 were years in which interest rates were low, credit was easy to obtain and asset prices were increasing. This period saw banks creating £1 trillion of new money, accompanied by a doubling of debt. Indeed, there was a 'herd effect', which resulted in people buying assets in the hope of future capital gains even though these were unjustified in terms of their real worth.

Externalities

REVISED

The activities of agents in the financial markets could cause asset bubbles, for example, in the housing market. This could be an external benefit to people who own houses but would be an external cost to those wishing to get onto the property ladder.

Market rigging

REVISED

One example of market rigging was that of the Libor rate. This is a benchmark interest rate based on the rates at which banks lend unsecured funds to each other on the London interbank market.

In another case, the Financial Conduct Authority accused traders at HSBC of colluding with traders from at least three other firms in an attempt to manipulate the sterling–dollar rate.

Now test yourself

TESTED

3 How does asymmetric information cause market failure in the banking industry?

Answers on p. 223

The role of central banks

Implementation of monetary policy

REVISED

Central banks are responsible for implementing the monetary policy of governments, which may involve inflation targeting with the use of interest rate policy and quantitative easing (see Theme 2).

Banker to the government

REVISED

From the beginning, the Bank of England was the government's banker, which means that it manages the government's accounts and arranges loans to the government. However, with the decision to grant the Bank operational independence in 1997, responsibility for government debt management was transferred to the new UK Debt Management Office in 1998.

Banker to the banks — lender of last resort

REVISED

A central bank is usually willing to offer loans to financial institutions which are experiencing financial difficulties and which are unable to obtain the necessary funds elsewhere, so helping to maintain the stability of the banking and financial system.

The scale of the 2008 financial crisis meant that a number of governments including those in the UK and Ireland had to bail out banks to keep them afloat.

Role of regulation in the banking industry

REVISED

Since April 2013, the UK has had two new financial regulators:

- the **Prudential Regulation Authority (PRA)**, whose main function is to ensure the stability of firms involved in financial services such as banks, building societies, credit unions and insurers
- the **Financial Conduct Authority (FCA)**, which is the City's behavioural watchdog and is designed to protect consumers, to promote competition and to maintain stability in the financial services sector

The Bank of England has also gained direct supervision of the whole of the banking system through its **Financial Policy Committee (FPC)**. The main objective of this committee is to identify risks and weaknesses across the UK financial system. If risks are increasing, it might ask banks to raise more money from shareholders as a buffer in case of a liquidity problem.

Some aspects of regulation

- By 2019, Britain's biggest banks must separate retail banking operations from their investment banking and overseas operations.

- The Bank of England subjects the UK's biggest banks to tests to measure whether they would survive a financial shock.
- Regulators in the UK, the USA and the European Union have fined banks more than $9 billion for rigging Libor, which underpins over $300 trillion worth of loans worldwide.

Exam tip

You will not be required to have detailed knowledge of bank regulations.

Now test yourself

TESTED

4 What function is a central bank performing when it changes interest rates?
5 What could the central bank do to reduce the risk of a bank going out of business?

Answers on p. 223

Revision activity

Draw a mind map to show the links between the key areas in this chapter and concepts covered in the other themes, e.g. market failures in Theme 1.

Exam practice

1 Evaluate the Bank of England's role as the central bank in the UK. [25]
2 Suppose the Bank of England and the UK government did not bail out a failing bank. Evaluate the likely effects of this on the UK economy. [25]

Answers and quick quizzes online

ONLINE

Summary

You should have an understanding of:
- The role and main functions of financial markets.
- Sources of market failure in financial markets.
- The role and main functions of central banks.

21 The role of the state in the macroeconomy

Public finance

There are three aspects to be considered:

- public expenditure
- taxation
- fiscal deficits (public sector borrowing) and national (public sector) debt

These are illustrated in Figure 21.1.

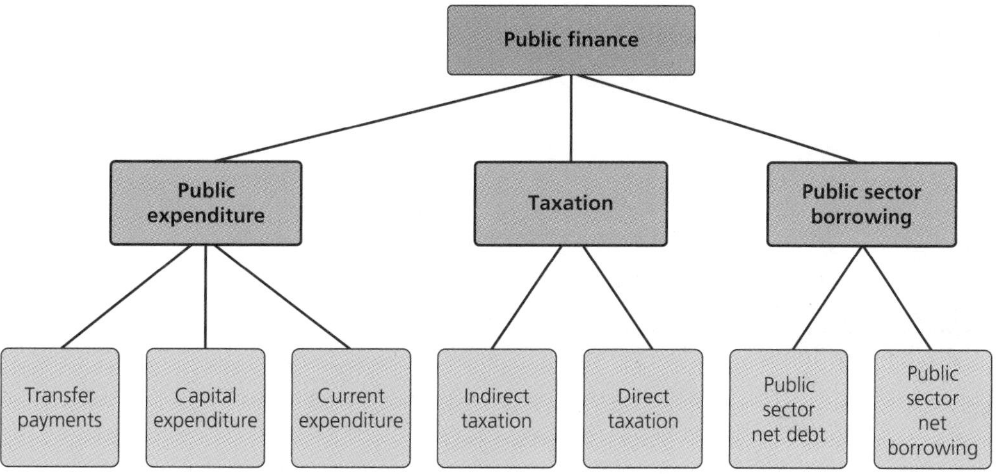

Figure 21.1 Key elements of public finance

These key elements of public expenditure are closely associated with the objectives of public expenditure, which are summarised in Figure 21.2.

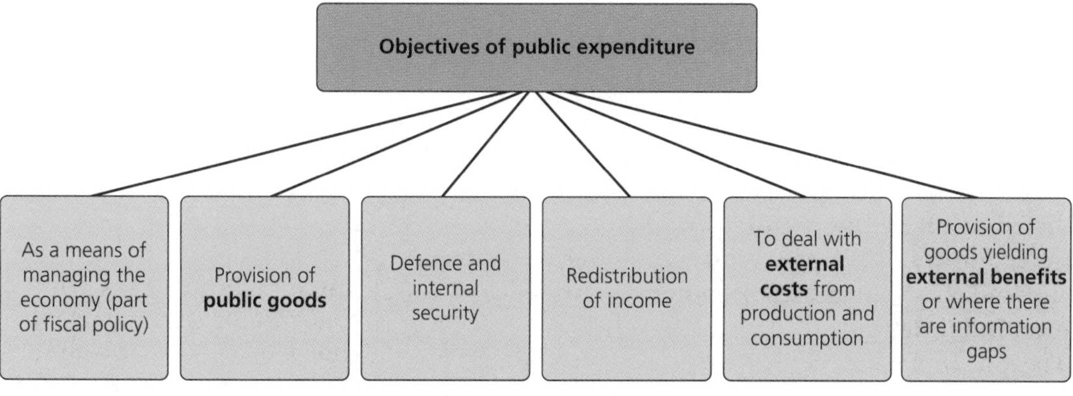

Figure 21.2 Objectives of public expenditure

Public goods are goods which would be under-provided and under-consumed because they have two key characteristics: non-excludability and the fact that they are non-rivalrous.

External benefits are benefits to third parties who are not part of the transaction between a consumer and a producer.

External costs are costs to third parties who are not part of the transaction between a consumer and a producer.

Public expenditure

There are three broad elements of **public expenditure**:

- **Capital expenditure.** This refers to long-term investment expenditure on capital projects such as HS2, new schools and new motorways.
- **Current expenditure.** This relates to the government's day-to-day expenditure on goods and services, for example wages and salaries of civil servants; drugs used by the NHS.
- **Transfer payments.** These are payments made by the state to individuals without there being any exchange of goods or services. They are used to redistribute income. UK examples include Universal Credit and state pensions.

Public expenditure relates to expenditure by central government, local authorities and public sector organisations.

Typical mistakes

Confusion between the three types of public expenditure.

Defining the term 'public expenditure' as expenditure by the public — this is incorrect!

Now test yourself TESTED

1 How might capital expenditure by the public sector affect GDP?
2 Give two examples of transfer payments.

Answers on p. 223

The changing size and composition of public expenditure in a global context

REVISED

The changing size of public expenditure

Several factors affect the size of public expenditure, including:

- **The level of GDP.**
- **Demand for public services.** Demand for many public services such as health and education is income elastic.
- **Size and age distribution of the population.**
- **The state of the economy.** When the economy is in recession, then public expenditure is likely to rise because of **automatic stabilisers**.
- **Interest on the national debt.**
- **The rate of inflation.** In nominal terms, public expenditure will inevitably increase during periods of inflation not least because many benefits are index linked, i.e. linked to the rate of inflation.
- **Political priorities**, e.g. governments might wish to improve public services.

Automatic stabilisers are changes in government spending or in tax revenue which occur automatically, without deliberate action by the government.

The changing composition of public expenditure

Figure 21.3 shows how public expenditure was distributed in the UK in 2015–16.

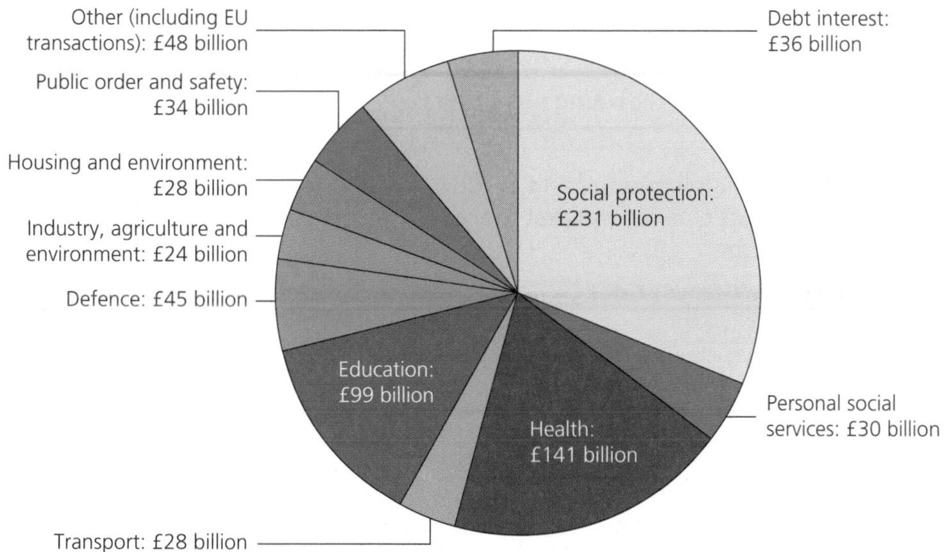

Figure 21.3 UK government expenditure, 2015–16

Source: Office for Budget Responsibility, 2015–16 estimates

Social protection (which includes the range of benefits), health and education have increased as a share of total government expenditure in recent years, partly because of:

- increased payments for housing benefits as a result of rising rents
- increased expenditure on tax credits
- the ageing population
- increased number of children of school age

However, austerity measures are designed to limit or reduce benefits in the future.

Now test yourself

TESTED

3 Why might expenditure on health as a proportion of GDP be expected to increase in the future?
4 Identify one other area of public expenditure which might also be expected to increase as a proportion of GDP in the future. Explain your reason.

Answers on p. 224

The significance of differing levels of public expenditure as a proportion of GDP

REVISED

Productivity and growth

If a country's public expenditure is a relatively high proportion of GDP, then its productivity and economic growth rates may be relatively low because of the absence of the profit motive and competition in the public sector.

Living standards

The impact will depend critically on the composition of public expenditure, for example the proportion of public expenditure spent on transfer payments and on health relative to the amount spent on defence.

Crowding out

Structural deficits could imply that the size of the public sector is increasing, which could cause **resource** or **financial crowding out**.

> **Resource crowding out** occurs when the economy is operating at full employment and the expansion of the public sector means that there is a shortage of resources in the private sector.
>
> **Financial crowding out** occurs when the expansion of the state sector is financed by increased government borrowing. This causes an increased demand for loanable funds, which drives up interest rates and crowds out private sector investment.

Level of taxation

If public expenditure is a high proportion of GDP then it is likely that taxation will also be a high proportion of GDP.

Equality

Much research suggests that higher public spending is associated with greater equality, for example in Sweden and Denmark. However, this is not always the case because some countries have both high public spending and a significant degree of inequality.

Taxation

Figure 21.4 summarises the main objectives of taxation.

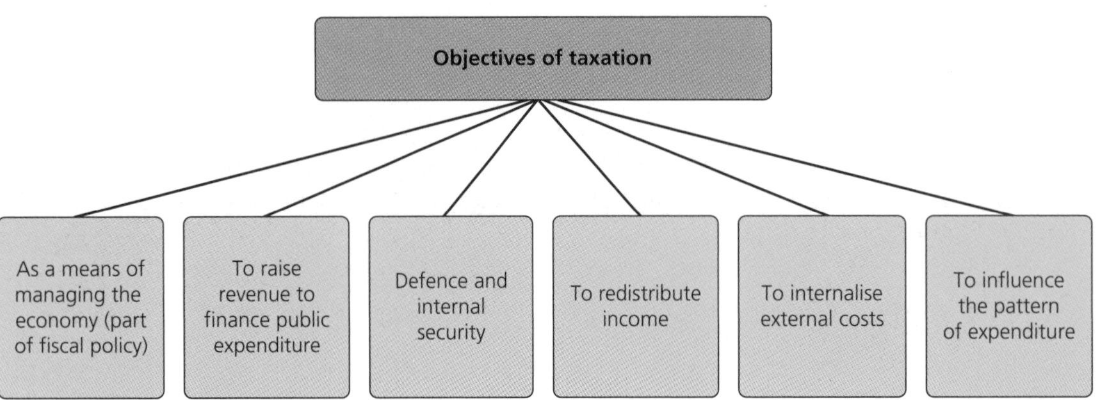

Figure 21.4 Objectives of taxation

Progressive, proportional and regressive taxes

REVISED

- **Progressive taxes** are taxes in which the proportion of income paid in tax rises as income increases.
- **Proportional taxes** are taxes in which the proportion of income paid in tax remains constant as income increases.
- **Regressive taxes** are taxes in which the proportion of income paid in tax falls as income increases.

Figure 21.5, where A is a progressive tax, B is a proportional tax and C is a regressive tax, shows the relationship between the proportion of income paid in tax and taxable income for the above categories of tax.

> **Typical mistake**
>
> Defining progressive taxes as follows: the more you earn the more you pay. This is imprecise because it also applies to *proportional* taxes.

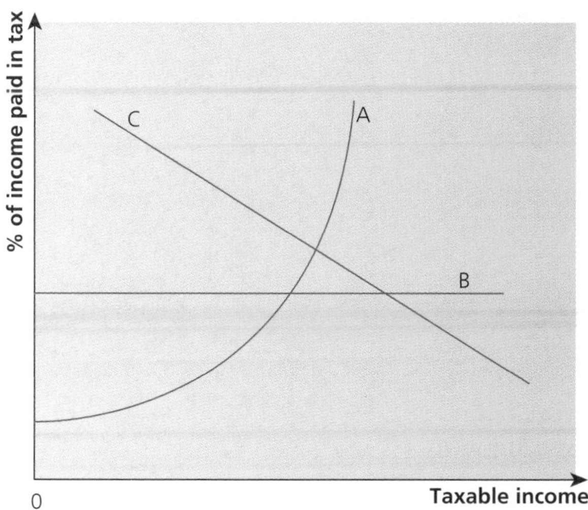

Figure 21.5 Categories of taxation

Direct and indirect tax rates

Direct taxes are those levied on incomes and wealth and include:

- **income tax** — a progressive tax levied at three rates: 20%; 40% and 45%
- **corporation tax** — a proportional tax on company profits, currently 20% in the UK but to be reduced to 17% in 2020
- **capital gains tax** — a tax on the increase in value of assets between the time they were bought and the time they were sold, e.g. on shares and investment property

Indirect taxes are taxes on expenditure and include:

- **value added tax (VAT)** — an ad valorem tax, i.e. a percentage of the price of the product
- **excise duties** — usually specific taxes, i.e. a set amount per unit.
- **tariffs**

Figure 21.6 shows the main sources of tax revenue and other sources of government revenue for the UK.

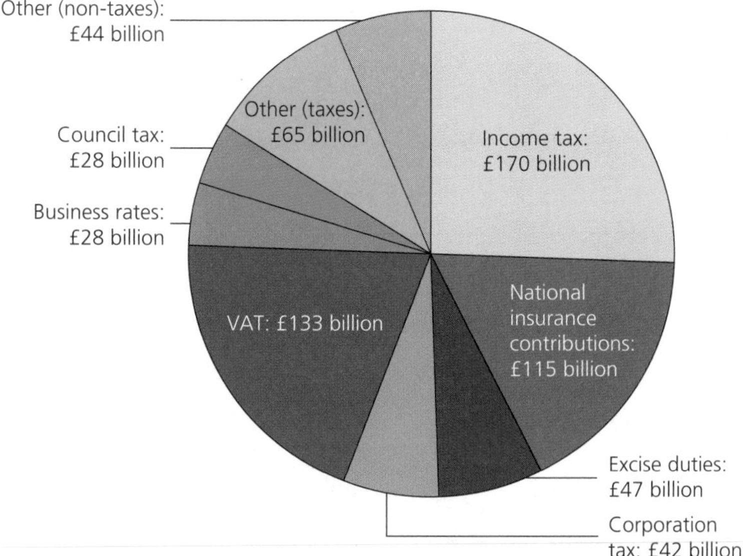

Figure 21.6 UK public sector receipts, 2015–16

Source: Office for Budget Responsibility, 2015–16 forecast

Direct taxes are taxes on income and wealth.

Indirect taxes are taxes on expenditure.

Exam tip

To determine whether a tax is direct or indirect, consider whether it is levied directly on a person's income or on their expenditure.

Typical mistake

Stating that VAT is a proportionate tax. This is incorrect because VAT is a percentage of the *price* of a product and is not based on *income*.

Now test yourself

TESTED

5 How does a progressive tax differ from a proportionate tax?

Answers on p. 224

Effects of changes in direct tax rates

REVISED

Incentives to work

An increase in income tax rates might cause a disincentive to work because:

- the unemployed and those currently 'inactive' would be less willing to take jobs
- workers currently employed may be less willing to do overtime, more likely to reduce their working hours, more likely to retire early and less willing to apply for promotion

Tax revenues

Increases in tax rates might cause tax revenues to fall. This may be explained using the **Laffer curve**, as shown in Figure 21.7.

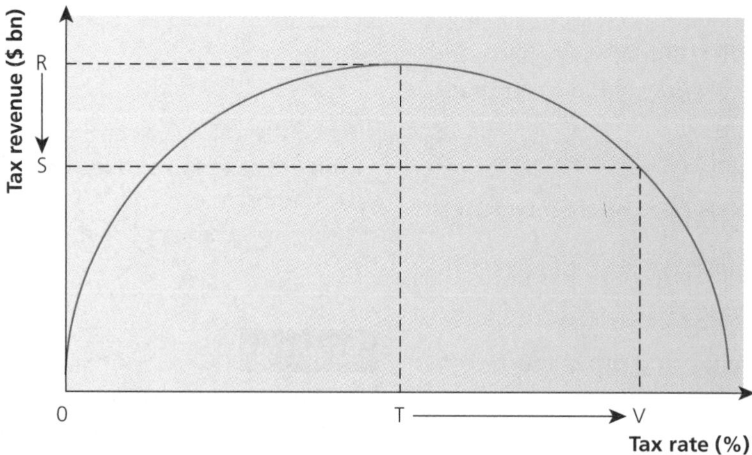

Figure 21.7 The Laffer curve

When the tax rate is increased up to point T, tax revenues increase. However, a further increase in the tax rate from T to V causes a fall in tax revenue from R to S. Several reasons might explain this phenomenon:

- increased disincentives to work
- an increase in tax avoidance, which is legal
- an increase in tax evasion, which is illegal
- a rise in the number of tax exiles

Income distribution

An increase in income tax rates will make the tax system more progressive, so making income distribution more equitable.

Real output and employment

Higher rates of income tax would cause a fall in disposable income, a fall in consumption and a fall in aggregate demand. The disincentive effects of higher rates of income tax might also cause a fall in aggregate supply. Consequently, there would be a fall in real output and employment.

The price level

The fall in aggregate demand following higher income tax rates would cause a fall in the price level. This may be partially offset by any fall in aggregate supply but the impact of the leftward shift in the aggregate demand curve is likely to be more significant.

The trade balance

An increase in income tax rates would reduce disposable income. In turn, this would cause a fall in consumption, resulting in a decrease in imports. Consequently, there should be an improvement in the trade balance.

FDI flows

An increase in direct taxes is likely to deter inward FDI. Further, an increase in income tax rates is also likely to deter inward FDI because disposable income would fall, causing a decrease in consumption.

Exam tip

Analyse tax changes with reference to aggregate demand and aggregate supply.

Now test yourself

TESTED

6 Why might an increase in income tax rates not result in an increase in government revenue?

Answer on p. 224

Effects of changes in indirect tax rates

REVISED

Incentives to work

An increase in the VAT rate might cause an incentive to work more because workers will try to maintain living standards by working harder.

Tax revenues

If the VAT rate is increased, then tax revenues will almost certainly increase because VAT is applied to most goods and services.

Income distribution

Research by the ONS in 2011 suggests that the impact of VAT is broadly regressive. Therefore, an increase in VAT would cause income distribution to become less even.

Real output and employment

A higher rate of VAT would cause a fall in real income, which would cause a fall in consumption and a fall in aggregate demand, leading to a reduction in real output and employment. For businesses, the higher VAT rate would raise costs, so causing a fall in aggregate supply, which would lead to a reduction in real output and employment.

The price level

The short-run effect of an increase in indirect taxes will be to increase the price level. However, it should be remembered that taxes are a leakage from the circular flow, so higher indirect taxes will cause a decrease in aggregate demand and, therefore, to a fall in the price level in the longer term.

The trade balance

Businesses can zero-rate goods exported outside the European Union (EU) or sent to someone who is registered for VAT in another EU country. Consequently, a change in VAT would only affect goods exported to someone in the EU who is not registered for VAT. Therefore, VAT changes by a country in the EU are likely to have very little impact.

FDI flows

If a government of a country raises its indirect taxes significantly, then global companies may be deterred from investing in that country because the tax rise might lead to a reduction in the domestic demand for the company's goods.

Now test yourself TESTED

7 What determines the incidence of an indirect tax?

Answer on p. 224

Public sector finances

Automatic stabilisers and discretionary fiscal policy

REVISED

Automatic stabilisers

These are changes in government expenditure and tax revenue which occur as GDP rises or falls without any change in government policy (see page 82). In a recession, unemployment increases, so the government spends more on unemployment benefits and other means-tested benefits. Such an increase in government expenditure is automatic. Further, tax revenues will fall because fewer people are working and therefore revenue from income tax will be lower. Meanwhile, VAT receipts will be lower because consumer spending is lower. In addition, there will be a fall in corporation tax receipts because company profits will be lower.

Discretionary fiscal policy

Discretionary fiscal policy involves deliberate changes in public expenditure and taxation by the government in an attempt to influence the level of economic activity (see page 82).

Distinction between the fiscal deficit and the national debt

REVISED

- A **fiscal deficit** implies that public expenditure is greater than tax revenues.
- The **national debt** is the cumulative total of past government borrowing.

The **national debt** is the total sum owed by a government to holders of government bonds (gilt-edged securities). In other words, it represents the total of a government's outstanding debt that it has accumulated over time.

Typical mistake

Confusing the fiscal (budget) deficit with the national debt.

Distinction between structural and cyclical deficits

REVISED

The government's finances change in line with the trade cycle, in other words they would usually be expected to deteriorate when the economy is in recession. These are referred to as **cyclical deficits**. A cyclical deficit is not regarded as a serious problem because it should disappear when the economy returns to its trend growth rate.

However, a **structural deficit** remains even when the economy is operating at a normal, sustainable level of employment and activity.

The **cyclical deficit** is that portion of a country's budget deficit that reflects changes in the economic cycle.

The **structural deficit** is the fiscal deficit which remains when the economy is normal, or when the output gap is zero.

Factors influencing the size of fiscal deficits

REVISED

The size of the fiscal deficit depends on factors which are similar to those which affect public expenditure and include:

- the state of the economy
- discretionary fiscal policy
- political priorities
- demographic factors
- sales of state-owned assets
- the efficiency of tax collection
- the degree of tax avoidance and tax evasion
- interest payments on the national debt
- the amount of government subsidies and financial support

In a particular year, a country's fiscal deficit may be reduced as a result of privatisations or telecoms spectrum auctions.

Now test yourself

TESTED

8 How might the following affect the size of the UK's fiscal deficit?
  (a) a significant increase in unemployment
  (b) an increase in the proportion of people aged over 65
  (c) an increase in tourism into the UK

Answers on p. 224

Factors influencing the size of national debts

REVISED

- fiscal deficits/surpluses
- wars
- economic crises such as the financial crisis of 2008
- measures adopted by the government which create immediate and long-term obligations

The significance of the size of the fiscal deficit and national debts

REVISED

The fiscal deficit as a proportion of GDP is more significant than the absolute size of the fiscal deficit because it gives a better indication of the ability of the country to finance the debt and eventually to repay it.

A persistent structural fiscal deficit and an increasing national debt might cause:

- **loss of the county's AAA credit rating**, which could mean higher interest rates when it borrows money
- **crowding out** (see page 204)
- **inflation**, because net injections will be increasing
- a **fall in confidence**, leading to a **fall in FDI**
- **rising interest payments on the national debt**

However, a fiscal deficit and rising national debt caused by significant investment on infrastructure and/or on education or health may not be regarded as a serious problem because such expenditure would increase long-run aggregate supply.

Now test yourself

TESTED

9 Explain the difference between a fiscal deficit and the national debt.
10 Suggest two reasons which might justify running a large budget deficit.
11 What might be the opportunity cost of an increasing national debt?

Answers on p. 224

Macroeconomic policies in a global context

Use of fiscal policy, monetary policy, exchange rate policy, supply-side policies and direct controls

REVISED

Measures to reduce fiscal deficits and national debts

To reduce a fiscal deficit, a government could:

- reduce public expenditure and/or
- increase taxes
- implement policies to increase economic growth. Some economists argue that these policies would have the effect of reducing the fiscal deficit and national debt *as a proportion of GDP*.

Now test yourself

TESTED

12 Why might deflationary fiscal policy not cause a fall in the fiscal deficit?

Answers on p. 224

Measures to reduce poverty and inequality

- Improved quality of education and training for the poor.
- Making the tax system more progressive.
- Higher inheritance taxes.
- Increasing the number and range of 'means-tested benefits'.
- Measures to reduce unemployment.
- Introduction of or increase in the national minimum wage/ **national living wage.**

The **national living wage** is a wage high enough for workers to have a normal standard of living, i.e. to be able to afford everyday things like food, transport and paying bills.

Now test yourself

TESTED

13 Identify one measure to reduce poverty and one measure to reduce inequality.

Answer on p. 224

Changes in interest rates and the supply of money

The impact of changes in interest rates and money supply are discussed in Theme 2.

Usually, central banks make independent decisions about changing interest rates in the light of inflationary expectations in their own countries. However, in October 2008, in response to the global financial crisis, central banks agreed a co-ordinated half-a-percentage-point cut in interest rates.

Quantitative easing is designed to make it easier and cheaper for businesses to borrow from banks. However, according to the **quantity theory of money**, this may cause inflation. Further, it could cause a depreciation in the country's exchange rate.

Quantitative easing involves the central bank buying securities from financial institutions, which has the effect of increasing the money supply.

The **quantity theory of money** states that there is a direct and proportionate relationship between changes in the money supply and the price level.

Measures to increase international competitiveness

Policies used to eliminate a balance of payments deficit on current account (see pages 76–77) would also be relevant as a means of increasing international competitiveness.

Now test yourself

TESTED

14 Why might currency depreciation not increase a country's international competitiveness?

Answer on p. 224

Exam tip

Subsidies may not be a relevant policy if they are outlawed by the WTO or the trading bloc to which the country belongs.

Use and impact of macroeconomic policies to respond to external shocks to the global economy

REVISED

External shocks to the global economy may take a variety of forms, including:

- a sudden increase (or decrease) in global oil or commodity prices in general
- a financial crisis causing a decrease in confidence in the banking system
- bursting of asset price bubbles
- extreme weather events causing major damage to infrastructure
- contagious diseases

- terrorist attacks or global conflicts
- cyber-attacks which could impact on communications, energy supplies, banking transactions and/or retailing

The macroeconomic policies used to respond to such external shocks will depend on the particular shock in question.

Now test yourself TESTED

15 What policies might be appropriate if there was a sudden fall in UK house prices?

Answer on p. 224

Measures to control global companies' operations

REVISED

The regulation of transfer pricing

It has proved very difficult for governments to control transfer pricing, although attempts are being made to seek international agreement to ensure that global companies pay a fair amount of tax in each of the countries in which they operate. For example, tax payable on turnover in each country might be levied.

Limits to government ability to control global companies

Global companies may:

- be 'footloose', i.e. they can move easily from one country to another in search of the lowest wage and other costs
- have a monopoly on technological and intellectual property
- threaten to withdraw investment

Problems facing policymakers when applying policies

REVISED

Inaccurate information

- Forecasts are notoriously inaccurate, e.g. of the future rate of inflation. This also applies to costs of major projects, e.g. HS2.
- Estimates of past data for a variety of indicators are frequently revised significantly in subsequent years, e.g. GDP and balance of payments on current account.

Revision activity

Make a chart showing the distinction between the following groups of terms.

(a) current account deficit; fiscal deficit; national debt
(b) structural fiscal deficits; cyclical deficits
(c) current expenditure; capital expenditure; transfer payments
(d) monetary policy; fiscal policy; supply-side policies

Risks and uncertainties

Risk is present when future events occur with measurable probability, whereas **uncertainty** is present when the likelihood of future events is indefinite or incalculable. Uncertainties cannot be eliminated or insured against.

Inability to control external shocks

Most of the external shocks described on page 211 are difficult to predict and, consequently, to allow for when applying policies. Therefore, policies being followed may no longer be appropriate.

Exam practice

1 (a) In 2015, the VAT rate in Greece was increased from 13% to 23% on many basic goods. This would only reduce Greece's fiscal deficit if:
  A Demand for these goods was elastic.
  B There was a negative rate of economic growth.
  C Demand for these goods was price inelastic.
  D Supply of these goods was elastic. [1]

(b) Explain the likely effect of an increase in a country's rates of income tax on the distribution of income. [4]

2 (a) Which of the following is most likely to increase a country's international competitiveness?
  A A decrease in public sector investment on transport.
  B An increase in the use of modern technology in manufacturing.
  C A decrease in the skills of the workforce.
  D An increase in environmental regulations. [1]

(b) Explain two reasons why deflationary economic policy might not have the impact intended by a government. [4]

Extract: The UK's Charter for Budget Responsibility

In 2015, the new Charter for Budget Responsibility (or Fiscal Charter) put into law that governments must run a fiscal surplus in 'normal' times. The Office for Budget Responsibility (OBR), an independent fiscal watchdog, will determine whether or not the situation is 'normal'. If the OBR judges that a negative shock has occurred, or will occur over the forecast period, the fiscal targets will be suspended.

Those in favour of this new Charter argue that it will encourage governments to act with greater responsibility with regard to public finances. Further, it will give business, markets and the public a clearer idea of the path of fiscal policy and help to restore credibility to the government's public finances. This follows the financial crisis, in which the fiscal deficit rose as high as 11%.

Fiscal rules for Eurozone members were enshrined in the 1997 Stability and Growth Pact, and were intended to ensure that national governments don't take advantage of their membership of the Eurozone to borrow excessively, and thereby threaten the stability of the currency area.

But the rules have been regularly broken since the euro was launched in 1999 and failed to prevent surges in borrowing that contributed to the currency area's debt crisis, which began in 2010 and continues to this day as Greece seeks an agreement with the rest of the Eurozone and the IMF that would enable it to repay its debts.

The combined debts of the Eurozone's member governments rose again in 2014, reaching 91.9% of gross domestic product, compared with an upper limit under the budget rules of 60%.

The IMF economists also said that the long-standing requirements that budget deficits don't exceed 3% of gross domestic product and that government debt should fall toward 60% of GDP are no longer consistent with each other.

The damage inflicted by the financial and debt crises mean the Eurozone's growth potential is much lower than it was when the rules were set down, so even deficits as low as 3% of GDP won't deliver the desired reduction in debt ratios. In fact, debts will probably rise if deficits aren't lower.

The IMF economists considered a range of alternative, simpler rules for fiscal policy, and concluded the best option would be a limit on the growth of government spending designed to bring down government debt as a share of economic output.

Table 1 Growth rates, fiscal deficits and unemployment rates in selected European Union countries

	Real GDP growth rate (%)		Unemployment rate (%)		Fiscal deficit (% of GDP)	
	2009	2014	2009	2014	2009	2014
Germany	–5.6	1.6	7.6	5.0	–3.2	0.3
Greece	–4.3	0.7	9.6	26.5	–15.2	–3.6
Spain	–3.6	1.4	17.9	24.5	–11.0	–5.9
UK	–4.2	2.2	7.6	6.1	–10.8	–5.7

3 (a) With reference to Table 1, explain how a fiscal deficit might affect a country's national debt. [5]
(b) Analyse possible reasons why the UK's growth rate was higher than that of Greece in 2014. [8]
(c) Assess the costs of unemployment to countries such as Spain or Greece. [12]
(d) Evaluate the view that countries should always run a balanced budget or budget surplus. [25]
Or
(e) Evaluate policies which Eurozone countries such as Greece and Spain might follow to reduce their unemployment rates. [25]

Answers and quick quiz 21 online

ONLINE

Summary

You should have an understanding of:

- Public expenditure: current, capital and transfer payments.
- Reasons for the changing size and composition of public expenditure as a proportion of GDP.
- Significance of differing levels of public expenditure as a proportion of GDP.
- Taxation: progressive, proportional and regressive taxes; direct and indirect taxation.
- Effects of changes in direct and indirect taxes rates.
- Distinction between fiscal deficits and national debts and factors influencing their size.
- Macroeconomic policies in a global context.

Now test yourself answers

Chapter 1

1 b, c and e are positive statements because these can be verified by reference to data.

a and d are normative statements because they are subjective and based on value judgements.

2 (a) Land because copper is a natural resource which is included in the economic definition of land.

(b) Enterprise because the woman has taken the risks to start a business.

(c) Capital because the robots are used to make other goods.

(d) Labour because the person is working for a business to makes goods and services.

3 (a) Capital good.

(b) Consumer good.

(c) Consumer good/service.

(d) Capital good.

4 Resources are scarce but wants are infinite, so choices must be made.

5 The holiday in Greece — this is the real cost of making a choice.

6 No resources are sacrificed in their use, so the opportunity cost is zero.

7 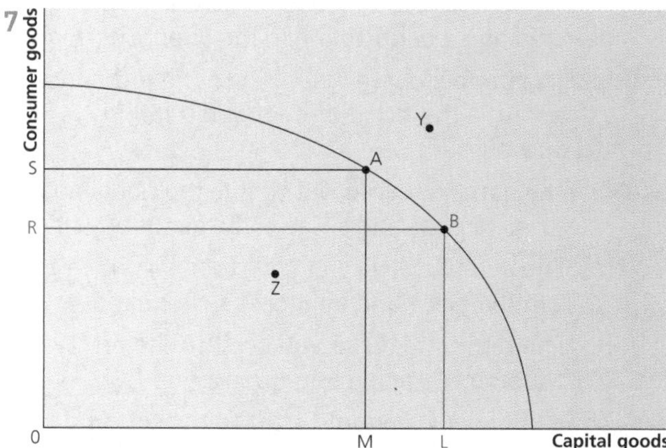

(a) At Z there will be unemployed resources because this point is not on the PPF.

(b) Point Y is currently unattainable. It could only be achieved if there was an outward shift in the PPF.

(c) LM capital goods.

(d) (i) Increasing the current output of consumer goods would increase current living standards.

(ii) However, future living standards may fall because fewer capital goods are being produced.

8 (a) An outward (rightward) shift because productivity would increase the productive capacity of the country.

(b) An inward shift on the PPF because productive capacity would have decreased.

(c) This would cause an outward shift in the PPF because the extra capital would enable output per worker to increase.

(d) This represents an increase in the working population causing an increase in the productive capacity of the country. Therefore, the PPF would shift outwards.

9 d: The demand for specialist products makes it very difficult to increase specialisation. Specialisation is best suited to the production of mass-produced goods, which enables the job to be broken down into small tasks.

10 Money enables a person to work in a highly specialist job. The money he/she is paid in can then be used to buy other goods and services.

11
- private ownership of resources
- profit motive
- competition between firms
- prices determined by the forces of supply and demand

12 Consumer sovereignty is the power of consumers to determine what is produced by their preferences. Firms respond to consumer demand by producing the goods and services which consumers buy.

13
- freedom to own resources
- efficiency associated with the profit motive and competition
- higher rates of growth than in command economies

14 There is freedom to own resources; those who own resources are likely to earn more income than those who do not own resources.

15 Any three of:
- Danger that there will be unemployed resources.
- The free market economy is likely to be subject to booms and slumps associated with the trade cycle.
- No account is taken of external costs and benefits.
- Danger that monopolies will occur.

16 The state.

17 ● The state can ensure all workers are employed.
● There is likely to be greater equality.

18 There is no profit motive and no competition.

Chapter 2

1 (a) The amount demanded at given prices over a certain period of time.
(b) (i) a rightward shift in the demand curve
(ii) a leftward shift in the demand curve
(iii) a rightward shift in the demand curve for houses because the substitute, rented accommodation, has increased in price
(iv) a leftward shift in the demand curve because it has become more expensive to buy a house

2 (a) PED = % change in quantity demanded/% change in price
$$= \frac{-10\%}{20\%} = -0.5$$
This implies that demand is price inelastic since the result is between 0 and −1.
(b) $PED = \frac{-15\%}{10\%} = -1.5$
This implies that demand is price elastic.
(c) $PED = \frac{6\%}{-6\%} = -1.$
This implies that demand is unitary elastic.

3 Total revenue will increase because the price will have risen by a larger percentage than the fall in quantity demanded.

4 Demand is price elastic because the rise in price must have caused a more than proportionate fall in quantity demanded.

5 Demand is unitary elastic because the increase in price must have caused an exactly proportionate fall in the quantity demanded.

6 There are many substitutes.

7 Inelastic because for many people there are no effective substitutes and coffee forms part of their daily diet.

8 Milk is a non-durable product and part of the everyday diet of many consumers.

9 (a) (i) +15% ÷ +10% = +1.5. Therefore, tea and coffee are substitutes since the result is positive.
(ii) −10% ÷ +5% = −2. Therefore, X and Y are complements because the result is negative.
(b) C

10 (a) −9% ÷ -3% = + 3. This implies that new cars are a normal good (the result is positive) and that demand is income elastic (the fall in income has led to a more than proportionate decrease in demand).
(b) −2% ÷ +5% = −0.4. Therefore, soya is an inferior good because the result is negative.
(c) +2% ÷ +10% = +0.2. Therefore, demand for oranges is income inelastic (the result is between 0 and +1).

11 The amount producers are willing to offer for sale at given prices in a particular period of time.

12 (a) Rightward shift of the supply curve because a subsidy reduces production costs.
(b) Leftward shift of the supply curve because higher wages would increase production costs.
(c) Rightward shift of the supply curve because output per worker has risen.
(d) Leftward shift of the supply curve because less tea will be available.

13 (a) 2% ÷ 20% = 0.1. Therefore, supply is inelastic since the result is between 0 and 1.
(b) 15% ÷ 5% = 3. Therefore, supply is elastic since the result is greater than +1.

14 Supply would be inelastic because tomatoes are perishable and cannot be stored, and there is a long growing period.

15 It is possible that the supply of butter would be elastic if there were stocks available in refrigerated warehouses.

16 Excess supply because the quantity supplied will be greater than the quantity demanded.

17 Market forces would cause an extension of demand and a contraction in the quantity supplied.

18 (a) The supply curve will shift to the left causing a rise in the price of beef and a fall in quantity.
(b) The demand curve will shift to the right causing a rise in price and a rise in the quantity.
(c) The supply curve will shift to the right causing a fall in price and an increase in quantity.
(d) The demand curve will shift to the left causing the price and quantity to fall.

19 The supply curve would shift to the left and become steeper.

Chapter 3

1 A market is said to fail if resources are not allocated in the most efficient way possible.

2 Externalities; public goods; information gaps.

3 The social marginal cost must be equal to the social marginal benefit.

4 Private costs: raw materials, wages; cost of fertiliser to the farmer.

External costs: waste discharge into river; loss of income to fishermen because these are fewer fish.

5 Private benefits: extra salary from gaining a degree; job satisfaction.

External benefits: increased economic growth; higher productivity of workers meaning goods are more competitive internationally.

6 Private goods are excludable, i.e. it is possible to prevent everyone from consuming the product and rivalrous — consumption by one person means that less is available for others.

7 Because it is impossible to exclude people from consuming the product.

8 By the use of detectors vans and hand-held detectors to ensure that those using televisions have a licence.

9 A dentist will usually have much greater knowledge and information about a person's teeth and dental hygiene than the patient. Consequently, it is possible that a patient may be given unnecessary treatment, e.g. a filling.

Chapter 4

1 It implies that the producer has to bear the cost of the pollution, so the negative externality is internalised by the producer causing it.

2 It may be difficult to (i) determine the extent of the external costs and (ii) to place a monetary value on the external costs caused in the production process.

3

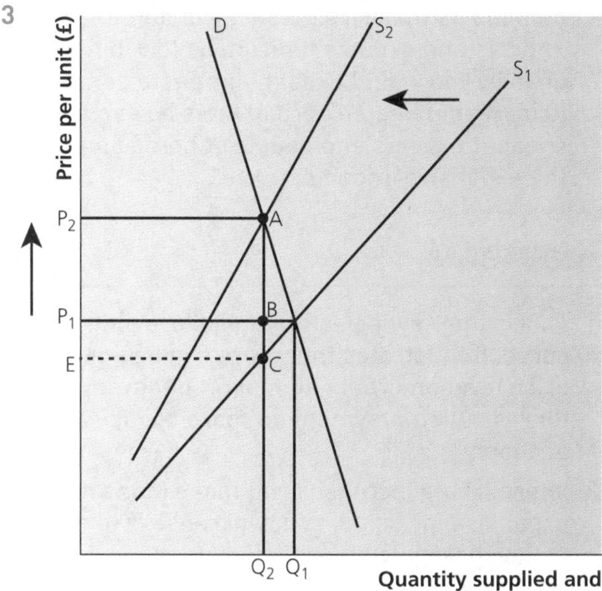

(a) Tax borne by consumer: P_1P_2AB

(b) Tax borne by producer: EP_1BC

4 This would cause the supply curve for those involved in electricity generation from wind farms to shift to the left. Consequently, there would be an increase in price and decrease in output.

5 To provide an incentive for farmers to increase production of wheat. Farmers would now know how much they would receive for the production of each kilo of wheat.

6 The quantity demanded by consumers would decrease because the price would be higher than the free market price. The quantity supplied would increase because the farmers would be encouraged to produce more as the price would be higher than the free market price.

7 The government can issue permits to pollute up to a certain limit. Those companies using clean technology can sell them to those using dirty technology. Over time, the number of these permits could be reduced forcing up their price so providing a growing incentive for firms to invest in new technology.

8 It may be very difficult and expensive to enforce laws and regulations designed to reduce pollution. Further, finding proof that a firm is responsible for pollution might not be possible without sufficient evidence.

9 Further away from the socially efficient output.

10 If the fishing quotas allow too many fish to be caught then it is possible that stocks will diminish and ultimately there may be no fish left.

Chapter 5

1 A recession means that incomes are falling, output is falling and spending is falling. The characteristics tend to be lower living standards, increasing unemployment, and many firms going out of business. From the government's point of view there tends to be more spending (on benefits) and reduced tax receipts.

2 It may mean that it could enjoy higher living standards, but this is not guaranteed. It might mean that people are working longer hours or live in much more crowded cities, for example.

3 Happiness takes into account the quality of life rather than the income alone. It is difficult to collect accurate data, but a picture can be built up over time of changes in happiness, and the ONS attempts to do this in its official statistics. Government policy can have a significant impact on happiness, for example by spending money on facilities for disabled people or providing efficient library services. However, some people think that the provision of these services is not the role of the government, and therefore policy should be focused on increased incomes for all, which will have indirect effects on other services as government revenues will increase as the economy grows.

4 No. If it is a one-off spike when prices go up sharply (and usually come down again) then it is neither general nor sustained. However, it could be a *cause* of inflation because when oil prices go up the cost of production rises for most firms, and this is likely to cause firms in general to raise their prices.

5 Similar items can be bought in high- and low-cost shops, so a selection of prices is gathered for each item. There are about 18000 separate price quotations used every month in compiling the indices, covering nearly 700 representative consumer goods and services. Prices are collected in about 150 areas.

6 High rates of inflation have impacts on other macro objectives of governments: to some extent they can worsen the distribution of income (people on low fixed incomes such as pensioners will see real wages fall), but a high rate of inflation can also narrow the distribution of income (real values of savings and debts decrease), so if those with high incomes have high savings and those with low incomes have more debts, the distribution of income will widen. International trade suffers if a country has higher inflation than its trading partners (exports become relatively expensive and imports relatively cheap) and there are adverse effects if interest rates rise to fight inflation because this often leads to an increase in the value of the currency.

7 Reasons might include: housing costs are excluded such as mortgage interest repayments and rent. The 650 items in the 'basket' are changed only once a year, but tastes and fashions change more quickly than this and 'special offers' temporarily change people's spending habits. For people with atypical spending patterns, such as vegetarians and non-drivers, the CPI will be unrepresentative. Quality and technology of goods change over time and this is difficult to incorporate in the measurement of CPI. For example, the quality of instant cameras has dramatically improved on a monthly basis and the basket of goods is not changed often enough to reflect this.

8 It falls by 3%.

9 It represents the people of working age who are economically inactive, e.g. students or those caring for dependants.

10 There are strict criteria for claiming JSA and many are not eligible. For example if you refuse work that you have been offered, have a high level of savings or have a spouse with a high income you may not be eligible.

11 The claimant count records people who receive a financial reward for declaring themselves unemployed, whereas in the ILO method there is no reward for saying that you are unemployed. So when times are hard and there is not much money around in the economy (in a recession) the JSA tends to rise relative to the ILO. People have a stronger incentive to claim the JSA payments, are less likely to have high levels of saving s or spouses with high incomes etc., which might have made them ineligible.

12 Because full-time students are not included in the official figures for employment or unemployment neither should change. However, many students do some paid work (EU students do not have any restrictions within the EU) so the level of employment might rise as casual vacancies are filled.

13 It is an import because money is flowing out of the country. Most people get confused with this because they think of themselves leaving the country as an exit not an entry. Remember to think about money flows, not the physical movement of goods or people.

Chapter 6

1 A movement along the AD curve happens when there is a change in the price level. This might be because all costs have risen, i.e. a shift in aggregate supply. A movement in AD occurs when one of the determinants of aggregate demand changes. For example, an increase in investment will increase AD. In this case, there is a **decrease in government spending (G)** so aggregate demand decreases (shifts to the left).

2 Consumption will rise.

3 Initially there might be a decrease in aggregate demand as the price elasticity of demand for imports and exports tends to be low, but as time goes by you would expect aggregate demand to increase. People abroad start buying the cheaper exports and people at home stop buying the expensive imports.

Chapter 7

1 This is the Keynesian method of drawing the AS curve. It illustrates that there can be equilibrium price level and real national output even when there is unemployment or spare capacity in the economy.

2 Interest rate increases will make loans more expensive for firms, so an increase is likely to make aggregate supply fall.

Chapter 8

1 It will rise more slowly. Government spending is an injection into the circular flow of income, so a fall in the injection means that incomes will rise less quickly than they did.

2 Equilibrium means there is a balance, and no tendency to change. It should mean that there are no surpluses or deficits, and markets are clearing. However, according to Keynes, equilibrium can occur while there is demand-deficient unemployment.
3 £2 million (2 × £1 million).

Chapter 9

1 You would expect a rise in both AD and AS. So growth rises.
2 The level of GDP has risen by 2%, whereas in the past it had risen more quickly at 3.2%. GDP has certainly not fallen even if growth rates fall.
3 High exchange rates make the price of exports expensive in foreign countries, so this may stop people buying them. If exports fall, AD falls because X is a component of AD and there are multiplier effects. Likewise, if exchange rates are high, imports are cheap and so if imports are increased, then because this is a negative component of AD, then AD falls with multiplier effects. However, a high exchange rate can have the reverse effect if the price elasticity of demand for exports and imports is low.
4 The increased import will worsen the balance of payments. If the car uses a lot of fuel, there will be increased carbon emissions, and the fuel itself will be an import.

Chapter 10

1 Deciles (10% slices of data) and quintiles (20% slices of data) help us to compare chunks of data rather than the extremes. For example, it is a more helpful measure of inequality if we are not too swayed by the extremely poor and extremely rich, as these make the results unrepresentative of most people.
2 The Phillips curve illustrates a negative relationship between inflation (on the vertical axis) and unemployment. The implication is that if you are prepared to forgo one you can achieve success in controlling the other.
3 Contractionary fiscal policy is when government spending and taxation is used to dampen demand, perhaps by cutting government spending or raising taxation.
4 Because deficits have to be financed by borrowing. Increased demand for loanable funds puts up interest rates.
5 Firms need to pay for resources which they then transform into goods and services that they can then sell. The time taken to transfer the resources into receipts for payment means that firms need to borrow.
6 Less bureaucracy means there are fewer rules and regulations for firms when they operate in a country. For example, it might mean that firms can take on more workers without doing full checks on their criminal records. This will cut costs for firms and mean they can increase output at a lower cost that it would otherwise be, but there are no direct payments as a result — except that those workers will start paying tax on their incomes more quickly.
7 Investment in people, such as spending on health or education, improves the productive potential of the workforce. Human assets are worth more to the economy.

Chapter 11

1 The main benefits are those of horizontal integration, i.e. economies of scale and increased market share. However, there are also advantages in bailing out a firm that might have been about to become insolvent.
2 The company is niche market, with a low minimum efficient scale. The cars are worth more to consumers partly because they are so rare!

Chapter 12

1 Yes and yes: profit maximisation is a balanced point which rational firms try to achieve unless the question tells you otherwise.
2 It is revenue maximising, which is rational because the costs become irrelevant when the stock has to be thrown away. The seller should make as much money as possible, ignoring the marginal cost in this specific example.
3 Lower, if the demand curve is sloping downwards. The firm needs to lower the price to sell more, and as it does so the marginal profit is negative — that is, it costs more to make each extra unit that is received from selling the extra unit.
4 The firms might have other objectives apart from short-run profit maximisation. If the owners can be kept happy with a certain amount of profits then other goals can be worked on.

Chapter 13

1 You should raise the price. Total revenue will rise, by definition.
2 It depends on the type of business as to how much money is needed to keep factors in their current use.

3 Normal profit is built into the cost curve. So if AC = AR or TC = TR you know that the firm is operating at normal profit.

4 It depends on the type of workers. If your workers are paid relative to the amount they produce, for example strawberry pickers, then they are variable costs. But if they are paid whether or not they produce anything, such as health and safety officers, they are fixed costs.

5 The law of diminishing returns sets in.

6 Yes. When the marginal product falls, it means that there is a smaller increase in output when one more factor is employed — that is, it means that the law of diminishing returns has set in.

7 8, that is 2 × 2 × 2. That's quite a big increase after doubling the lengths.

8 It should decrease output, which means the long-run average costs will fall.

9 Internal economies occur when the firm gets larger, and external economies occur when the industry gets larger.

10 Profit is maximised.

Chapter 14

1 Yes. If the demand and MR curves both pass through the lowest point of the AC curve then P = MC and MC = AC. This only happens in the long run in perfect competition.

2 Because they are covering AVC and making a contribution to the fixed costs. If all costs are variable, the firm will leave the industry, which is what happens in the long run as there are no fixed costs in the long run.

3 Yes, they make normal profit only. If there are supernormal profits in the short run, they will be eroded away by new entrants in the long run, and if there is a loss in the short run then firms will leave in the long run.

4 It is overt collusion because it is openly asking a question about future prices. However, it is not guaranteed that the firms will act on the information and it might be very hard to detect this.

5 Nothing for revenue. Both raising and lowering price causes revenue to fall. To raise profits the firm needs to cut its costs or diversify into new markets. Or it could collude with other firms.

6 Legally they can both be treated as monopolies. However, the fact that the two-firm concentration ratio appears to be 52% means this also meets the guideline for oligopoly. In this case we would call the market structure a duopoly because two firms are in control of the market.

7 Monopolies can make prices higher and choice restricted for consumers, among other things.

8 If there were no monopoly power, new firms could enter the industry and exploit the supernormal profits that are available when a price discriminator charges a higher price to consumers with a lower price elasticity of demand.

9 Monopoly power means that a firm has power over consumers, and monopsony means a firm has power over its suppliers.

10 No. In fact a firm could be the only firm in the market (monopoly) but have no barriers to entry. But it is unlikely to be making a profit, or other firms would enter.

11 Contestability brings the benefits of competition or removes some of the problems of monopolies without other firms actually having to enter the market.

Chapter 15

1 No. If cutting JSA does have a positive influence on the labour market it is because some people think it means people will make more of an effort to find a job. However, moving from being unemployed to employed has no effect on the size of the labour force because *unemployed people are part of the labour force*.

2 If everything else remains the same then the worker will be able to be paid more. However, there is a huge assumption that the same amount will be sold, and if the demand for the product falls the worker might lose her job!

3 A competitive market exists if there are many buyers and sellers of labour. In a non-competitive market there is *market power* — either buyers have monopsony power (the employers, for example the NHS, can force prices or wages down) or suppliers have monopoly power (trade unions, for example, force up wages).

Chapter 16

1 Competition can lead to lower prices and more choice for consumers.

2 Symmetric information in this context means that the regulator knows as much about the business as the firm that it is trying to regulate. Asymmetric information means that the firm knows more and can shield information from the regulator, which might mean that the firm will face penalties.

3 While there are problems with the CMA picking up cases (such as tacit collusion or because of regulatory capture), it must also be true that the heavy actions such as fines and imprisonment of directors must *deter* other firms from taking anticompetitive action.

Chapter 17

1
- Structural changes, e.g. developed economies bringing back manufacturing to their own countries; China rebalancing its economy away from exports towards domestic production.
- Global economic downturn; increased protectionism.

2 Reasons include:
- Continued fall in protectionist measures as more countries join trading blocs and the WTO negotiates lower trade barriers.
- Further specialisation by countries based on the law of comparative advantage.
- Growth of emerging economies that will both export more and import more, as real incomes increase.

3 Firms can access world markets more easily by advertising on the internet; it is easier for consumers to buy goods from other countries.

4
- Larger markets, enabling firms to benefit from economies of scale.
- Lower labour costs.
- Can source raw materials more cheaply.

5 Absolute advantage implies that one country can produce more of a product than another country. Comparative advantage means that a country can produce a product at a lower opportunity cost than another country. Even if country A can produce more of all products than country B, specialisation and trade will still be beneficial if country B has a relative or comparative advantage in one of the products.

6 Advantages: more choice; lower prices and, therefore, increased consumer surplus.

Disadvantages: consumers may face less choice in the long run if domestic firms are unable to compete and so go bankrupt. In turn, this might imply that workers in the domestic industries are made redundant.

7 Advantages: lower cost of imported raw materials; larger market for the goods produced which might enable firms to benefit from economies of scale. Both these factors might enable firms to increase profits.

Disadvantages: inability to compete with foreign competitors; lower profits and the possibility that firms might go bankrupt.

8
- Change from inward-looking strategy to outward-looking strategy, leading to foreign direct investment (FDI).
- FDI combined with low labour costs leading to development of manufacturing industries and increased exports.
- Rising real incomes in emerging and developing economies, creating extra demand for goods produced in China.

9 (a) $T/T = \frac{120}{110} \times 100 = 109.09$

(b) $T/T = \frac{110}{90} \times 100 = 122.2$

10 Living standards will fall because more must be exported to gain a given quantity of imports.

11 The primary aim of the WTO is to promote free trade and the theoretical basis for free trade is the law of comparative advantage.

12 These terms are usually applied when considering trading blocs. Trade creation relates to increased trade with other countries following the removal of trade barriers. Trade diversion occurs when trade barriers are imposed. This usually means trade flows being diverted from low-cost producers to high-cost producers.

13 Because dumping causes an artificial distortion of comparative advantage.

14 To allow its infant industries to develop and reach a size which will enable firms to benefit from economies of scale. In turn, this will enable the firms to compete internationally.

15
- Tariffs bring in tax revenue for the government whereas a subsidy will cause an increase in government expenditure.
- Tariffs cause a rise in the price of goods whereas subsidies to domestic firms will not.

16
- Consumers will have less choice and higher prices.
- Domestic producers will benefit from less competition but overseas producers will face a reduction in demand.

17 (a) Visible export: inflow into the trade in goods balance, which is part of the current account. Positive effect on balance of payments.

(b) Invisible import: outflow from the trade in services balance, which is part of the current account. Negative effect on balance of payments.

(c) Inflow into the financial account. Positive effect on balance of payments.

(d) Visible import: outflow from the trade in goods balance, which is part of the current account. Negative effect on balance of payments.

(e) Outflow from the current account under the 'investment income' balance. Negative effect on balance of payments.

18 (a) Answer A: these countries will have more money to spend on UK exports.

(b) Not because this will make the UK's goods less competitive and so less attractive to other countries, causing a fall in UK exports and an increase in imports.

(c) Not because this will make the UK's goods less competitive since average costs and prices of UK goods will increase.

(d) Not a deterioration because UK consumers will have more disposable income, causing a rise in imports and so leading to a worsening in the current account.

19 150 – 165 + 60 – 50 – 25 – 10 = –$40 billion

20 Demand-side policies relate to those which affect aggregate demand. Either fiscal or monetary policy may be used.

- Fiscal policy: to reduce a current account deficit, public expenditure could be reduced or taxes increased. Both of these would reduce aggregate demand within the country and so cause a fall in consumption and a fall in imports.
- Monetary policy: an increase in interest rates would increase the incentive to save. In contrast, there would be less incentive to borrow because a higher rate of interest would be payable on loans. Again, the overall effect would be to decrease imports.

However, it should be noted that an increase in interest rates could cause an increase in the value of the country's currency, which would cause a fall in competitiveness of its goods (because the foreign currency price of exports would increase and the price of imports would decrease).

21 (a) Yes, because inward investment causes an increase in demand for US dollars.

(b) No, because the purchasing power of the dollar would be falling relative to other countries' currencies.

(c) No, because money is likely to flow out of the USA to foreign banks where the interest rate is higher.

(d) Yes, because this is likely to increase the demand for dollars by foreigners.

22 Likely effects:

- Fall in competitiveness of the country's goods.
- This could cause a deterioration in the current account of the balance of payments.
- If the country's goods are less competitive then unemployment may increase and real output may fall.
- The fall in the price of imported raw materials will help to reduce cost-push inflationary pressures.
- Possibility of an increase in living standards because less has to be exported to gain a given quantity of imports — the terms of trade will have risen.

23
- The central bank could reduce interest rates to make it less attractive for foreigners to place surplus cash balances in the country's banks.
- Also, it could sell its own currency on the foreign exchange market.

24 (a) Increase

(b) Increase

(c) Decrease

(d) Increase

(e) Increase

Chapter 18

1 No. It is possible for there to be significant falls in absolute poverty while relative poverty is increasing. Remember that relative poverty involves making a comparison with others in that country, so even if a country has a very high GDP per head, there will always be people in relative poverty and that level could be increasing.

2
- An increase in benefits from the government
- A decrease in unemployment

3 The Lorenz curve would move further away from the 45° line.

4
- Inheritance: inherited assets are a major source of inequality.
- Ownership of assets, e.g. property: those owning property have enjoyed substantial increases in their wealth in most countries over the last 50 years.

5 The owners of resources are likely to earn higher incomes and be able to accumulate wealth more easily than those who do not own resources.

Chapter 19

1
- Health (life expectancy).
- Education (expected years of schooling at age 4; and mean years of schooling at age 25).
- GNI per capita.

2
- Proportion of the population employed in agriculture.
- Proportion of the population with access to clean water.

3 (a) Terms of trade $= \dfrac{\text{index of export prices}}{\text{index of import prices}} \times 100$

$$= \frac{104}{112} \times 100$$

$$= 92.86$$

(b) The terms of trade have decreased, which implies that more must be exported to gain a given quantity of imports. In turn, this suggests that living standards have fallen. However, the fall in the terms of trade indicates that the country's goods are more competitive. This could result in an improvement in its balance of payments, which could lead to an increase in growth.

4 Supply and demand are very price inelastic, so any shift in either the supply or demand curve would cause a significant price change.

5 With low incomes, the marginal propensity to consume would be high because people would tend to spend much of any increase in their incomes. Consequently, savings would be low so that funds for investment would be limited.

6 A shortage of foreign exchange would mean that there would be insufficient funds for importing capital goods or essential raw materials and oil or healthcare products. In turn, it may be difficult for the country to achieve economic growth and generate tax revenues which could be used to improve education (and literacy rates); healthcare (and life expectancy); and improvements in access to clean water etc.

7 If population is growing at a faster rate than the growth in real GDP, then GDP per head will fall.

8 To service the debt, i.e. to make interest payments on the debt, the country will have to pay in foreign currency, meaning that there is less available for purchasing capital goods, oil, food etc.

9 Reduction in trade barriers such as tariffs and quotas so that the country is more open to trade.

10
- If an economy is open to trade, it is more likely that transnational companies will invest in the country. This will generate economic growth and, with higher real incomes, development might occur, e.g. in terms of improved education and healthcare.
- Removal of trade barriers will act as an incentive for domestic firms to become more efficient and productive. With higher growth, economic development is more likely.

11 Inability of potential entrepreneurs to access funds from the banking system; or absence of a readily available financial system with the ability to extend credit.

12 To reduce price fluctuations.

13
- If all the major producers are members of the scheme.
- If there is no 'cheating' by individual members.
- If the floor and ceiling prices are realistic, i.e. neither too high nor too low.
- If there are no close substitutes.

14 (a) There will be an increasing proportion of the population in urban areas.

(b) Inequality is likely to increase because earnings in manufacturing are likely to be higher than those in the agricultural sector.

(c) Increased levels of pollution and environmental degradation.

15 There are several possible reasons:
- Demand for tourism is critically dependent on the state of the world economy because demand is income elastic.
- Many developing countries dependent on tourism are subject to extreme weather events such as hurricanes.
- Demand for tourism in some countries may be seasonal, so foreign currency earnings fluctuate between seasons.

16
- Only a small proportion of the retail price may be paid to producers.
- It could encourage more farmers to grow bananas, so increasing supply and putting a downward pressure on prices.

17
- Corruption — money diverted from aid to government officials.
- Might create a dependency culture and stifle entrepreneurial spirit in the country.

18 Aid is the free transfer of resources from one country to another. FDI is investment by a TNC in another country whose shareholders expect to make a profit from the investment.

Chapter 20

1
- Banking sector
- Insurance
- Foreign exchange
- Derivatives

2 (a) Stock market

(b) Foreign exchange market

3
- Savers/lenders to those in the financial system have less knowledge than those working in the banking industry.
- Regulators may have less knowledge than bankers.

4 Implementation of monetary policy.

5 Regulations to increase liquid assets held by banks; or to raise more capital; or to impose restrictions on mortgage lending.

Chapter 21

1 Capital expenditure (investment) is an injection into the circular flow. Therefore, it will have a multiplier effect on GDP.

2 State pensions; housing benefit

3
- The UK has an ageing population. The elderly tend to make much greater demands on the NHS.
- New medical technology, e.g. CT scanners.
- New drug treatments.

4 Possible areas:
- Transfer payments (social protection), because expenditure on state pensions will continue to increase as the population ages.
- Aid budget, because the government is committed to increasing aid so that it is 0.7% of GDP
- Debt interest, because the size of the national debt is increasing and so interest payments are likely to increase significantly

5 With a progressive tax, the proportion of income paid in tax rises as income rises, whereas with a proportionate tax, the proportion of income paid in tax remains constant as income increases.

6 Disincentive effects may mean that workers withdraw from the workforce, do less overtime, or may move to another country (tax exiles). The Laffer curve may be used to illustrate the effects of changes in tax rates on tax revenues.

7 The price elasticity of demand and price elasticity of supply of the product. For example, if demand is price inelastic, then consumers will bear a larger proportion of the tax than producers.

8 (a) This is likely to increase the fiscal deficit because government expenditure on benefits will increase while tax revenues (from income tax, national insurance, VAT and corporation tax) will decrease.

(b) This is likely to increase the fiscal deficit because government expenditure on state pensions and other benefits will increase along with higher expenditure on healthcare. If fewer people are working then tax revenues (especially from income tax and national insurance) will decrease.

(c) This should reduce the UK's fiscal deficit because:
- the government would receive increased tax revenue from VAT receipts (from expenditure by tourists in the UK)
- more employment in the tourist industry would increase tax revenues from income tax and national insurance contributions

9 A fiscal deficit occurs when public expenditure exceeds tax revenues in a particular year. A national debt refers to the cumulative total of a government's past borrowing (previous fiscal deficits).

10
- If it is being used to finance increased investment.
- If it is being used to stimulate aggregate demand during a severe recession.

11 With an increasing national debt, there will be an increase in the amount of interest which has to be paid servicing it. Therefore, the opportunity cost may be new hospitals or schools. These would have to be sacrificed to pay the interest.

12 Higher taxes and reduced public expenditure could cause a fall in aggregate demand and so lead to a fall in real output. With lower GDP, tax revenues could fall, for example if there is a significant increase in unemployment.

13
- To reduce poverty there could be an increase in means-tested benefits.
- To reduce inequality, the progressiveness of the tax system could be increased by raising the higher rates of income tax.

14
- It could cause imported inflation, i.e. the cost of imported raw materials would increase, raising the costs of production for firms which might then increase their prices.
- Also, if net exports increase, then there would be an increase in aggregate demand, which could also be inflationary.

15
- Cut in interest rates.
- Reflationary fiscal policy, e.g. reduction in taxes.